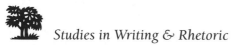

Studies in Writing & Rhetoric

Other Books in the Studies in Writing & Rhetoric Series

African American Literacies Unleashed

African American Literacies Unleashed

Vernacular English and the
Composition Classroom

Arnetha F. Ball
and
Ted Lardner

With a Foreword by Keith Gilyard

SOUTHERN ILLINOIS UNIVERSITY PRESS

Carbondale

Publication partially funded by a subvention grant from The Conference on College
Composition and Communication of the National Council of Teachers of English.

Library of Congress Cataloging-in-Publication Data
Ball, Arnetha F., date.
   African American literacies unleashed : vernacular English and the composition
classroom / Arnetha F. Ball and Ted Lardner ; with a foreword by Keith Gilyard.
   p. cm. — (Studies in writing & rhetoric)
Includes bibliographical references and index.
1. African Americans—Languages. 2. English language—Rhetoric—Study and
teaching—United States. 3. English language—Composition and exercises—
Study and teaching—United States. 4. English language—Study and teaching—
United States. 5. African Americans—Education. 6. Black English—United
States. I. Lardner, Ted. II. Title. III. Series.
PE3102.N44B35 2005
808'.042'08996073—dc22
ISBN 0-8093-2659-0 (alk. paper)
ISBN 0-8093-2660-4 (pbk.)   2005008770

Printed on recycled paper. ♻

With enormous gratitude to Fred Ball and Helen Lardner for their patient understanding throughout our collaboration, we dedicate this book to writing teachers everywhere who envision possibilities for themselves, their profession, and especially for their students.

Linguistic change is the result and
not the cause of social change.

—James Sledd

To make a difference you've got to
be different.

—Keith Gilyard

Contents

Foreword

The book that puts an end to excuses. That was not exactly the claim that professors Ball and Lardner made for their evolving project as we ate breakfast during an annual convention of the Conference on College Composition and Communication. But my opening sentence captures both the spirit of their talk and the way I began to think about their book. In other words, we noted during our discussion the positive research strides that have been made in the study of African American Vernacular English. In fact, over the past thirty-five years, it has been the most studied and written about language variety in the world. As the valiant linguist Geneva Smitherman often exclaims when a new/old language controversy comes around, "Ain we done been here before?" No doubt. Yet in most corners of academe, linguistic findings seem to run far ahead of changes in pedagogy. According to several indicators, African American students remain underserved.

As Ball, Lardner, and I kept talking that morning, we sensed that lore, the stories that folks pass along about teaching, stories steeped (really deeply) in tradition, perhaps circulate more widely, consistently, and powerfully than empirical evidence. Research findings have to be introduced formally to each new generation of teachers. Lore, basic assumptions and dispositions, travels freely all the time. And it usually arrives first on Monday morning. Given that realization, we saw the most expeditious approach to improved practice to be the circulation of counterstories that could gain discursive force. This prospect is what excited my two colleagues. They felt that they were, in fact, going to produce a text so practical, so connected to everyday teaching that it had a chance to become lore. It will be the good fortune of all of us if they prove to be right.

In *African American Literacies Unleashed,* Ball and Lardner, award-winning collaborators, distill their combined insight and teaching experience into a narrative that is truly a gift to the profession. They write with eloquence, and at times elegance, as they urge us to broaden or reconsider our thinking about African American students (about all students, actually), pedagogy, and the professional development of teachers. They do theorize, as they should, but such ruminations remain firmly linked to personal engagement and classroom know-how. Much of the strength of the book derives from personal anecdotes and case studies drawn both from campus and community experiences.

Ball and Lardner know that addressing knowledge deficits is not enough. Why a general progressive impulse concerning educational access and equity often turns to strict conservatism when the issue is language diversity in the classroom has more to do with an attitude gap than an information gap. As such, the authors are vitally concerned with how teachers assimilate new information and how new information becomes generative. They pay particular attention to the question of "the cumulative impact of our knowledge and experiences on our feelings about our students' ability and our ability to teach them." They understand, too, that teachers, to serve any students well, must feel some connection to them and their communities. So while Ball and Lardner take us on a whirlwind tour of disciplinary knowledge——sociolinguistics, race theory, whiteness studies, Bakhtin, Vygotsky——they focus ultimately on the empathy and commitment exemplified by their lives and teaching careers and, most importantly, the wonderful and *ordinarily* brilliant students that they have met along the way.

African American Literacies Unleashed is a slim volume with a wide and crucial embrace, in the manner of, say, John Rouse's *The Completed Gesture*, Robert Brooke's *Writing and Sense of Self,* and Tom Fox's *Defending Access.* It is an extremely important intervention, a succinct and heartfelt appeal, a call that we should affirm with our response. As a group, we can teach better, definitely unleash some literacies in the quest for an improved democracy. No excuse not to.

Keith Gilyard

Preface

Over the decades, the teaching profession has stood as a vanguard on issues of justice, freedom, equity, and access. Yet we find our professed values at odds sometimes with institutional practices, particularly when it comes to issues related to using varieties of English in our students' written and oral discourse in our classrooms. Since the 1960s and 1970s, sociolinguistic research on African American Vernacular English (AAVE) has provided a complex profile of the linguistic practices of AAVE-speaking students. More recent work examining African American rhetorical traditions has added to the knowledge base concerning AAVE as a language system. At the same time, writing and composition teachers have become cognizant of the situated nature of writing. Scholars theorize the interplay of identities, literacies, and power relations as elements of composition pedagogy and indeed as elements of the writing process.

While the impact of this work has been far-reaching, it appears that these developments have not led most teachers to implement changes in their classroom practices. In spite of considerable efforts on the part of the linguistic research community since the 1960s and 1970s, accumulating information concerning diverse rhetorical traditions and new theoretical sophistication, we find that linguistically based research knowledge has yet to be translated into widespread educational application. Institutional routines and individual teachers' habits have proven to be resistant to applications of this knowledge. Understanding why this phenomenon persists and how it can be changed is the focal message we address in this book.

In "Dispositions toward Language: Teachers' Constructs of Knowledge and the Ann Arbor 'Black English' Case," we attempted to identify the road of change that writing teachers (and writing program administrators, researchers, and teacher educators) would need to take to respond more thoroughly and thoughtfully to the

needs and experiences of all of our students. In that article, we spoke
of a critical disconnection between knowledge and application in
writing and composition classrooms. In "Dispositions," we spoke
of competing constructs of teacher knowledge, focusing on the 1979
Ann Arbor court decision to explore the implications of these constructs as teachers confront racially informed language attitudes.
Noting lack of application of linguistic research-based knowledge
on writing pedagogy, we shifted focus to teachers' constructs or
interpretations of knowledge. In our reading, the Ann Arbor decision stands as an intervention into the institutional status quo by
holding the school system partially responsible for the educational
underachievement of African American students. The court held the
Ann Arbor school district and King School teachers responsible for
rethinking pedagogy and curriculum in light of existing information about AAVE. At the conclusion of the court-ordered twenty-hour
in-service program, the King School teachers reported improved
knowledge of substantive issues, but they were "less positive" about
the pedagogical applications (Howard 17).

The 1979 Ann Arbor "Black English" case spotlights the complicated task faced by teachers seeking to assimilate new knowledge
about race and language in order to translate that knowledge into
classroom practice. History shows that transformations in the teachers' instructional practices never really materialized. As we envision
a transformation of literacy instruction in today's schools that moves
toward more inclusive pedagogy, we believe it is important to analyze and offer new angles on teachers' constructs of knowledge. Our
audience is teachers of writing and composition who have little
knowledge of AAVE and linguistically diverse students. Our purpose
is to argue that needed changes in theory and practice can be addressed by refocusing attention from strictly teachers' knowledge
deficits to the processes through which teachers assimilate information relevant to culturally informed pedagogy and the development
and maintenance of a high sense of teaching efficacy and reflective
optimism. We extend the meaning of "teacher efficacy" to refer to
a teacher's belief in her or his ability to connect with and work effectively with all students. By "reflective optimism," we mean a

teacher's informed expectation that all of his or her students have the potential to succeed.

In this book, we take the opportunity to say, Look. Calling ourselves progressive teachers is not enough. If the status quo in our own classrooms is less than optimal, we need to do something about that, to change the status quo. We need to unlearn our own racism if that's what's involved. We need to remedy our knowledge deficits regarding AAVE. We need to transform our attitudes in order to transform our practice. This is not easy, but if we want to be successful teachers to linguistically diverse and/or African American students, we must begin taking these steps.

Our message calls for a three-part change in the way composition specialists approach diversity in the classroom:

1. Knowledge. While in itself it is insufficient to catalyze the needed changes, knowledge of AAVE is indispensable. As we say in "Dispositions," teachers are not free to ignore facts. Knowledge that we argue is essential includes linguistic knowledge of AAVE and AAVE rhetorical patterns; knowledge of cultures and communities of all students, but particularly of African American students; knowledge of students as persons; and knowledge of critical race theory and power relations.

2. Self-reflection. In light of the knowledge being gained, teachers should explore and analyze their own racism and prejudices— interrogate their own beliefs. Teachers should also reflect on their teaching style(s) and its effects, as well as their relationship to those power relations.

3. Personal and professional/classroom change. The application of self-reflection will lead teachers to give attention to building a sense of efficacy and positive optimism and motivate them to create teaching practices that reflect these attitudes. The specific, practical advice given throughout this book, and particularly in chapter 5, should be linked directly to this sense of efficacy and positive optimism.

In chapter 1, we provide context for our project, establishing it on the central issues of understanding the work that has gone before us, identifying the differences between AAVE theory and critical race theory, and using our own personal narratives as evidence.

In chapter 2, we show the need for teachers and teacher educators to draw the line between learning about AAVE, unlearning racism, and transforming their attitudes. Using a student text as a frame to set the terms for what knowledge(s) need to be gained, we argue that teachers will not be able to do much for AAVE-speaking students until this knowledge deficit is rectified. Teachers need to position themselves as learners of AAVE. At the same time, they need to be self-reflecting and give attention to building attitudes of self-efficacy and reflective optimism.

Chapter 3 shifts focus from student texts to interactive discourse, drawing extensively on examples from community-based organizations to show teachers' knowledge being appropriately used, and to show their positive attitudes and high efficacy in the transformed pedagogies/curricula in these community-based organizations.

Chapter 4 focuses on self-reflection in the process of readjusting attitudes. Using our own personal stories, we identify the applications we are modeling in the move beyond internalization. Reflecting on our own journeys toward efficacy, we reanalyze personal beliefs and assumptions that underlie our teaching. The "re-negotiation" of our teaching identities, the shifting of who we are and how we operate in the classroom, that results from self-reflection sends us down familiar curricular/professional paths. It also sends us down paths through formative experiences that are extracurricular, extraprofessional in nature.

In chapter 5, we spell out what our reflections on efficacy suggest for teachers who want to know where and how to begin the process of implementing a transformed pedagogy. We present twelve changes teachers can initiate and monitor as they reflect on, analyze, and change their classroom practice.

Chapter 6 extends the invitation to writing program administrators, teacher educators, and researchers to apply the constructs of efficacy and reflective optimism to their practices as well.

Because we approach the issue of AAVE and writing in terms of teacher knowledge, attitudes, and attempts to change, we speak as teacher educators. In spite of a widely repeated assertion that the classroom forms the center of our field, the discourse of teacher education seems to articulate oddly with composition studies. This point was dramatically brought home in the course of working on our article, "Dispositions toward Language: Teachers' Constructs of Knowledge and the Ann Arbor Black English Case." We took a draft of it to the writing workshop led by Richard Larson at the 1997 Conference on College Composition and Communication CCCC in Phoenix. When it came time for the group to discuss the draft, members delved into the subjects of dialect, teachers' responses to diversity, and student writing, but the responses seemed tentative. The article was different from others submitted. It wasn't about rhetorical theory. It wasn't a historical analysis of early modern writing by women. It was about teachers. And, yes, it was a rough draft, uncertain of its voice and focus. But what finally seemed to explain the vague responses from the group crystallized in a comment by one of the participants: "But isn't this more suited to an education journal? It's about teacher training, and composition isn't as interested in that." This experience crystallized for us the concern that composition is perceived as not being interested in issues of teacher professional development.

We know our profession espouses a commitment to equitable access and racial justice. Yet we experience writing programs such as one at a modestly sized midwestern urban university, where fifty-five to sixty sections of first-year writing courses will be offered each semester. Almost all sections will be staffed by part-time or adjunct faculty, most of whom work hard in contrast to the poor rate of compensation they receive. Little incentive is afforded them by their institution to pursue professional development opportunities. Program review in their home institution is a maintenance task routinely deferred. On average, in the sections of first-year writing offered each term, 12 percent of the students will be African Americans. For many of these students, their stances and primary discourses position them at difficult angles with the presumptions of the teachers charged with the task of initiating them into the academic discourse community. In general, the underachievement of many of these African American students will remain unnoted by a critical mass of teachers or writing program administrators. The majority of students do all right, so why should teachers change—for to reach these students, changes in teachers' lives and teaching practices (and in writing programs, as well) would have to be significantly noted, sufficiently prioritized. And even if the motive were there, how would such change proceed?

In this volume, we take some risks in the hope of moving forward the dialogue on teacher professional development in composition. Building from our own experiences and observations, we present concepts and reflections on how individual composition teachers can become confident in the realization that they can teach AAVE-speaking students without referring to a "crib sheet" of politically correct terms or "multiculturally appropriate" reading and writing assignments. We take these risks in the hopes that individual writing and composition teachers will come to understand that possessing an understanding of their own passion to teach, a willingness to use multiple voices like those illustrated by the teachers in many community-based organizations, and a commitment to become agents of change will move them away from "business as usual" at the risk of displaying what John Baugh refers to as "feelings" (91). We are convinced that if writing teachers, program administrators, researchers, and teacher educators will do what needs to be done to open our classrooms to experimentations with the unvoiced aspiration of taking on composition as "serious business," then changes in the profession will begin to occur. As we consider these issues, we find that teacher efficacy can be the key vehicle that opens up the possibilities for reenvisioning composition classes for AAVE-speaking students.

Acknowledgments

For their generous reading and valuable feedback on drafts of this manuscript, we express deep gratitude to Keith Gilyard, Maria Montaperto, Andrea Lunsford, Beverly Moss, Christine Stewart-Nunez, and Smokey Wilson. For their assistance preparing the manuscript, we thank Rhonda Haddix and Julie Wilson. For his patience and encouragement, we thank Robert Brooke.

We incorporate as illustrative matter numerous examples of effective, powerful writing by students with whom we have been fortunate to work over the past fifteen years. Wherever possible, we have gotten their permission to include their words. In every case, we are grateful for the lessons we have learned from them.

Some material in this book appeared, in different forms, in other publications: portions of "Community-Based Learning in Urban Settings as a Model for Educational Reform," by Arnetha Ball, have been reprinted from *Applied Behavioral Science Review*, vol. 3, no. 2, pp. 127–46 (1995), with permission from Elsevier; "Dances of Identity: Finding an Ethnic Self in the Arts," by Arnetha Ball and Shirley Brice Heath, appeared in 1993 in *Possible Selves: Achievement, Ethnicity, and Gender for Inner-City Youth* (Teachers College Press); and "Text Design Patterns in the Writing of Urban African-American Students: Teaching to the Strengths of Students in Multicultural Settings" was published in *Urban Education*, vol. 30, no. 3, pp. 253–89 (1995). We gratefully acknowledge the consent of these publishers to include this material in *African American Literacies Unleashed*. We also gratefully acknowledge the photo team of Ashley Allen and Alina S. Ball for the cover photo, "An African American Writer."

African American Literacies Unleashed

1 / How We Got Here

The story of our coming together centers around the fact that we have been grappling with some perplexing issues related to having African American Vernacular English (AAVE)–speaking students in our writing and composition classrooms for a long time. Now, we are reflecting upon these experiences, and we would like to share the theoretical frames and the principles, practices, and processes that have helped us to make the most sense of these experiences. The message in this book concerning language diversity in the writing and composition classroom has been evolving in our lives for over a decade and serves as the unifying force that brings us together in this project. Our observations and reflections in our own classrooms along with our reading of ongoing work in the fields of composition, literacy, and teacher preparation inform our discussion here. A commitment to our belief in writing as a tool for personal and professional change was the catalyst that brought us together in our initial collaborative efforts, and it continues to sustain our work. A commitment to our belief in writing as a vehicle for societal transformation was our motivation for writing this book.

We have both worked with AAVE-speaking students in writing and composition classrooms for some time, and our puzzlement about why a disproportionate number of these students fail to thrive was one of the reasons we came together to write this book. And so, our audiences include writing and composition teachers and those who have the opportunity to or are charged with the responsibility of preparing writing and composition teachers through preservice training or through professional development programs.

For more than fifteen years, we have also taught courses that examine language diversity in the context of teaching writing and composition. These courses have taken the form of English department offerings, licensure courses in colleges of education, inservice teacher workshops, and writing intensive courses taught by Arnetha to inner city students, and to teachers in South Africa. These courses and workshops have enrolled English or communications or other majors seeking to round out their electives, preservice teachers, and graduate students—some who are inservice teachers updating credentials, others who enroll as a condition of employment as tutors or teaching assistants. The content of these courses includes sociocultural perspectives on literacy and learning, sociolinguistic information about AAVE, and critical analyses of theory, pedagogy, and schooling. These courses represent areas of inquiry with which we are intensely involved professionally and personally.

Yet, as fulfilling and engaging as this material may be, we have found that working with it can be emotionally draining: the highs are high, but the lows can be very low. Our own emotional take on teaching these courses, we believe, is reciprocally related to our students' emotional responses to material that remains contentious, provocative, and unsettling at times. When we foreground AAVE as a feature of power relations in society and in the classroom, the material is threatening. Such talk disrupts a cultural narrative of color-blind schooling with literacy as the means to socioeconomic mobility. When we talk about AAVE in relation to school literacy and power relations, we complicate a professional narrative that portrays teacher knowledge as a skill set based on cognitive universals, readily adaptable to the needs of different students. In these courses, we reexamine some closely held beliefs about American education and the individualist ideology that explains student success or failure. What does it mean to work as a writing teacher of AAVE-speaking students in a given institution? What core values structure our sense of ourselves as writing teachers? Sociolinguistically, in the moment-to-moment verbal exchanges that constitute the interactive discourse of our classrooms, where do we meet these students? What spaces for learning do we open with them? Where may we lead them as we attempt to foster a positive relationship to writing in school? And, if actions speak louder than words, do we offer opportunities or do we foreclose options?

Needless to say, there are few easy answers to these questions. However, this book is an effort to work out some answers to these persisting challenges to our field, and in composing it together, we hope to create one example of cross-cultural examination of issues of mutual import to us as teachers. By exploring these issues, we aim to do justice to possibilities for literacy for students whose home language or language of nurture is not Standard English. We aim to do justice to the epistemic possibilities and the latent counter-hegemonic power available in the varieties of English that wash through society everyday. "It is the asymmetries," Clifford Geertz has written, "between what we believe or feel and what others do, that makes it possible to locate where we now are in the world, how it feels to be there, and where we might or might not want to go" (114). In these circumstances, Geertz asserts, one thing we need is "fluency in an enlarged vocabulary." The "reach of our minds, of what we can say, think, appreciate, and judge, the range of signs we can manage somehow to interpret, is what defines the intellectual, emotional, and moral space within which we live" (113). As writing teachers, we aim to do justice in pursuit of knowledge of the "asymmetries" that define our cognitive, affective, and sociocultural locations; we aim for justice in the many vocabularies needed to articulate it. We aim to do justice to the ongoing work of becoming *better* writing teachers—knowing what works, visioning what might work *better*—and taking the intellectual and emotional leaps of faith to bridge the difference.

This book represents a coming together of two worlds—Ted's middle-America, suburban/rural world and Arnetha's West Coast inner-city/urban world. We come together around issues of language, literacy, race, and teacher efficacy in our personal and professional lives. Our thoughts have developed and merged around issues of identity that society and our early school experiences have offered to us. In *Lives on the Boundary*, Mike Rose recounts his realization of an important influence in his life:

> MacFarland . . . tapped my old interest in reading and creating stories. He gave me a way to feel special by using my

mind. And he provided a role model that wasn't shaped on physical prowess alone, and something inside me that I wasn't quite aware of responded to that. Jack MacFarland established a literacy club, to borrow a phrase of Frank Smith's, and invited me—invited all of us—to join. . . . My linguistic play moved into the world . . . link[ing] my mind to something outside it. . . . Jack MacFarland, Frank Carothers, and the others created the conditions for me to use my mind to engage the world. What I wanted strongly now was a program that would further develop my intellectual tools and equip me . . . to teach . . . to change the lives of others. . . . (33–34, 67)

Just as Mike Rose realized that a turning point occurred for him when the school offered a way for him to use his mind to engage the world and perhaps even to change the lives of others, this was the case for both of us. Somewhere in our early academic experience, teachers offered us a way to use our minds to engage the world, only in different ways—in ways that were different from the schools' agenda. If we may characterize it this way, the school's agenda is, generally, to use students' AP scores and test results as admission criteria to the better colleges, and these colleges train scholars and produce a teaching force that will maintain the status quo. Our agenda, however, was to locate tools with which to see into and change the defining shape of the worlds from which we each emerged. Although we come from very different worlds, we have found that we both fought against the pressures to stay within our designated tracks and resisted the lessons designed to teach us conformity, knowing that there could be consequences for such actions. And there were.

Personal Context for This Work

Ted

When I think what brings me to this project, I go home. I see the Mississippi River, I picture it Mark Twain's river, but with late history written in high-water lines staining flood walls and buildings downtown. When I think of that place, I remember my grandfather, smell black willows, water's edge, cigarette smoke where men waved hello as they fished for food in the evening. I think of the name Rock Island. From thirty-one thousand feet, it is the fly-over country of hog barns, soybean and cornfields. I remember foreclosures, rural depopulation, well-paying jobs lost from shuttered implement factories. I remember the public high school there—"Go, Rocks!" Perched on the river bluff, it overlooked the site of the Sac and Fox village where the west end of town reaches for water. I think about classmates who stayed (my best friend) and others, like me, who left.

What future in academia is foretold in this record? What concern for race, literacy, and pedagogy? From a locker in the basement, I retrieve a binder. It holds papers salvaged from notebooks and school folders. I flip from Mrs. Foss's sixth grade to grade 7 English with Mrs. Carson. A page of spelling corrections is a record of rough accommodation (see figure). I would call it careless, but it is not only that. There are multiple attempts to correct then recorrect "mission," "going," "lieutenant," and "curb." The handwriting seems overdetermined, as though shaping each letter were a struggle for consensus among brain, eye, and hand. When I look at the page headed "Incorrect Incorrect," I remember Mrs. Carson's glasses and posture. In my memory, she seems always to look down from a far height. I read through eight different assignments. What you cannot see directly is the social distance the boy felt from Mrs. Carson. He did well enough (see table).

But these assignments became kind of a tug-of-war. Those As and Bs did not come from Mrs. Carson's encouragement or useful feedback, of which there was little. At grade 7, at least, my primary relationship to writing was forged largely independently from school instruction, and instruction in school writing seemed kind of like a threat.

In high school, I knew kids in "vo-tec" and more in the college track. I negotiated a place between, just enough math (a semester of Algebra II) to fill a requirement, three years of French because my sisters took French. "Regular" English, where I earned Bs, and Creative Writing, where I earned As.

Ted Lardner

Incorrect	Incorrect
michen'n	machine mission
g10n	giant going
leutenet	lieutenant lieutant
disapieR iNa	disapearing
Sapose	supposed
wAted	waited
closeseR	closer
spce	space
slamed breaks	slammed
	brakes
mARshon	martian
snAped	snapped
ofcoRse	of course
turture	future
carb	card care CURb

Grade 7 spelling list of a European American boy

From the high school expository writing class, "Composition and Perception," another cache of work. We had a student teacher. One warm day, she led the class outdoors. "Take out a sheet of paper," she said. "Start in, keep writing no matter what. It's called 'freewriting.' It's stream-of-consciousness. Write as much as you can. I'll tell you when to stop. We'll exchange with the other class for peer feedback." Freewriting? Peer feedback? I remember how I got caught up. The next Monday I got my paper back and read, astonished, words Eric Johnson had written on the back: "Hot damn! Good poetry!"

Poetry? I knew Eric, an AP English student, a jazz drummer. Whatever my page was, Eric admired it, and that counted. It was not that I loved suddenly to write. It is that I became conscious of

Total Feedback on Grade 7 Writing Assignments

Title	Grade	Comment
Wild Horse Island	A	Good story. A little messy.
My Goal	B-	I believe a beginning to show your desire to swim could be added. Also, a better ending is needed.
Getting Up in the Morning	B-	Quite brief.
My Camelot	B+	Excellent word choices. Incomplete sentences.
Our Visitors	B	[No feedback]
Happy Thanksgiving Memories	B+	Sounds as though you had a great time.
My Duck	B	[No feedback]
My Exile, or Where I Went to School after My Parents Kicked Me Out	B+	Good imagination. Needless mechanical errors. Wrong sheet.

myself as someone writing. I knew I could do it. This sense for writing was my first anchor as a writing teacher. But what exactly is it about writing that compels my involvement with it?

In a book of essays, Diane Ackerman explores the concept of deep play in a range of familiar contexts. (Clifford Geertz's essay on Balinese cock fights, familiar to composition teachers from a popular reader, is not mentioned.) Reading Ackerman, I feel the resonance. "According to rules freely accepted, and outside the sphere of necessity or material utility," Ackerman begins, quoting Johan Huizinga, "the play-mood is one of rapture and enthusiasm, and is sacred or restive in accordance with the occasion. A feeling of exultation and tension accompanies the action" (3). In her essay "Remembered Rapture," bell hooks describes writing in similar terms: "I am still transported, carried away by writing and reading," she says (36). Citing her words, I identify with their meaning: "All academics write," says hooks, "but not all see themselves as writers. Writing to fulfill professional career expectations is not the same as writing that emerges as the fulfillment of a yearning to work with words when there is no clear benefit or reward, when it is the experience of writing that matters" (37).

I had a poetry teacher in college who had a knack for describing what he expected in terms we could understand. Metaphors. "You go into the water," he said. "You swim out to the middle, then you dive to the bottom, and you grab a handful of *it.*" (*It* was the muck on the bottom.) He was saying you have to ask the questions, to swim down where the light is dim and stir things up. Bring it from below the surface, bring it to the light, regardless of the consequences. The metaphor struck deep as an image. His explanation helped lay out a course of action. When you write, he said, don't write what you know. Write what you don't know about what you know.

Therein, I think, lies the clue to the other, the part that reveals my involvement with matters of race in relation to literacy. When I color the outlines of my story, the places gain contours, the figures gain voices. The "west end" was a code. "The hill" marked a social dividing line. So, even as the "metaphor" of literacy (Scribner 73) I imbibed with that freewriting lesson that long-ago day was as white, perhaps, as color-blind can be, race was not far from my consciousness. I heard the diversity of voices in my home community, that same mix of common American speech Twain put to work in the service of interrogating the ideology of slavery.

Deeper in the folder of old school work, I examine work produced for Creative Writing I with Mrs. Anderson and Creative Writing II with Mr. Fessler. The paper smells musty. I wonder who this was: *Who wrote this?* Who did my teachers see between the lines? One story, for Mrs. Anderson's class. I try to read as I would read one of my own student's drafts: What is he trying to do? What strengths are evident, that the writer might build on? Knowing him as I do, I recognize that some strengths, of course, are not "in" the paper. They are "behind" it, for example, in the positive relationship the writer had to the story (its imagined characters, its time and place, the events that plot its shape). Another strength is the positive relationship the writer had to the writing (his purposes, including taking pleasure in manipulating elements of craft like descriptive detail, conflict, and dialogue.)

The story takes place on a farm where, during hunting season, the family supplements its income by opening its land to hunters. The protagonist is Caleb Collins, the son of "Smitty" Collins, who owns the farm and operates the hunting business. Clients come in, pay money to hunt. Told in third person, the story begins as Caleb wakes one cold autumn morning. The financial standing of the Collins family is fragile, and hope resides in gaining one client's interest in purchasing the whole spread. The story includes three registers of speech: the narrator's voice, which delivers exposition and description, the home language of Caleb and his father rendered in the dialogue they share, and the voice of Mr. Walurt, a "city dude" who is the high-paying client who plays the pivotal role in the plot.

The narrator's voice sounds like this:

> He was a lanky boy. Tall and skinny and rather frail looking. Strong though, strong enough to chuck hay bails [sic], and carry sacks of feed. In fact, farm chores had strengthened him.
>
> He leaned up on his elbow and peered out into the early morning light. . . . Frost had built up on the inside of his windows. Outside, a solitary leaf turned over, spinning slowly by the window in the frozen air.

Caleb's and his dad's voices sound like this:

> "I know, I know," his father assured him. "Only I was thinkin. You know how my helth's been goin' out on me. And I figured that it was time you started takin' on some adult sized responsibility. Naw I ain't sayin' it's gonna be easy, but I think that it would be best."
>
> "Oh no! No way! You ain't never said anything about this b'fore! Na!"

In another passage, Mr. Collins explains the two kinds of clients. One is a real hunter, he says,

"But then you got chur city dude who thinks he is a fine shootin' man. He's the kind that flips through them expensive cat'logs, buyin' a passel of parephenalia, hopin that all that stuff will kill hisself a bird. Them's the ones that you'll make your dollar off of."

Mr. Walurt's voice is hardly presented through direct discourse. However, it is described by the narrator as "curt" and "business-like." The narrator, in other words, is sympathetic to the Collins family, and especially to Caleb. Their nonstandard speech is valorized in the context of the plot.

Stapled to the story is a peer-response sheet. On it are the names of nine classmates. Their comments praise the story's descriptions and use of "conversational" dialogue. Also on the cover sheet, feedback from Mrs. Anderson. Her note reads:

A well-written story—it had characters, plot + conflict all woven together to make a fast-paced readable story. Excellent descriptive language—you took the reader there. It is not easy to sustain dialect; however, you did it very well—one or two places you missed.

And the grade(s): A/B+. Then a P.S. from Mrs. A.: "Ted, I would like to submit this story to Cavalcades. See me."

I'm not claiming the story is particularly well written. The story embarrasses me a little—to write about it. But it stands as evidence of an early interest and appreciation of variation in language (the social stratification of "heteroglossia," in Bakhtin's term). The story shows evidence of the effort to represent the sounds of spoken language realistically in the medium of written discourse. Before I had heard of sociolinguistics, before I had heard the term "nonstandard English," I had—I see now, looking at this story—taken a step on the journey that brings me here.

Arnetha
When I think of what brings me to this project, I see the faces of

inner-city African American students who bring rich language resources to the classroom, I see students who resist uncritical conformity, and I see glimpses of myself in them. You see, I have been interested in language and literacy for as long as I can remember. I grew up in an inner-city, African American community in South Central Los Angeles, and I can recall developing an appreciation for the power of language as my peers established positions of power and prestige through uses of "the word" in the African American rhetorical tradition. Verbal duals occurred on the playground daily, including exchanges of playin' the dozens, boastin', and signifyin'. I avoided most of these encounters because I just could not think quickly enough to emerge as a victor in these verbal competitions. I also avoided many of the lures that so often sidetrack poor, inner-city students of color. Instead of getting involved with petty drugs, teenage pregnancy, or yielding to the peer group pressure of avoiding looking smart because it was not cool, I became immersed in the pursuit of academic success and fascinated with literacies and language use within the classroom setting. Similar to Mike Rose's experience, my mentors tapped my interests in reading and writing as they gave me a way to feel special by using my mind. They invited me to join the "literacy club," and they created the conditions for me to use my mind to engage the world.

When I reflect on my early educational experiences, I can remember walking to school every morning with a small group of friends. We maneuvered our way through a nearby housing project where I secretly marveled at how young kids could find their own houses—since every one of the front doors looked exactly the same. Then we made our way down block after block of single-family dwellings and storefront churches, stopping occasionally at the neighborhood corner store that was owned by Jeannie Kyda's mom and dad. I also marveled at how it just so happened that Jeannie (the only nonblack student in our college-track class) was always the one who was chosen by our teachers and administrators to receive the classroom awards and school scholarships. While inside the doors of the school, I vigorously resisted the role that society had reserved for the kids coming from the east side of town.

I insisted on assuming a different role at every turn. My girlfriend Sheila and I would go to the fabric store regularly and purchase the fabric we needed to make the clothes we wore so we would have a new look, a distinct look—one that was different from all of the other girls in class. I graduated in a high school class of 650 students; most of them were from lower-middle-class backgrounds. It would have been very easy to just fade into a background of mediocrity in a school with almost three thousand students. But looking at the senior class picture in our high school yearbook, I see that our images stood out. We were different and we liked it that way. We were different, not only in our physical dress, but also in our thinking.

I remember how disappointed I was when our class chose *Los Conquistadores* as our class name—a name that had been used several times in recent years, and they voted to select burgundy and blue as our class colors—very typical class colors in our day. Once again, I was forced to conform. But whenever I could, I resisted conformity and mediocrity—in my classwork, in my dress, and in my way of thinking. You see, like bell hooks,

> I wanted to become a critical thinker. Yet that longing was often seen as a threat to authority. Individual white males who were seen as "exceptional" were often allowed to chart their intellectual journeys, but the rest of us (and particularly those from marginal groups) were always expected to conform. Nonconformity on our part was viewed with suspicion, as empty gestures of defiance aimed at masking inferiority or substandard work. (5)

The pressure to conform was noticeable in almost every academic setting I entered. One exception was the college prep writing class. I excelled in this class. There we were often allowed to express our ideas in creative ways. There we found the freedom to engage the world; we found a way to be ourselves and to be different in our worlds of writing. There I could express my ideas and not be penalized for not adhering to the "party line"—that is, as long as I wrote those ideas in standard academic English.

Years later, I entered the teaching profession because, like bell hooks, I feel that "the classroom remains the most radical space of possibility in the academy" (12). I began my teaching career as an ethnic studies resource teacher in an inner-city school—determined to challenge the legacy of academic failure that plagued many of the schools' AAVE-speaking students. I brought to my teaching an interest in helping these students find an outlet for sharing their voices. Because of my own school experiences, as a teacher I have always been energized by the nonconforming students in my class. I brought to my teaching an interest in the language resources of culturally and linguistically diverse students that had not been particularly nurtured or cultivated in my own K-12 schooling experiences, nor in the preservice teacher education program that I had attended, one that at times seemed blind to issues of race. My teacher education courses reminded me of the experience Patricia Williams recounts in her article, "Aren't We Happy Yet?" There she notes,

> On a recent radio program, I heard a woman describing a reunion of family and friends that had been planned for a resort in South Carolina during a time when the NAACP had called for tourism boycott until the Confederate flag was removed from state property. She said that the extended family had "never" discussed race before, and so they consulted with one another about what to do and whether to go. . . . I didn't hear the woman reveal her race, but it's a safe bet that group was white. How else do you go through life "never" thinking about race? (11)

Well, race has always been real for me. It is always there for people of color. But not necessarily in a negative way. Quite the opposite. My interests in using my students' heritage languages as a resource in their writing stemmed from my own experiences as an African American bidialectal female. Throughout my developmental years, I harbored both a fascination and a curiosity about the seemingly contradictory reports that African American students possessed great agility with the spoken word in the tradition of the African

American *griot,* yet they were generally considered to be "poor writers" in most academic settings. And the saddest thing about this was that, because of their educational experiences, most of these AAVE-speaking students considered themselves to be poor writers—even those who actually expressed themselves quite well in writing. In my experiences as part of the teaching staff at several inner-city schools, I frequently heard the murmuring complaints of teachers who were frustrated by what they perceived to be a failure on the part of their African American students to communicate their ideas effectively in writing. My own teaching experiences, however, provided me with countless examples of culturally and linguistically diverse students who demonstrated strong writing abilities, particularly in non-school settings. My decision to investigate the writing of African American students in grad school grew out of these experiences and out of my desire to seek answers to complex questions about the oral language and written literacies of culturally and linguistically diverse students, and the development of teachers who are eager and prepared to work with them. I wanted to become active in programs in which "prospective teachers [could] be educated as transformative intellectuals who are able to affirm and practice the discourse of freedom and democracy"—a "discourse that unites the language of critique with the language of possibility, so that social educators recognize that they can make changes" (Giroux 159, 128).

My sense of self as a writing teacher is summed up in the slogan "Teaching to Change the World." My passion for teaching writing is closely tied to the work that I do with youth and young adult students of color who will be populating freshman composition classes in a very short period of time. I want to do my best to instill in them a vision of the possibilities of taking on the identity of a successful (or even competent) writer of academic texts. In a recent survey I conducted with a group of inner-city students of color that I worked with, I found that only five of the twenty-three students felt confident about themselves as writers all the time. These students felt even less confident about their writing in academic settings. Survey responses from fifty percent of the students in our writing class revealed that they felt confident about their writing only "sometimes" or "not very often." A recent discussion with a colleague—an experienced writing teacher who works predominantly with AAVE-speaking students—revealed that she held deep concerns about her students' perceptions of themselves as writers. A survey she conducted with her students revealed that over 65 percent of them "do not enjoy writing at school" and over 75 percent "do not think of themselves as good writers at school." When asked what information they would like to share with future writing and composition teachers, several students noted that they would like their teachers to "focus more on getting to know them as individuals." One eleventh-grade student of color wrote, "I would also like my teachers to assess me in a way that can help them understand me better as a person rather than [just as] a writer." This student indicated that she is not college bound, although the talent and the potential is there. Another tenth-grade student of color wrote that she wanted her teachers to read her writing in ways that will help them to "read it and know the real me." This request was written by a student who is very active in class and involved in sports teams at school. Most of the students in my classes will never set foot in a freshman composition classroom unless they change their perceptions of themselves as writers and unless they can be turned on to the possibilities of writing. Accordingly, my sense of self as a writing teacher is linked to issues of social justice. The spark that sustains me is the possibility that at any moment a student might get turned on to writing. I construe my work as a writing teacher in terms of the potentiality of writing. I feel like my academic survival depends on being able to write. And I hope that my students will come to realize this too.

Scholarly Context for This Work

Although much work has been done that speaks to issues of the achievement of students of color in writing and composition classrooms (which we cite and refer to), we have come to recognize a need to make explicit the link between AAVE-speaking students, race theory, and teacher efficacy. We feel that a coming together of these three areas of study can help us to explain what we have been seeing. The coming together of these domains of study can help us in three areas: it can help us understand teachers who overgeneralize about AAVE speakers and culturally influenced mechanical variations found in their writing—teachers who think all errors by African American students are AAVE related; it can help us explain the success of many AAVE-speaking students in community-based organizations—settings in which these students often thrive; and it can help us explicate what teachers need to be taught through teacher education or professional development programs in order to reimagine new possibilities for AAVE-speaking students in the composition classroom and to develop the sense of efficacy that is critical for becoming successful teachers of these students.

Ultimately, we believe that for most teachers, the journey toward unleashing the literacies of AAVE-speaking students in writing and composition classrooms begins with seeing with new eyes. We propose that most teachers need, first, to examine their attitudes toward nonstandard language, and the unspoken, sometimes unconscious, prejudices they possess to some degree as products of the racially divided society in which we participate. Recognizing a need to make the link between AAVE-speaking students, critical race theory, and their own success will help teachers to begin the journey toward changed attitudes. That journey will begin as writing teachers come to analyze their own knowledge of and practice in dealing with AAVE-speaking students through the lens of their own sense of efficacy and reflective optimism. Most helpful will be the perspective taken from critical race theory. Teachers must ask themselves, "How can efficacy theory, which puts race at the center of teachers' constructs of knowledge, help us reimagine the possibilities for AAVE-speaking students in the writing or composition classroom?"

In our prior work together (Ball and Lardner), we noted that teachers' unconscious negative attitudes toward AAVE have been named as one barrier to academic achievement faced by African American students. The recognition of "language attitudes" as a barrier suggests what some other barriers to achievement might be. Structural factors such as socioeconomic status have been shown to play a significant role in school success. As a cause of different achievement levels, teachers' attitudes may prove less proximate than constraints resulting from mis-educative curriculum mandates including testing policies and inadequate school funding as it adversely affects class size, the availability of extracurricular or enrichment resources, and the recruitment and retention of highly qualified teachers. All this being said, we believe that identifying teachers' unconscious negative attitudes toward students' uses of AAVE still offers a useful point of entry. For, conjoined in an individual's attitudinal barrier toward Black English, we find interwoven issues of race and efficacy, played out institutionally in practices of literacy and evident personally in the affective stances we take toward participation in those literacies.

At the same time, defining the problem of some degree of students' academic underachievement in terms of teachers' negative language attitudes toward African American English requires a new paradigm for thinking through solutions and action. Dissemination of existing information about AAVE is an important factor in overcoming ineffective pedagogical approaches, but evidence suggests that in and of itself, adding information to the mix does not consistently produce change in pedagogy. Three decades of scholarly discussion punctuated by crises like the 1979 Ann Arbor "Black English" case and the 1996 Ebonics controversy in Oakland seem to bear this out.

For too long, attention has been focused on teachers' knowledge deficits. The needed changes in practice and theory can be addressed by shifting the focus to processes through which teachers assimilate information relevant to culturally informed pedagogy and the development and maintenance of a high sense of teaching efficacy and reflective optimism. These two notions have guided our inquiry in our classrooms and in the process of writing this book. Teacher efficacy refers to our belief in our ability to teach writing to all of our students. Reflective optimism refers to our belief in our students' ability to succeed. We come to this conclusion through our own professional autobiographies and through years of study and work with African American students. In essence, then, we want to share with our readers in this book the lessons we have learned from community-based organization as a model for classroom reform and what we have learned from a study of the development of efficacy in our own lives about improving the experiences of AAVE-speaking students in writing and composition classrooms. We want to share our carefully theorized position based on our experiences working in settings where race-related cultural differences were an acknowledged part of the scene. Thus, the major focus in this book is to shed light on how teachers may cultivate a high sense of efficacy—belief in their own capability as teachers—and reflective optimism—belief in their students' ability to achieve—even when we are teaching at the limits of our own cultural zones of comfort. In *Teaching to Transgress*, bell hooks tells of her desire to "add [her] voice to the collective call for renewal and rejuvenation in our teaching practices" (12). In this book, we also want to add our voices to the collective call for renewal and rejuvenation of the teaching practices in our field. We urge our readers to have open minds and hearts so that everyone can know beyond the boundaries of what currently is, can think and rethink, and create new visions. Like hooks, we celebrate teaching that enables transgressions against and beyond boundaries. According to hooks, these are the movements that make education the practice of freedom.

Literature Consulted

Two significant bodies of scholarship inform our project: scholarship in writing pedagogy and critical race theory. Scholarship in writing pedagogy in composition forms the primary context for our work. This scholarship includes critical literacy (Freire; Gee; Giroux; Berlin; Street); postprocess conceptions of writing and writer (Faigley; Gray-Rosendale; Harris; Welch; Brooke); studies of language and multicultural rhetorics and literacies (Delpit; Gilyard; Fox; Ball; Balester; Moss; Prendergast; Richardson; Scott); and studies of classroom life (hooks; Foster; Jordan; McLeod).

Across disciplinary boundaries, we invite composition teachers and college writing program administrators (including those who mentor new teaching assistants) as well as preservice teachers, teacher educators, and teachers in the extracurriculum to engage in this exploration. Therefore, we throw our arms open to the rich literature on teacher education. In our study, we draw on work that addresses how teachers construct knowledge of their professional identity (Ashton and Webb; Bishop; Harrington; Hillocks; Royster and Taylor; Ritchie and Wilson; Stenberg and Lee). In addition, we refer to studies of teachers' constructs of literacy and language arts in the context of multicultural classrooms (Baugh; Ladson-Billings; McCracken; Meier; Pang and Sablan; Rosen and Abt-Perkins). Re-marking on the ill effects of "the silence surrounding the demands of teaching outside one's immediate cultural frame," McCracken states, "It has not been easy to find a discourse to address the ways that unexamined attitudes about race, class, language, and gender perpetuate failure in schools" (247). As Pang and Sablan argue, "When the overwhelming majority of the teaching force in this country is not from underrepresented groups, the need to look at teacher misconceptions of African American culture, customs, his-tory, and values is essential" (16).

In this book, practitioners and scholars working in composition are invited to reconsider how this field, so grounded in the classroom, can more carefully articulate its processes of teacher preparation and mentoring so as to contribute to a reshaping of mainstream practices and attitudes encountered in the teaching and learning of African American students. This pedagogy would emphasize the inclusion of culturally relevant reading and writing assignments. But crucially, such pedagogy would be predicated again and again on the kind of reflection John Baugh suggests is needed when he argues,

> Teacher education needs to come to terms with issues of teachers' feelings about their students. Most states regulate teacher education without substantial regard to student di-versity and with even less regard to a student teacher's com-fort zone with respect to teaching under circumstances where the majority of students come from backgrounds that are substantially different from those of the teacher. (91)

Critical here is the issue of dealing with teachers' feelings about their students. Whether in teacher preparation programs or college writing classrooms, this affective dimension of teacher knowledge and professional identity can no longer remain a hidden variable in our quest for our students' educational success.

The second significant body of work that informs our project is the effort, from a variety of disciplines, to theorize race. Among scholars in sociology, history, anthropology, and the hybrid disciplines associated with critical theory, the notion of race as a socially constructed category has been widely recognized. As a social construct in a hierarchy of power relations, race has served to define identity and difference both as "a matter of individuality, of the formation of identity" and as "a matter of collectivity, the formation of social structures" (Omi and Winant 66). Extensive theorization of race is not the main concern of this book, because this has already been done sufficiently well by others (West; Gilyard, *Race;* Bell). Nevertheless, briefly posed, some general outlines drawn from critical race theory (CRT) will be helpful.

One premise of critical race theory is that racism is pervasive in our society. In "Just What Is Critical Race Theory and What's It Doing in a Nice Field Like Education," Gloria Ladson-Billings states,

> Critical race theory begins with the notion that racism is "normal, not aberrant, in American society" (Delgado, 1995, p. xiv) and because it is so enmeshed in the fabric of our social order, it appears both normal and natural to people in this culture. Indeed, Bell's major premise in *Faces at the Bottom of the Well* (1992) is that racism is a permanent fixture of American life. Thus, the strategy of critical race theorists becomes one of unmasking and exposing racism in its various permutations. (12)

Ladson-Billings touches on a second premise of CRT when she refers to Toni Morrison's contention that race is a ubiquitous presence, traceable through all aspects of our social lives (10). Amplifying the point, David Roediger observes, "Even in an all white town, race was never absent" (3). More significant than the omnipresence of race, however, is the notion that "whites reach the conclusion that their whiteness is meaningful" (Roediger 6). Thus, according to Ladson-Billings,

> It is because of the meaning and value imputed to white-ness that critical race theory . . . becomes an important intellectual and social tool for deconstruction, reconstruc-tion, and construction—deconstruction of oppressive structures and discourses, reconstruction of human agency, and construction of equitable and socially just relations of power. (10)

Ladson-Billings discusses CRT "to speak to innovative theoretical ways of framing discussions about social injustice and democracy and the role of education in reproducing or interrupting current practices" (10).

We write to speak to innovative theoretical ways of framing discussions about social injustice in writing and composition class-room. We want to question the role our profession has played in reproducing these practices and the role we are willing to play as professionals in interrupting current practices. CRT is very helpful to us in our attempts to investigate these questions. It "provides a perspective from which to critique our liberalism, our stance on racism, and our approach toward a long, slow, upward pull toward racial equality. CRT argues that the elimination of racism will not require a long, slow, upward pull toward racial equality, but rather, sweeping changes" (Roithmeyer 1).

According to Roithmeyer, "Critical race theory . . . is an excit-ing intellectual movement that puts race at the center of critical analysis" (1). It has its roots in critical legal scholarship that emerged during the civil rights movement but represents a significant depar-ture from it in several ways. While critical legal scholarship focused on universalisms, objectivity, and the race-neutrality of concepts like "equal opportunity," "merit," and "basic writers," they saw racism as an irrational deviation from race-neutral norms and sought to use legal approaches to eradicate those instances of race consciousness in social decision making, leaving behind an otherwise race-neutral way of distributing opportunities and resources. CRT articulated a deep dissatisfaction with liberal legal ideology and proposed that not only was it not being used to transform society's structures and to advance the political commitment to racial emancipation, but it was actually benefiting whites more them blacks, and white women in particular. In a compilation of CRT writings, Crenshaw, Gotanda, Peller, and Thomas noted that although critical race theorists have no canonical set of doctrines or methodologies, they are unified by two common interests: (a) to understand the relationship between ostensibly race-neutral ideas and the structure of white supremacy, racism, and how the subordination of people of color has been created and maintained in America, and (b) to change the bond that exists between law and racial power and use it to advance the political commitment to racial emancipation.

The work of these scholars helps to frame three significant tendencies occurring in writing and composition that need to be pointed out and addressed.

1. The tendency to "essentialize" race, reducing members of a group to a stereotyped, single racial identity. McCarthy and Crichlow caution against the tendencies of essentialism and reductionism, that is, to portray race in terms of a stable, homogeneous group identity "as though members of these groups possessed some innate and invariant set of characteristics that set them apart." Reductionism tends to "locate the 'source' of racial differences in schooling in a single variable or cause" (xviii).

Some readers will note that we seem to equate discussing race in the classroom with focusing on African American students, and that in doing so we commit the further error of essentializing African American identity. We say, "Not so." A large portion of our concern throughout this book is to shift the discussion so that it includes the teacher and the teacher-student relationship in order to understand how race-related cultural differences might become a catalyst for dynamic learning interactions rather than a (hidden) barrier to students' academic achievement and teachers' professional well-being. We posit that race matters in the relationship between white teachers and black students in the classroom, and acknowledge that it is this particular racialized relationship that concerns us. At the same time, recognizing from our own interactions in the field that "race" is an overdetermined category, Anthony Appiah's analysis helps to keep us on track. Noting that "race" remains probative even if, as a category of difference founded on supposed biological traits, it no longer stands scientific scrutiny, Appiah says, "What exists 'out there' in the world—communities of meaning, shading variously into each other in the rich structure of the social world—is the province not of biology but of hermeneutic understanding" (36). Of the Africanness of African American identity and culture, Appiah says what remains is "a subtle connection mediated not by genetics but by intentions, by meaning" (31). Similar arguments accenting the socially constructed basis of identity have been made concerning the racial identity of white writing teachers who contend sometimes with the hermeneutic misunderstandings that confound the formation of communities of meaning in the writing classroom (Trainor; T. West, "Racist Other"; Marshall and Ryden).

Let us declare at the outset then that we use terms like "race" and "white" and "black" or "African American" and in doing so run the risk of totalizing, essentializing, and reducing the subtle complexities of subjectivity and positioning with the blunt instruments of common speech. It is not our intention to do damage this way, but until a new discourse is invented that renders these terms obsolete, we do the best we can, placing these terms in quotes when needed to indicate their problematic usage.

2. The tendency to disconnect race from power relations. Critics of multiculturalism have attacked the tendency to celebrate difference while overlooking or denying the reality of the affective, nonrational politics of identity. Thomas West and Gary Olson's generative critique of the terms "negotiation" and "hybridity" in theoretical discourse offer a representative diagnosis. West and Olson challenge the commonplace use of "negotiation" as a rhetorical practice in writing classrooms because, they suggest, it seems to refer to a kind of "genteel" discussion, too often leaving out "the role and effect of emotion and passion" (150) in negotiation: "Dealing with

difference in the real world is not neat, contained, and rational; it is often messy, sprawling, and emotional" (151). They want to reimagine the negotiation of differences, including racial differences, "not merely as the trading of pre-given objects or positions but as a moment of self- and co-definition that may be turned to advantage" (152). Pushing farther to recognize that categories of difference, specifically race, are constructed, West and Olson go on to say that "hybridity" is the condition we are all already in, but "hybridization involves more, however, than eating ethnic foods or sharing exotic stories and experiences; such a position, typical of much uncritical academic multiculturalism, still posits ordinary elements that are merely traded or shared, but not 'translated,' often within highly asymmetrical power relations" (154).

In the context of asymmetrical power relations, played out in terms of racial and other differences in the writing classroom, we should take account of the affective dimension of teaching and learning. Lynn Worsham's intense scrutiny of "pedagogic violence" makes a persuasive case for the idea that while "critical social theories helped to shape an intellectual understanding of the practices and costs of othering," still, "the discourse of emotion is our primary education" (216). Worsham continues, "Grief, hatred, bitterness, anger, rage, terror, and apathy as well as emotions of self-assessment such as pride, guilt, and shame—these form the core of the hidden curriculum for the vast majority of people living and learning in a highly stratified capitalist society. This curriculum holds most of us so deeply and intimately and yet differently within its logic that our affective lives are largely immune to the legislative efforts of social critique and to the legislative gains of progressive social movements" (216). We know from experience how readily the affective, specifically emotional, dimension of learning and teaching can intrude on and upset, so to speak, the apparently smooth proceedings in any classroom. At such moments, we are reminded how much (else) can be at stake in the apparently straightforward exchanges that constitute educational practice.

3. The tendency to assign race as a category of difference signifying others, that is, to overlook "white" as a category of racial

identity that conveys significant privileges: "White people don't know they're white. / *Newspaper. Coffee. Gosh-whataday!*" So writes poet Tim Seibles in "The Case." Peggy McIntosh's widely known inventory of the "invisible" privileges of whiteness fills in the picture. An engagement with critical race theory leads one to see what gets left out, what is not talked about, what remains silenced. Silence about white racial identity is the norm in the white community. The essential ingredient in white skin privilege, therefore, is the option a white person possesses to avoid contending with race. This brings us to the relationship between race and racism. Discussions of race and racism are closely intertwined. If we think race is a power-infused category of social difference, racism is the process of extracting advantage from it. A significant material condition frames race and racism as grist for theory and practice in teaching writing: the persistent social self-segregation of white people. Measurements of residential location to television viewing preferences to perceptions of race relations show remarkable separation(s) of black and white people (and other groups) in our society. This insight holds true for an analysis of institutional practices as well as for individual teachers' critical reflections on their own actions and predispositions. "Racism is so deeply ingrained in the fabric of American institutions, it is easily self-perpetuating. All that is required to maintain it is business as usual" (Tatum 11).

Because racism is such a charged topic, we do well to carefully consider the meanings of this term. One common definition equates racism with prejudice, seated in individuals, that results from ignorance (if we believe "ignorance" is a necessary and sufficient explanation for hate crimes loosely defined). This view of racism portrays it as a psychological defect in individuals and ties its origins to individuals' (bad) intentions. Other definitions delink racism and individual intention, portraying racism as a system, that is, a system of advantage based on race (Tatum). Finally, some explorations of racism have begun to tease out relationships between individual actions and systemic or institutional racism. Barbara Trepagnier, for example, refers to "routine actions that go unquestioned by members of the dominant group which in some way discriminates against members of a racial or ethnic category" (144). Trepagnier thus points out how "well-meaning white people who are sensitive to race issues and who see themselves and are seen by others as not racist nevertheless perpetuate institutional racism, albeit unintentionally" (144).

So what has racism of the sort Trepagnier investigates got to do with teaching writing in school? According to NPR education reporter Claudio Sanchez, 90 percent of teachers today are white women. The majority of college writing teachers today lack the socialization that would lead to fluency in AAVE (Meier) or to a fluent understanding of the day-to-day cultural experiences of African American students. (Parallel claims can be made for other "Other" students.) Meier goes on to say, "Many of these teacher characteristics and strategies are rooted in African American oral and literary traditions and depend for their implementation on the kinds of linguistic abilities and insights fostered through socialization in those traditions" (106). While granting that non–African American teachers can be effective with African American students, Meier nonetheless asserts that lack of familiarity with African American oral and literary traditions makes it "extremely unlikely" that a teacher will "inspire African American students to reach their highest potential" (106). Adopting the first-person singular recasts the systemic view offered by Meier as an individual viewpoint: *I do not have sustained, informal interactions with people of color, nor much if any systemic help or ready cultural incentives to see the racialized aspect of my white self in a hierarchy of power.* Teachers in writing and composition classrooms who hold these attitudes can have devastating effects on students.

Arnetha

I learned about these effects from a student who shared the following story with me. It was a story that broke my heart. The story illustrated the student's experience with a teacher who did not have sustained informal interactions with people of color nor systemic help or cultural incentives to see the racialized aspect of her teaching on her students, which had a long-term effect on this student's perception of herself as a writer. This experience is shared by many AAVE-speaking students and illustrates one teacher's missed opportunity to establish a vibrant relationship with her student. The teacher was unwilling to frontally engage ethnically different ways of expressing ideas as a meaningful sociopsychological dimension of the writing classroom. While I have shared this story many times, I thought it deserved repeating here.

> [Students' oral comments on the tape recorder as she prepares to begin a writing assignment: "Okay, now I'm gonna be like telling a story, and I know what it's about and everything. I just don't know how to get it started. Okay, I'm just gonna write it out." The student begins writing:]

> *I'd been given an assignment by Mrs. Brakett, my fifth grade teacher to write a creative story. I decided to write a story about my shoe. Well, it wasn't actually my shoe but an evil shoe that had the power to make me extremely clumsy. After having completed the story, I discovered it was a masterpiece (I mean that in the most humble way).*

> *Unfortunately Mrs. Brakett didn't share in my enthusiasm. She praised the story, but said that the use of language was unsatisfactory because of the word "ain't." That one little word, that I only used once in the entire four pages of brilliant creativity "forced" her to give me a B-. Now I would've been able to understand her judgment if this had been a book report. But this was supposed to be a creative story. So it wasn't really me saying ain't, but it was my shoe saying ain't. Now I don't know about you, but I've never met a shoe with good grammar.*

> *I think it took me a good three years to finally put that behind me, and start taking creative risks again.*

In her oral discussion of the incident, the student concluded, "Well anyways, I think that was bad for my writing because I didn't want to express myself anymore. I started writing like what I thought the teacher would like instead of what I wanted to say. But I have no idea how to put that on paper." I have realized that such encounters contribute to many AAVE-speaking students' perceptions of themselves as poor writers. And, as much as I would like to think this happens only rarely in the academy, I have collected numerous narratives from AAVE-speaking students with similar story lines.

With current statistics indicating that approximately 75 percent of all black college students attend predominantly white colleges (Tatum 228), the realization sets in that more students than we would like to imagine have had a similar experience. Under these circumstances, we need to talk about what it means to be a writing teacher who is committed to activating the potentials for literacies that are present in the language resources and cultural resources of AAVE-speaking students. Though there has been much scholarly and public debate about multiculturalism in higher education, there is as yet little evidence to suggest wide-ranging, effective changes in writing and composition classrooms. Yet exciting theoretical work is being done to explore race, ethnicity, and identity from postmodern and postcolonial perspectives. Meanwhile, we observe the persistent underachievement of African American students as a continuing challenge to us as educators and as citizens (Spenner, Buchmann, and Landerman). At the college level, Claude Steele, for example, cites black-white differences in both drop-out rates and final grade-point averages as evidence of an achievement gap (110). We wonder how schools can continue to function for the benefit of some at the expense of others, and recognize a need to identify steps, however modest, toward changing this situation.

The Need for Storying

Critical race theory departs from mainstream legal scholarship by sometimes employing storytelling to "analyze the myths, presuppositions, and received wisdoms that make up the common culture about race and that invariably render blacks and other minorities one-down" (Delgado xiv). According to Barnes, "Critical race theorists . . . integrate their experiential knowledge, drawn from a shared history as 'other' with their ongoing struggles to transform a world deteriorating under the albatross of racial hegemony" (1864–65). Thus, the experience of oppressions such as racism or sexism is important for developing a CRT analytical standpoint. According to critical race theorists, to the extent that whites experience forms of racial oppression or feel its effects in the lives of those who are important to them, they may develop such a standpoint, too.

Almost everyone, at some time, has been unfairly judged by appearances. In this book, we have made a conscious decision to include our own personal narratives. In the discourse of our narratives, we find a counterpoint language to the authoritative professional discourses we interact with as teachers and scholars. In addition, we purposefully pose our narratives as counterpoints to one another. At the risk of essentializing and reducing our experiences, at the risk of overlooking that our narratives are "composed" rather than mirror images of our lives, we assert significance in the similarities (and differences) reflected in our stories. Additionally, we use narratives interwoven here to enact the multimodal, multidimensional thinking that we argue is the engine of change that leads to high teacher efficacy and reflective optimism. Incorporating personal narrative in the discussion opens a space where we explore and reflectively test our subjective beliefs about ourselves as teachers and where we can model what we hope readers will do.

To complement this subjective inquiry, we also incorporate stories from observations made in community-based organizations. We draw these stories from research on community-based educational organizations to inform our discussion of innovations in the use of pedagogy in writing and composition classrooms. Through the example of these organizations, we show how teachers may respect, value, and integrate into classroom practices our students' diverse cultural and linguistic backgrounds. We have seen in these organizations examples of how literacy learning events can be structured as highly participatory, energetic, and culturally informed engagement with personal growth in the context of community and communal involvement. The evidence is clear that in these sites, African American students who in the routines of traditional school feel shut out, cut off, disaffected, or neglected come alive and thrive. Vibrant engagement is the norm rather than the exception. Four sites are the focus of our stories: Operation "Together We Can Succeed," a job training program, Upward Bound, also a job training program, and Ujima, an Afrocentric rites-of-passage program, all located in an urban metropolitan community in a midwestern city; and Troop, a dance program for inner-city girls in a West Coast city. Participants in these groups represent a small portion of the many African American youths who come together in inner-city community-based organizations to take part in language, literacy, and learning related activities outside traditional classroom walls.

Some will sense a tendency in our writing, when we do address teachers, to talk to white teachers primarily or even exclusively. We realize that there are many teachers, including African American teachers, who are unaware of the untapped potentialities and rich linguistic resources AAVE-speaking students bring into the writing and composition classroom. These teachers are limited by their predisposed notions about language and unaware of the subtle features that characterize AAVE as a distinct and viable linguistic system. Generally, we have found that those who have not had experiences with AAVE rhetorical styles, linguistic creativity, uses of African and English words and grammatical constructions, or African American preaching, cannot help but fail to fully understand how these experiences influence the linguistic practices of AAVE-speaking students. Regarding the ability of these students to succeed academically, these teachers' sense of efficacy is often diminished. Realizing this, we address our comments to all teachers who may find them applicable.

Carried on in the lingering momentum of public controversy over Ebonics, or AAVE, or Black English, some will approach this book wondering whether this is a language or a dialect we are talking about, and whether we are advocating that teachers teach it. We'll get back to the latter issue. As to the former, according to Ball and Farr,

> the term "language" is used to refer to the abstract system underlying the collective totality of the speech and writing behavior of a community; the term "dialect" refers to a regional or socially distinctive variety of a language, iden-

tified by a particular set of words and grammatical structures. (436)

In this book, when we speak of Ebonics or AAVE or Black English, we draw on Smitherman's definition to refer to the totality of the Africanized form of American English, the language system used at some time to some degree by most African Americans today (*Talkin and Testifyin*). Encompassing a range of informal and formal registers and embodied in characteristic phonological, grammatical, lexical, and discourse patterns, in its totality as a language system, African American English possesses stylistic and speech-act components that define the linguistic competence of its speakers as participants in a long-lived and thriving cultural tradition. As educators claiming expertise in "language arts," we recognize this variety of English as part of the repertoire of linguistic resources that contribute to the communicative competence of the diverse members of our English-speaking community.

Conclusion

Moving beyond internalization is indeed a transformative process. It is the process of coming in generative ways to understand something independently of someone else's thoughts or understandings, yet building upon one's own thoughts and experiences. Teachers' mimicry of information is not enough to increase teacher efficacy. The Ann Arbor case suggests that the key to effective uses of language diversity in the classroom relates fundamentally to teachers' dispositions toward literacy—that is, it depends upon teachers' affective stance toward themselves, their work environment, and especially their culturally diverse students. More current research seems to confirm this. Addressing disposition as the most important variable, we have begun to push beyond internalization of knowledge about AAVE in the teacher education programs we are involved in (Ball, "Preservice"). In doing so, we have found ourselves observing the ways preservice teachers encounter and contextualize the pedagogical ramifications of language diversity. Some research suggests that preservice teachers who attempt to address the complex issues relating to this topic may do so by examining personal experiences of crossing borders from one speech community to another (Lardner; Okawa). Given these observations, we have begun to consider occasions for knowledge making that appear—not only in "extraprofessional" sites, but also within our own professional development sites where teachers become aware of their own culturally influenced dispositions toward literacy. To accomplish this, we find that teachers must begin to explore ways of talking about their own professional development that help them connect to parts of their experience that conventional academic, theoretical frameworks seem to silence.

In the next chapter, we take up the construct of efficacy, situating it in the specific "teaching moment" of reading a student composition that makes extensive use of AAVE discourse. The chapter moves to show how "knowledge about" AAVE—the usual remedy prescribed for teachers—in and of itself can leave a teacher short in terms of changing practice. Offering the counterexample of one teacher in a community-based organization, the chapter shows what high-efficacy, culturally informed teaching can look like.

2/ Knowledge and Efficacy: Teachers' Dispositions Toward Classroom Change

In this chapter, we would like to set forth an important claim: certain kinds of knowledge are critically important to writing and composition teachers who want to work successfully with students from diverse cultural and linguistic backgrounds. Acquiring an awareness of the need to gain that knowledge can be one of the major turning points in a teacher's journey to efficacy. We both can remember turning points in our own lives—points at which we came to a realization of the need to move from a tacit awareness of AAVE to a technical understanding of forms and functions of language—points at which we realized that we would need to understand perspectives on language and the knowledge needed to understand the attitudes of mainstream and academic Americans toward AAVE. For both of us, the heightened awareness resulted from unexpected encounters while in graduate degree programs.

Arnetha
In 1998, I began an article in the following way:

> Often, teachers encounter what Richard Wright refers to as a "secret language"—one that, although similar to academic English in many ways, is extended to include new words, new shapes, colors, order, and tempo. Wright expounds on his notion of a "secret language" by explaining that many lower- and working-class African Americans have developed a language that, among other things, "assigns to common, simple words new meanings" (1941, p. 40)—meanings that enable AAVE speakers to actually communicate in the presence of non-AAVE speakers without their being

aware of subtle meanings. Most teachers, *including many African-American teachers* [emphasis added], are unaware of the subtle features that characterize AAVE as a distinct linguistic system.

Although I grew up in an AAVE-speaking community, I was once one of those teachers who did not possess this explicit knowledge. While I had grown up using African American rhetorical styles, knew the African American preaching tradition well, and was adept at code switching as an academically successful student, I had only tacit knowledge of the underlying structure of AAVE, and I'd given little conscious thought to the reaction of mainstream Americans to the language used by AAVE speakers. This state of uninformed bliss was interrupted by an experience I had with one of my professors while working on my masters degree. This experience motivated me to actively seek out a more explicit, more nuanced understanding of language usage by diverse populations and to gain a more technical understanding of the rules that governed the use of AAVE in various contexts. Most importantly, I wanted to gain a better understanding of the attitudes held by mainstream and academic Americans toward the use of AAVE.

Near the close of my masters program, I began preparation to seek a job in the area of speech and language pathology. I requested a letter of recommendation from one of my professors who agreed without hesitation. Some weeks later, I found out that the professor had written words of commendation about my skills and knowledge as a speech pathologist; however, he closed the letter by alerting the potential employer that the only weakness he could speak of was my need to gain a clearer and more articulate command of Standard English. I felt betrayed by this professor. He had never expressed such a concern directly to me. And I realized that such a statement in a so-called letter of recommendation was the kiss of death in terms of my ever being offered a job. Hurt and dejected, I requested that the letter be removed from my career file, and I tucked this memory away in the back of my mind. I wish I had secured a copy of that letter, for it marked a turning point in my

professional life. It marked a loss of innocence. I had been forced
to learn about what Lisa Delpit refers to as an unspoken culture of
power that exists in the academy and in society in general ("Silenced"). Since few of my teachers had read the works of Franz
Fanon, W.E.B. DuBois, or Malcolm X, they were ill-equipped to educate me about the arbitrariness of the codes of the culture of power,
about the power relationships they represent, or the consequences for
me not knowing them. This lesson was learned through my experience with this professor, and the hidden curriculum that accompanies that lesson remains with me today. When I began doctoral studies years later, the stinging pain of that memory still lingered in my
subconscious mind, and I decided to complete a minor in linguistics so I could gain an explicit and deeply nuanced understanding
of AAVE and the research documenting the negative attitudes held by
many Americans regarding the vernacular and its users.

Ted

I went through two TA-training programs, worked in a writing center, and taught composition courses as a TA (later as a part-timer) at
three colleges, went back to graduate school and got halfway to
candidacy before I heard the terms "Black English," "Black English
Vernacular," or "African American English." I was a college writing teacher. I was twenty-nine years old. I had by then passed or
failed some hundreds of students.

Actually, I read the terms, since no one I spoke with was using
them. No one with whom I had sustained, informal interactions was
using AAVE, except for the crossover terms, lexical items that passed
for hip white slang among my lefty grad student crowd.

Then, in the space of a school year, I was introduced to Zora
Neale Hurston (*Their Eyes Were Watching God*), William Labov's
"The Logic on Nonstandard English," and James Sledd's "Bidialectalism: The Linguistics of White Supremacy." There was more,
to be sure. Bakhtin's "Discourse in the Novel." *Marxism and the
Philosophy of Language*. Brian Street's *Literacy in Theory and Practice*. Scribner and Cole. Shirley Brice Heath. And Geneva Smitherman's *Talkin and Testifyin*, which, because of its use of AAVE, was the

most engaging (with a close second going to Sledd, because his writing was funny, mean, and antiestablishment).

About this flurry of reading, I note two points. First, the sociolinguistic information about AAVE came mixed with analyses of hegemony, language, literacy, and schooling. For example, the margins of my now-quite-worn-out copy of *The Dialogic Imagination* are strewn with penciled references to Labov, Smitherman, and other sociolinguists. What grasp I gained of sociolinguistics of AAVE, in cluding its grammatical, phonological, and rhetorical aspects, I gained along the way of investigating power relationships manifested in practices of schooling, including my own practices as a writing teacher.

Second, the impulse that initially propelled me into this literature was hardly organic. It did not arise in me as felt need in a deep sense; that is, it did not result from immediate experience as something I was compelled to deal with. I could have gone on being a white guy speaking more or less Standard English, knowing little about AAVE except what I picked up from media and crossover, and done fine, I imagine, as a composition teacher. Except at the end of the seminar one night, the professor wrote "bidialectalism" on the edge of a very full chalkboard and mentioned in an offhand way that it would make a good topic for a paper, and I needed a topic for a paper. With the professor's further direction to "add Sledd" to my list of readings on bidialectalism, the dice were cast.

History has shown that even when teachers have this information about AAVE, the pedagogical applications remain unclear. And so, the question remains: Once teachers have a critical turning point, become aware of their need for explicit knowledge about AAVE, and they have taken steps to gain some knowledge in that area, how might they best support the aptitudes for literacy their AAVE-speaking students bring to the classroom? In chapter 1, we introduced the significance of "storying" as a method employed by practitioners of critical race theory to analyze, deconstruct, and reconstruct dominant narratives. In this chapter, we use this methodology to explore this question, probing what it means to be a (white) teacher of AAVE-speaking students—a white teacher who has taken the first two of these three steps. The stories we tell illustrate the need to move from gaining information *about* AAVE to efficacy and reflective optimism in classrooms. We offer them to analyze the situation of teachers who want to gain a better understanding of how they can help AAVE-speaking students achieve academic success in the writing classroom.

Keith Gilyard asks, "How do the socially constructed 'races' of teachers and students make a difference in the writing class?" ("Higher Learning" 47). With reference to race and racism present in writing classes when students speak or draw on AAVE in their writing, we see white privilege arbitrating the codes of power (Delpit, "Silenced") and the "everyday racism" (Trepagnier) of white supremacy. This white supremacy is most often manifested as silence, an inability to see the miseducative effects of well-intended pedagogical expectations, such as the expectation that AAVE speakers must code switch to Standard English in their speaking and avoid the use of AAVE rhetorical styles in their writing. Many scholars have observed the correlation of schooling with white hegemony (Fordham; Prendergast; Perry; Villanueva). Within pedagogical routine, facts about racism collide with facts about language diversity. When the socially constructed races of students and teachers appear to teachers to be peripheral, we see a need for teachers to become alert to limitations in their practice, their sense of efficacy, and the expectations they hold and communicate to their AAVE-speaking students.

Lisa's Paper

The following paper was written by an AAVE-speaking student. We call her Lisa. It was written for an assignment in ENG 101, the first of a two-course, first-year requirement at a midwestern urban commuter university. This course was structured around a set of four major assignments in a ten-week quarter, using a midterm portfolio and a final portfolio to gather the drafts and revisions of the major papers along with students' reflective writing on their own work. In the university curriculum, ENG 101 focuses on academic reading and writing, so its assignments ask students to offer engaged readings of challenging texts. The text used in Lisa's section was a custom-published anthology of readings selected by the instructor. At intervals during the term, students were given the opportunity to choose among the readings for their writing assignments. Lisa's paper is a response to an assignment that asked students to read two pieces, the story "Theft," by Joyce Carol Oates, and Alice Walker's essay "In Search of Our Mother's Gardens." Students were given the choice to compose an essay responding to either piece or to synthesize a response to both. Through whole-class discussions of each reading as well as informal, in-class conferencing and peer-group discussions on early drafts, the students were helped to formulate a thematic response. Within a set of general parameters (such as approximate essay length, purpose and audience, the need to form a specific response that is developed throughout the essay), the assignment left specifics for the students to work out. The student writes (paragraphs are numbered by the authors for ease of discussion later):

1. "Theft," by Joyce Carol Oates tells the story of a girl name Marya who has something taken from her. In the beginning Marya had her favorite pen and wallet stolen from her drawer. She did eventually get her wallet but her pen she didn't see anymore. Imogene who's another girl in this story has nothing taken from her. Yet, she becomes Marya's friend and eventually tries to steal her image.

2. The meaning of "Theft" in this story can be explained in two different ways. One was when Marya had her wallet and pen taken from her. The other was when Imogene her supposed to be friend, tries to take away Marya's image. It's one thing to steal someone's belongings. It's another when you steal someone's image, identity or reputation. And this story "Theft" is a good example of both.

3. Imogene was the most popular around the campus. Marya was not. Imogene had nice clothes and was very pretty. Marya on the other hand was not. Marya did not have fancy clothes and she wasn't as pretty as Imogene was. What Marya did want was the kind of things Imogene possessed.

And there's nothing wrong with that. I would want to have those nice things myself. But what seemed to be the problem was that Imogene pretended to be Marya's friend.

4. See a person like Imogene is phony to me. The reason I say this is for the simple fact that Imogene would only want to be around Marya when no one was around. When you think about it Marya and Imogene really couldn't be friends. They seemed to be going in opposite directions. For example, Imogene would ridicule Marya in front of all their other friends. Now if Imogene was a real friend she wouldn't do or say things that would hurt Marya's image. I personally know of people who had tried to do me the same way. I don't know which one hurts the most. Especially, if you're the kind of person that basically stay to yourself. Somewhat like myself. It makes you mad when people try and do things of this nature to you.

5. As, I mention before on how Imogen would say things about Marya in front of their friends. She was also the type of person who would spread a rumor around. But what happens is those things like that catch up with you eventually. You can't just go around treating people anyway that you will like. You should treat people the way you want to be treated. And I personally feel that Imogene wasn't that kind of a person.

6. Imogene, I feel didn't know any better. The reason I say this is because she would laugh about the little smart statements she made about Marya. And later on when no one was around she would apologize. There was this one incident that happened between the two that was really interesting. Imogene one day gave Marya her favorite coat. She came over to Marya's room and said "I don't want the coat any longer because I have so many. Anyway here it is; I think it would look nice on you." (pg. 445)

7. Although Marya thought that Imogene was giving it to her for the sake of Marya having it she was wrong. Because when Marya did not do the things that Imogene

wanted her to do she would tell all their other friends that "Marya borrowed money from her and the coat. Because she didn't have one of her own and she was so poor." (pg. 452)

8. Now if that's not a friend I don't know what is. I don't see how Marya was putting up with this pathetic behavior of her so called friend Imogene. I personally feel that what goes around comes around and eventually Imogene will get exactly what is coming to her. I really feel bad for people like Imogene because of the simple fact, they don't know how to treat people. And in this day and time we need the help of each other. So that's why I say it sometimes benefit you to treat people the right way.

9. Imogene had gotten to the point of starting a rumor about "Marya had been attacked—that is raped—in a black neighborhood near the foot of Tower Hill." (pg. 451) And that's all Marya need was for her to totally destroy her reputation around the school. Now the way it turned out was that Marya felt that she had to pay Imogene back for all the rotten things she had said or even done to ruin her overall image around the campus.

10. Yet, Imogene succeeded at spreading the rumor. She got what was coming to her in the end. Marya approached her so called friend, in essence to resolve the problem, but it didn't work. I think most normal people would try to talk it out before fighting occurs. But that didn't work for this Imogene character, because she still tried to pretend that she never meant anything by it. You know as well as I know that you can't just say anything about people and they find out it was a bunch of lies, and expect them not to be happy. I personally know I would be very upset.

11. Well anyway, it led up to a physical incident between Marya and Imogene. However, Marya came out on top. The reason is that she wanted to show her friend Imogene how it feels to have something taken away from you. I know as far as I'm concern, I wouldn't want my reputation ruined or my identity, by someone I thought or wanted to be my

friend. So, therefore Imogene got what she deserved. And that was no better treatment for her.

12. It was just like I mention before: you can't treat people anyway. You can't say what you want to say about people and expect them not to respond in some way or another. It's the simple fact that Marya felt that she was having her identity taken away. And she was. You don't have to have something material taken from you for it to be called theft.

13. Let me say, that everything taken from you is not always material. It could be something more personal like your image or identity. See it's one thing to steal someone's things. It's another when you start dealing with people's image, identity, or reputation. And when you don't treat other people the right way, then people will start treating you in the same way. Because what goes around comes around. And that was the case in this story "Theft," by Joyce Carol Oates.

This paper has been used as a sample in numerous college courses and staff-development workshops. It has served in workshops that bring high school and college writing teachers together to examine assessment issues in students' transition from high school to college. Typically, the responses generated in these venues have fallen in the "deficit" category (see Scott for a discussion of deficit responses to students' uses of AAVE in their writing). For example, recent discussion generated the following comments: "The writer cannot write properly." "There is a conversational tone as to a friend, rather than to a professor." Among the teaching points, the following were named: "You shouldn't use informal language." "Generate an actual thesis and develop it beyond the obvious." "Examples should support your argument." "Work on sentence structure. Vary it, so it is not so awkward." "Be consistent in use of 'I,' 'you,' point of view." "Elaborate on quotes." "Proofread." Participants in these discussions tend to evaluate the paper negatively, and the paper's organizational features and level of formality (register) consistently draw the most attention.

Most teachers, including many African American teachers, are unaware of the subtle features that characterize AAVE as a distinct linguistic system. Generally, those who have not had socialization experiences with AAVE rhetorical styles, traditions of linguistic creativity, uses of African and English words and grammatical constructions, or African American preaching fail to fully understand that these experiences influence the linguistic practices of AAVE-speaking students. Sarah Michaels refers to some of these practices when describing some of the oral strategies African Americans use, including implicit linking of topics in the discourse, shifts in focus, and topic relationships that must be inferred by the message receiver. Teachers encounter these linguistic practices every day when they serve students who are native speakers of AAVE and many wonder how they can best evaluate or respond to these students' written texts. Although linguists and anthropologists have assured teachers that AAVE is a logical language with systematic patterns of expression, many educators have trouble seeing and appreciating these patterns. Instead of patterns, they see only mistakes; instead of efficacies—powerful resources that are part of an oral tradition that students can use to produce an effect—they see errors. This is sometimes understandable since the writing of AAVE speakers, like the writing of any group of students, may indeed contain errors—features of language or organizational patterns that are, from any perspective, mistakes that need to be corrected. But sometimes what seems like a error may be more than that. It may be part of a linguistic code that has considerable social or cultural value.

Variations in the writing patterns of many diverse students are not random but are rather influenced by the patterns of the students' spoken linguistic system in predictable ways. Of course, students, although members of culturally and linguistically diverse communities, are individuals, and their individuality will also be reflected in their writing patterns. Some of the variations in students' writing, therefore, will be attributable to cultural influences while others will not. As pointed out in Ball ("Evaluating"), it is the teacher's responsibility to distinguish between these kinds of variations based on the teacher's knowledge of the student's cultural and linguistic practices and patterns.

Ball leaves teachers and evaluators with two questions: How can they distinguish between random instances of inept writing and valid, predictable, and systematic patterns that are a part of students' cultural and linguistic backgrounds? And how can they best work with students whose writing displays these patterns? We can all agree that our ultimate goal is to enable all students to express their ideas in a wide range of registers and discourse styles. But the question remains, how to accomplish this goal without causing some students to feel negative about the linguistic resources they bring from home?

Significant scholarship exists showing the use of AAVE discourse patterns in essays written for school (Ball, "Cultural Preferences"; Ball, "Text Design Patterns"; Richardson, "Rhetorical"; Richardson, *African American*; Smitherman, "Blacker"; Canagarajah). We see this way of reading demonstrated in Valerie Balester's *Cultural Divide: A Study of African-American College Level Writers,* which alerted us to some of the personal politics that may confront African American students as they negotiate their learning and their identities in the university writing class. In one instance, Balester portrays a student who in oral interaction in the classroom is characteristically self-confident, even aggressive. In her essays, however, this same student was described by her European American raters as lacking engagement with her subject; her writing seemed tentative and distant. Balester argues that the teaching issue raised by this student's underachievement in her writing requires finding ways to help her tap the power of her persona in oral discourse and infuse her writing with it. Balester analyzes the written and spoken discourse of the African Americans in her study, drawing on research concerning African American Vernacular discourse as well as a theory of social identity construction in considering the way writers in university courses may attempt to "use language to assume an ethos, by modeling their style of speaking on their stereotyped conceptions of the groups with which they wish to be identified" (xi).

Some scholars have critiqued Balester's study for taking for granted and leaving uncontested the goal of assimilating seemingly "outsider" students into the voice of academic discourse (Royster and Williams, "History"). This line of critique further proposes that *Cultural Divide* too readily equates AAVE with a fixed conception of a unitary black identity (Royster and Williams, "A Response"). Both criticisms have some validity. Nevertheless, we find Balester's research helpful in pointing to the tension between teachers' constructs of appropriate voice in academic writing, and the voice(s) students adopt in their writing. Such a focus shifts attention from exclusive concern with discrete uses of AAVE or discourse patterns toward catching a sense of the overall performance of the paper. Reading such a text, the goal becomes noticing how its gestures, including the uses of AAVE and oral-based discourse, come together to produce specific effects—some of which may fit the writer's purposes (including the construction of an ethos), some of which may unintentionally subvert or undercut those intentions.

The following analysis shows the systematic use of AAVE and oral-based features throughout the student paper presented above.

> Two word-level errors in the essay: typos, probably: "anyway" for "any (which) way" (para. 12), and "Imogen" for "Imogene" (para. 5).
>
> AAVE rendering of verb forms: an omitted final -s in "stay" (para. 4) and "benefit" (para. 8); omitted final -ed in "mention" (para. 5), "concern" (para. 11), and "mention" again (para. 12). Rickford describes research that tries to determine the role of dialect interference in errors with Standard English. "We have lots of anecdotal evidence that Ebonics is somehow relevant to these errors," he writes.
>
>> But Labov . . . reported that an African American legal transcriber in Chicago made many errors with SE plural s-marking and few with verbal (third person singular) s-marking. This pattern is the opposite of what we would have predicted from the frequency with

which these features occur in spontaneous Ebonics
speech. (16)

Rickford states, "as far as I know, we do not have systematic scientific analyses of the extent to which the errors that
Ebonics speakers make in speaking and writing sε reflect
interference or transfer from Ebonics (in terms of which
features are affected and how often)" (15–16).

Except for some errors in the use of punctuation, for
example, missing or misplaced use of commas, the essay
is free of mechanical errors. Allowing for AAVE syntactical
features, the essay has no errors in grammar.

AAVE and Oral-Based Idioms

Para. 2   "Imogene her supposed to be friend"
Para. 4   "See, a person like Imogene is a phony to me."
           "The reason I say this is for the simple fact that"
           "I personally know of people who had tried to do
           me the same way"
           "Especially, if you're the kind of person that
           basically stay to yourself."
Para. 5   "As, I mention before on how Imogene would say
           things"
           "the type of person who would spread a rumor
           around."
Para. 8   "Now if that's not a friend I don't know what is"
           "I personally feel that what goes around comes
           around."
           "feel bad for people like Imogene because of the
           simple fact"
           "in this day and time we need to help each other"
           "So that's why I say it sometimes benefit you to
           treat people"
Para. 9   "And that's all Marya need was for her to totally
           destroy her reputation."
Para. 10   "You know as well as I know that you can't just say

anything about people and they find out it was a
bunch of lies, and expect them not to be happy."

Para. 11 "Well, anyway . . ."

Para. 12 "It was just like I mention before: you can't treat
people anyway."

Para. 13 "Let me say, that everything taken from you"
"Because what goes around comes around."

As we trace the writer's use of AAVE and oral-based idioms
in this essay, we also need to take notice of phrases that
seem to strike a different key. Three examples should be
sufficient to alert us: the phrase "ridicule Marya" in para.
4; the phrase in para. 10, "in essence to resolve the problem"; and the phrase in para. 11, "a physical incident."
These stand as much more formal locutions than other
phrases used by this writer, such as "they find out it was a
bunch of lies" or "people who had tried to do me the same
way," and this should be noted as well.

Still, what impresses us most is the ubiquity of AAVE and
oral-based idioms in the paper. In the context of other
observable features of this text, even without having extra-
textual cues to draw on such as familiarity with the student-
writer and the scene in which she composed, a teacher has
strong evidence to conclude that the choices are purpose-
ful. In other words, a teacher has evidence to warrant thinking about responding to this writer by working to understand
her choice to use AAVE and oral-based idioms to the extent
she has. It will do no good to regard their appearance in her
text as errant or misguided or accidental. They are one of
the defining stylistic features of the whole utterance.

Organization: Patterning and Devices
The essay is an exposition with interpretive commentary
on the content of the story. The essay follows the order of
the story straight through from beginning to end, using key
events in the plot of the story to define its structure. The

key events referenced are in para. 3, the beginning of the friendship between Imogene and Marya; para. 4, Imogene's ridiculing of Marya; para. 6, Imogene giving Marya the coat; para. 9, Imogene starting a rumor that Marya had been raped in a black neighborhood; and para. 11, the "physical incident" between Marya and Imogene. These incidents provide a cue for Lisa to extrapolate or "speak on" the meaning, incorporating references to communal experiences and to her personal experiences of the hardships of friendship betrayed. This expository essay adheres to the research findings of Ball ("Organizational Patterns") when Lisa uses what Ball refers to as narrative interspersion—the insertion of narratives within the context of the expository text in the tradition of the African American oral tradition in order to achieve particular effects or purposes. For example, in para. 4, Lisa offers her own testimony, referring to personal experience: "I personally know of people who had tried to do me the same way. I don't know which one hurts the most. Especially, if you're the kind of person that basically stay to yourself. Somewhat like myself. It makes you mad when people try and do things of this nature to you." Into her ongoing exposition of the theme of "Theft," these lines interject a personal referent, punctuating the unfolding analysis. They suggest, albeit indirectly, the outlines of a story from direct experience, experience that lends credibility to Lisa's discourse. The essay also coheres as an extended act of signifyin' by Lisa who, as in the lines just cited, obliquely refers to the hurtful behaviors of "supposed to be" friends.

The essay is highly patterned. Lisa uses repetition as a patterning device. The first sentence and the last read almost like mirror images of each other: "'Theft,' by Joyce Carol Oates tells the story of a girl name Marya who has something taken from her." "And that was the case in this story 'Theft,' by Joyce Carol Oates." The essay's key idea, used to open up the idea that "Theft" has two meanings, is introduced in para. 2 with the reference to theft of "someone's image, identity, or reputation." Variations of this phrase appear again in para. 9, para. 11, and para. 13, the conclusion.

Finally, a well-conceived use of transition devices at the beginning of paragraphs helps move the essay from point to point. For example:

Para. 4   See a person like Imogene is phony to me.

Para. 5   As, I mention before on how Imogen would say things about Marya in front of their friends.

Para. 10   Yet, Imogene succeeded at spreading the rumor.

Para. 11   Well anyway, it led up to a physical incident between Marya and Imogene.

Para. 12   It was just like I mention before: you can't treat people anyway.

Para. 13   Let me say, that everything taken from you is not always material.

We presented deficit responses and assessments this paper has generated from writing teachers and preservice teachers, and we have begun to answer these responses with a detailed analysis showing the use of AAVE-based discourse features. We believe teachers need to gain knowledge of AAVE and AAVE-based discourse features. We also believe teachers need to regard these features as potentially powerful rhetorical resources for students' academic writing. Familiarity with AAVE discourse patterns should help teachers more effectively assess their students' ability to shape written discourse for varying audiences and purposes. We include "mid-process" assessment as especially important, so that teachers become better able to read drafts with a more discerning eye in helping students toward goals of academic literacy and writing proficiency. Of course, we acknowledge our experiences working with teachers and preservice teachers: sometimes identifying instances of AAVE discourse features did not improve teachers' overall responses to the paper. For these teachers, identification of AAVE features meant essentially telling the writer to code switch or "translate" her or his ideas into Standard

English and/or "appropriate" academic discourse (cf. Howard, "Great Wall").

We have noticed also that for many teachers, identifying features of AAVE in sample texts like this one does not in and of itself help them to figure out how to respond in a way that will facilitate some kind of productive revision and equip students with additional strategies toward competency as skilled writers. Building on our own experiences working with diverse students in academic settings and synthesizing recent scholarship in composition, we believe what is needed is a stance for reading that accepts the shifts in voice or register where AAVE features are used. We think this stance of reading would regard these moments not as unfortunate signs of the writer's lack of mastery of academic conventions but as potentially significant formal elements in the composition and perhaps a key to its strength. This stance of reading acknowledges that some important dimensions of intended meaning probably cannot be "translated" from AAVE to Standard English. In other words, an important element of an essay's potential for impact on an audience results from the choice of using AAVE-based discourse features such as those detailed above.

Teachers who lack any familiarity with the cultural-rhetorical resources their AAVE-speaking students bring with them to the classroom are at a distinct disadvantage when it comes to skillfully responding to their students' writing. Our effort to reconstruct the responses of teachers to writing like that found in Lisa's paper brings us to examine (later in this chapter) the approach taken by one teacher in a community-based organization who exhibits a high sense of efficacy and reflective optimism in regard to his students.

We are helped to this view by scholarship from compositionists that (a) pushes toward pedagogical application and (b) moves away from "essentializing" AAVE-speaking students' writing voices by (c) focusing attention on the intermingling of discourses. In this context, teachers can form responses that will support this student in her efforts to gain fluency in conventions of academic writing while at the same time recognizing and reinforcing strategic uses of rhetorical stances in African American culture.

Responding to Mary Louise Pratt's call for "pedagogical contact zones," Joseph Harris underlines her emphasis on classrooms that seek "not to erase linguistic and cultural differences but to examine them" (118). Harris argues that Pratt remains vague "about how one goes about making sure [diverse] voices get their say" (118). Harris concludes by citing our need "to learn not only how to articulate our differences but how to bring them into useful relation with each other" (120). As a practical matter, Harris asserts, these issues need to be examined, analyzed, and reattempted in "the details of classroom work" (121), which include "how teachers set up and respond to what students have to say" (121). Toward this end, however, Catherine Prendergast considers an "agenda of socialization" to be "insufficient for enfranchisement" (50). Moreover, in reference to AAVE as one language found in classrooms as cultural contact zones, Prendergast cites critical race theorists who reconstruct "voice" in terms of double consciousness. "It is not tied to a posited 'oral' culture of people of color, nor to the assertion of any existence of a separate black English," Prendergast argues (40). Instead, the discourse of double consciousness "embodies contradiction, ambiguity, and even irrationality as it reflects the experience of discrimination in a society which professes to be colorblind" (40).

Prendergast is interested in problematizing assimilationist teaching (38), and she examines the textual practices of critical race theorists such as Patricia Williams, Derek Bell, Mari Matsuda, and others in order to show by contrast how composition's "colonial sensibilities" might be reflected in our own texts as well as the texts of our students. Key to her analysis is the pressure placed by systemic racism on the available means of persuasion: "So much of racism in this society is unconscious—the norm rather than a deviation from the norm—there is no language with which to expose and punish it. . . . The words just aren't there" (39). Thus, while race may frequently appear "as a category to delineate cultural groups that will be the focal subjects of research studies," Prendergast argues that in composition, "the relationship of race to the composing process is seldom fully explored" (36). Prendergast defers pedagogical applications of these insights, leaving that burden for others to take up. Thinking about how we as teachers can productively respond to students' uses of AAVE discourse patterns in their writing seems like a good place to begin that work. Of course, having some familiarity with AAVE and AAVE discourse features is a prerequisite. In *Defending Access*, Thomas Fox lays out a persuasive case that as college writing teachers committed to the potentials of truly multicultural education, we need to take measures "in the meantime" to ensure that we "stop doing harm": "as writing teachers, we are institutionally positioned to gatekeep, to do harm. To create access, we must go against the grain" (17).

Mary Ann's Letter

So what happens when teachers take up the burden of exploring the relationship between race and the composing process? What happens to teachers' constructs of knowledge when the theoretical concepts of teaching across racial or cultural comfort zones fail to yield clear changes in practice? Christine Sleeter has shown, for example, how teachers in her study resisted and eventually abandoned a staff-development project focused on thinking about school as a racially marked ideological space. At such a juncture, teachers' encounters with high-powered theory were insufficient to produce a transformed outlook, much less a transformed pedagogy. To understand this situation, we find it helpful to think in terms analogous to David Bartholomae's refiguration of the composing process, seeing teacher development "not as an internal psychological drama . . . but as an accommodation of the discursive positions (the roles or identifications) that can produce" a writing teacher (9). What we refer to as a teacher's sense of efficacy and reflective optimism becomes an index of the success of these accommodations.

The sociological construct of identity negotiation has been an important part of composition theory for fifteen years, and a forceful trope in learning theory more generally for much longer. In composition studies, much of the attention to identity negotiations in the classroom has focused on students, making visible the varied locations that students occupy in their composition courses, and, crucially, drawing attention to students' own evaluations or dispositions toward writing and school (Brooke). Because identity negotiation is a dynamic process, identity is ever in flux; it is never finished off in an act of self-definition. As we interact with others, we play roles that preexist us and work to shape our self-understanding. Students entering our writing classrooms are occupying institutional as well as social and personal locations, and the construct of identity negotiation allows teachers to take into account these locations in student learning. We contend that teachers face our own negotiations as we enter the writing classroom. When we shift the focus to teachers, the construct of identity negotiation helps us examine how the ideology of race shapes our sense of self, including our professional identity as educators.

Noting that "as professionals, we are all racialized, gendered, and political subjects in classroom space" (27), Royster and Taylor call on writing teachers to examine "the relationship between who we are and the work we make possible for our students" (31). Among many factors (including institutional location, a point we will return to in chapter 3), race, gender, and class shape "who I am as a teacher in my classroom" (32). Royster and Taylor call on teachers to reconsider how institutional, social, and personal identities together inform our understanding of ourselves as "writing professionals" with consequences for how we construe the literacy possibilities of all of our students (44). Scholars in writing studies have taken up the nexus of race and pedagogy from a variety of perspectives. Harkening back to debates about bidialectalism from the 1960s, Jerrie Cobb Scott notes the "recycling of deficit pedagogy in basic writing and other programs," linking it both to "technocratic definitions of literacy" and "attitudes that pervasively but persistently resist change" (47). Scott refers to this constellation of attitudes and practices as "uncritical dysconsciousness" and defines it as the "acceptance, sometimes unconsciously, of culturally sanctioned beliefs that, regardless of good intentions, defend the advantages of insiders and the disadvantages of outsiders" (47). Calling on teachers to reconsider not only the content of the writing curriculum but also "the attitudes that ultimately determine how the content will be delivered," Scott argues that we will need to reflect on "how our individual processes of self-identity interplay with the self-identity of students" (50–51).

Familiarity with oral and literate traditions is one of degree; teachers may be more or less "familiar" with these traditions with more or less consequence for their patterns of interaction in their classrooms. How familiar must one be? And if one lacks familiarity, how is that overcome? What motivates this overcoming? From whence does the commitment come? As an example, we present an assignment by one of our students. Mary Ann was a European American woman in an English course called "Language Diversity and Teaching English." Here, Mary Ann speaks through a reflective letter written at the conclusion of the course. Mary Ann was a tutor in the writing center. The course was designed to prepare writing and composition teachers for the challenges and possibilities that lie before them in universities or secondary-school English language arts classrooms. This future freshman composition teacher, in fact, has a knowledge base about the features of AAVE-speaking students. In her concluding reflections on the course, she composed a letter to her teacher, excerpts of which follow:

Dear Ted:

Over the last eleven weeks, I have had many thoughts coursing through my mind, not the least of which is personal writing, hence the form of this essay. Perhaps the subject of personal writing seems disconnected from the subject of language diversity, and the subject of this class, but I think they are connected in a most important way. When a composition teacher encourages students to write a personal essay, the teacher should expect writing samples from many different forms of English. If the teacher demands only standard English, he or she takes the personal out of the writing. The problem with my writing is that it has no "personal-ity" what-so-ever, at least not a natural, unforced one. So, I create something artificial, like a letter. . . .

My response to the class, or more specifically its second half, is despair. In your assignment for this second essay, you say that the "latter half of our course has been concerned with the application of social linguistic knowledge about Black English, language and literacy to the teaching of English," and you wanted comment on the significant ways that Keith Gilyard's Voices of the Self and Lisa Delpit's Other People's Children "shed light on teaching in a multicultural society." But after reading these two books and listening to some of the comments in class, especially during the presentations, I am more in the dark than ever before. I keep asking myself, "is there anything I, as a middle-class, white, Anglo-Saxon female, can do besides feel guilty for being born as I was?" The general answer out there seems to be "NO!"

When I tell friends and acquaintances that I am studying Black English, I am often confronted with "When my family came over from the old country, they learned to speak English. Why can't these people do the same thing?" I never quite knew how to answer them, but now Gilyard's "immigrant-success fallacy" has given me a logical response: "Your ancestors could just assume the clothing and the language of the dominant group and live undetected in its midst. African Americans cannot blend in so easily." From an educational aspect, Gilyard also points out that mastery of the dialect of the dominant group does not in and of itself lead to outstanding academic progress. Nor can one instructional method alone guarantee student success, because proponents of any one method of instruction forget to include the family's role in instruction.

For his own part, Gilyard credits his success to his family, specifically his sister, and not to his teachers. . . . The message I got from Gilyard's book was stay out of the way and try not to do too much damage. So much for what a teacher can do. Delpit's book did, however, focus on what a teacher could do: more harm than good. . . . While I agree that it is helpful to see where and how educators are failing, I also think some positive role models would be just as helpful, particularly a few white role models. I think that finding white role models is important because of the statistic Delpit herself points out: "the current number of teachers from nonwhite groups threatens to fall below 10 percent" (105). If more

than 90 percent of future teachers are white, they need to be
educated on how to be better teachers of diverse cultures rather
than discouraged from being teachers at all. Delpit, in trying, I
suppose, to educate future teachers by showing past and current
teachers' mistakes, has no shortage of examples. Delpit begins with
her "culture of power" (24) and ends with the clash between
school culture and home culture (167). But Delpit's attitude seems
to be re-enforcing the culture clash rather than reforming it. The
term "well-meaning white liberal educator," which is used in one
form or another in several places, feels like a slap in the face to
me. . . . I can honestly say that after reading Geneva Smitherman's
Talkin and Testifyin and James Paul Gee's Social Linguistics and
Literacies, I do have a deep appreciation for, not just a tolerance
of, language diversity. Many of the historical and linguistic
features of Black English that Smitherman enumerated were very
enlightening for me. Showing the ties that Black English has to
Western African languages really legitimized the dialect in my
mind. Gee, for his part, raised my consciousness to a new level.
His idea of Discourse (with a Capital D, meaning more than
language) was and still is fascinating to me. But is this apprecia-
tion of diversity enough? . . .

It seems to me that this subject of language diversity is as much
emotional as it is academic, so, on that note, I hope you will
understand and be tolerant of my diverse response.

    Sincerely,
    Mary Ann

Mary Ann's letter reveals another example of what was reported in Ann Arbor: exposing teachers to information about AAVE will not in and of itself lead to improved efficacy. On one hand, it may not serve to open up teachers to their own unconscious negative racial beliefs and attitudes. Nor will it help them to understand their own racialized identity and relative position in a society that distributes privilege along a power hierarchy defined in part by racial difference. On the other hand, simply knowing about signifyin', styling, or boasting, for example, does not necessarily give teachers a new teaching paradigm to implement in the writing classroom. Socio-linguistic information may initiate transformation in a teacher's thinking, but it cannot be the only ingredient. Similarly, to the extent a writing teacher has immersed herself in the literature, socio-linguistic information about AAVE exists in dialogue with other discourses that together constitute the conceptual vocabulary of pedagogical theory. Actively reflecting on and interpreting her work in the classroom—her students, herself as a writing teacher, her constructs of literacy—involves a dialogue that traverses the boundary between professional and personal categories of experience.

What is needed is a vocabulary within which teachers may address their own affective responses to students' writing, including low expectations and disrespect, which are the chief means through which pedagogical racism is manifested. When we acknowledge the presence of unconscious negative racial stereotypes as an issue in pedagogical theory, we immediately confront the need for a language—a set of terms—and a context—a set of roles and relationships—with which to move forward. We will not find it in the curriculum guides written by the state, nor the policy formulations of "education governors." We need a new story.

Teacher Efficacy and Reflective Optimism

To shape greater teacher success or efficacy, the crucial variable is the teacher's stance toward his or her role as a teacher. Pang and Sablan show that teachers' sense of efficacy goes down when they work with students of color with whom they have little experience interacting. In terms of the influence of institutional identity, an additional finding in the research is the effect that professional socialization seems to have on teacher efficacy. Survey research conducted by Pang and Sablan suggests that "preservice teachers [were] more positive about their ability to reach African American children than inservice teachers . . . We believe socialization of new teachers by the system is so strong that they come to emulate negative feelings about African American students which they find in their more experienced colleagues" (14). One barrier to effective

teaching of AAVE-speaking students is negative attitudes, com-
pounded by lack of information about the language system and effective techniques for teaching language skills, all of which is manifested in an unwillingness to adapt teaching styles to students'
aptitudes and needs. A second barrier to change, though, is lack of
alternative models. Teachers' subjective perceptions of their work
are difficult to change due to lack of role models. Smitherman notes
that changing language attitudes means changing worldview. This
can be a very difficult task. That being the case, we need to think
more carefully about the dynamics of that change.

In education and sociolinguistics, there is abundant literature
describing teachers who excel with African American students and
literature that recommends the establishment of teacher preparation
programs that better prepare teachers to meet the needs of diverse
students (Grant; Ladson-Billings). Scholarship in composition
leaves some gaps in regard to teacher preparation, yet Wendy
Bishop's study of teacher change stands as one exemplar. Focusing
on the way teachers selectively adapted a whole-language writing
workshop approach to teaching basic writing, Bishop maps the
public/private binaries that mediated pedagogical changes these
teachers adopted. Asking, "How do teachers, and individuals, create
and maintain social, professional, and personal identities?" (129),
Bishop concludes that the teachers she studied "reflected an interactive process which included affective, cognitive, *and* pedagogical development in patterns that were not easily isolated" (130). They fil-
tered the whole-language writing workshop approach they were
taught "through personal constructs that affected the way their classrooms actually developed" in the subsequent school year (130). Citing R. B. Parker's construct of public and private theories, Bishop
traces how teachers responded, resisted, assimilated, and transformed
the authoritative discourse of public theories they encountered with
the internally persuasive discourse of their private theories. As Bishop
makes clear, the negotiation of public and private theories coexisted
with, and provoked a renegotiation of, the private and professional
identities. According to Bishop, private identities "included teachers' being parents and/or spouses, and many had non-teaching or

non-graduate school identities—as creative writers, or bicycle or music enthusiasts, sportspersons, and so on" (134).

Other compositionists have turned to teacher narratives to plumb the connections among public/professional and private/personal domains of teacher knowledge. Joy Ritchie and David Wilson turn to professional autobiographies to examine how personal and professional identities become integrated: written portrayals of teachers' lives serve to "illuminate . . . the inextricable connections between . . . personal and professional development" (6). The examples they offer range across several cultural and ideological boundaries, including class, gender, sexual orientation, and ethnicity. Ritchie and Wilson's work makes explicit use of the concept of ideology as part of its analysis, noting the constraints on teacher change resulting from belief systems that inform institutional routines and so shape teachers' sense of professional identity.

The "ecology" of teacher efficacy offered by Ashton and Webb portrays a matrix organized into four spheres of influence and interaction. The first is the classroom, including student characteristics such as perceived ability to learn, teacher characteristics and beliefs about their role, class size, and the nature of the activity in the classroom. The second sphere is the school, including size, demographics, home-school relations as a factor in school achievement, including discontinuity between modeling and problem-solving, information processing modes; and discontinuity resulting from racial and socioeconomic differences. The third sphere includes social structures external to the school, exemplified in characteristics of the school district and mandates for education resulting from judicial or legislative action. The fourth sphere is constituted of "basic cultural beliefs." These include conceptions of the learner and the role of the teacher, for example, or reference to concepts like intelligence and ability as innate and therefore unchangeable characteristics of learners. This cultural frame also includes narratives that encourage teachers to blame students for failing to learn and the role of education as the path to advancement and the gateway to opportunities (17–34). The construct of efficacy represents teacher knowledge as dynamic, changing over time in relation with factors within the classroom and outside the classroom walls.

A teacher's sense of efficacy varies according to factors that include curricular and pedagogical know-how, extra-professional experiences, and the types of exposure an individual experiences in order to facilitate their development of efficacy. In *Self-Efficacy: The Exercise of Control*, Bandura identifies four sources that inform an individual's sense of efficacy: mastery experience, vicarious experience, verbal/social persuasion, and affective/physiological arousal.

Enactive mastery experience. The efficacy source of enactive mastery experience is defined as an individual's past successes and failures. Efficacy develops as a result of personal experiences that resulted in successes and failures. This source includes the person's appraisal of the effect of an outcome or a process or how she/he performed. Enactive mastery experience is the most influential source of efficacy information because it provides the "most authentic evidence" of whether the individual is capable of successfully completing the task (80). Many studies suggest that enactive mastery experience is the most powerful and salient efficacy source for many teachers. They also suggest that mastery experience is the type of experience that teachers value most. Accordingly, teachers report that classroom experiences are their most valuable teacher education experiences.

Vicarious experience. Vicarious experiences are those in which the skill in question is modeled by someone else. Bandura pointed out that, in some instances, vicarious experience can subordinate mastery experience when a person fails but remains efficacious because she/he sees another person succeeding in a similar situation. The degree to which the observer identifies with the model moderates the efficacy effect on the observer (Bandura, "Self-Efficacy: Toward a Unifying Theory"). The more closely the observer identifies with the model, the stronger will be the impact on efficacy. Bandura writes, "Vicarious experiences [are] mediated through modeled attainments" (*Self-Efficacy: The Exercise of Control* 86). Vicarious experience seems to occur in two forms. The first and most powerful form of vicarious experience is often the observation of a mentor teacher. But, in instances when the mentor teacher is absent or deficient, the teachers' second vicarious source is theoretical texts, narratives, or videos.

Physiological and affective states. Even though it is believed that people rely only in part on somatic (bodily) information conveyed by physiological and emotional arousal to form judgments about self-efficacy, how people interpret this information is of major importance. According to Bandura in *Self-Efficacy: The Exercise of Control,* perceived aversion arousal can hinder performance, which results in feelings of personal intolerance, leading to feelings of personal incompetence. How one perceives and interprets his/her somatic state directly affects coping with stressors within a specific domain as well as healthy functioning in general. Simply put, teachers cannot work effectively if they experience prolonged feelings of discomfort in the presence of the students they serve or in the environment in which they work. A teachers' interpretation of his/her psychological and affective responses directly influences his or her ability to learn and to teach well.

Verbal/social persuasion. Verbal/social persuasion is encouragement or constructive feedback by an individual who is perceived by the recipient to be knowledgeable. Persuasion can contribute to successful performances to the extent that a persuasive boost in self-efficacy leads a person to initiate the task, attempt new strategies, or try hard enough to succeed (Bandura, "Self-Efficacy Mechanism in Human Agency"). The potency of persuasion depends on the credibility, trustworthiness, and experience of the persuader (Bandura, *Social Foundations*).

The models Bandura offers play themselves out in the efficacy development of writing and composition teachers. Ashton and Bandura both speak of feedback loops. On the one hand, these are processes by which teachers are given messages about their ability to work well with students. For example, Mary Ann refers to friends and family who question her interest in studying Black English. On the other hand, these are processes by which teachers can reconstruct a sense of themselves as having high efficacy. In the narrative that follows, we offer as a model of vicarious experience a story about a European American teacher working very effectively in a racially diverse community-based setting. Teachers who confront the racialized power relations of their work in the writing classroom frequently need help in figuring out a satisfactory story for themselves. Through such stories, teachers interpret their efforts on behalf of all students and the communities they serve. These stories serve to mediate teachers' internal role definitions and the role definitions already in place. As a teaching story, the narrative below offers a reconstruction of the paralysis articulated by Mary Ann. In the example of Philip, an instructor in a community-based dance troupe, high efficacy and reflective optimism come as a result not of ignoring, denying, or wishing away racial and ethnic diversity but from embracing it. That we turn to a community-based location for this model of a high-efficacy teacher may reflect a dearth of similar models in college or university writing programs. In the next chapter, we will have much more to say about patterns of participation in community-based sites of literacy learning. In the context of this chapter's focus on analyzing, deconstructing, and reconstructing our own narratives about what it means to be a (white) teacher of AAVE-speaking students, the example of Philip illustrates what high-efficacy teaching looks like. This narrative first appeared in Ball ("Community-Based Learning"), and we repeat it here as an important lesson in vicarious experience for writing and composition teachers.

Troop

Nestled between two storefront businesses on a busy downtown street stands the Troop dance program for inner-city girls. Ayana, a twenty-year-old graduate from the Troop program remarks, "I really loved the program and I still love to dance. The teachers in this program had such a huge impact on my life. I learned a lot and still apply what I learned there in my current college level performances!" Ayana effectively summarizes why she and the other participants came to this after-school dance program on a voluntary basis and continued to come week after week and, in many cases, year after year.

The dance program was established for students living in low-income, inner-city areas predominantly populated by African Americans, Hispanic Americans, Pacific Islanders, and recent immigrants to this country who are at risk for educational failure. With unemployment rates above 20 percent and school drop-out rates above 40 percent, this community is plagued with myriad family and school-related problems that are not uncommon to many contemporary urban areas. The Troop dance education program, however, was created to counteract the widespread social and educational problems that afflict students from these types of communities. Its program was designed to reach at-risk students by developing personal, social, physical, and academic skills through dance as an enjoyable art form that appeals to youth. The learning exchanges that take place at this site bear witness to the uses in positive ways of literacies, complex problem-solving activities, and capacities to function within local communities from other parts of the students' lives. As students practice each dance, they focus on skills necessary to master the art form. However, they are also learning to watch and listen attentively, taking risks, attempting new tasks, self-composing, self-revising, and publishing what they have learned in a variety of forms and mediums.

These principles—essential in the development of a successful dancer—are also essential principles in the development of a successful writer: learning to scan a text attentively to discover emerging themes and patterns, experimenting with new forms of expression, composing, revising, and demonstrating what they have learned in subsequent drafts. The language used in Troop focuses the students' attention on the future, on hypothetical situations, and on problem identification and solutions. Focus on these types of activities has proven to be of particular interest to this predominantly African American group of students. Between practice sessions, participants work on homework assignments and write down their plans for upcoming Troop activities—what they will wear, when and where they will meet, and notes to one another. As the students change and adapt their language, literacy is put to a wide variety of uses and develops more forms. Conceptual ideas and program themes that have their beginnings in oral or written forms may come to be represented as visual literacies in pictorial forms or symbols that are then transformed into physical motion and musical representations. Those themes and ideas that survive the artistic process may ultimately be represented in yet another written form during the group's preparation and publication of their annual performance programs and handouts.

Although portrayals of local literacies in the lives of African American populations within sites of the extracurriculum have received little attention in the literature, the acknowledgment of such biliteracies and multiliteracies is a growing phenomena (Street, "Struggles"; Barton). Activities and achievements that go on outside formal education often celebrate practices and values that exist away from formal schooling. One primary encouragement for recognizing these diverse literacies is Barton's notion that "when people take hold of literacy, they actually transform it for their own uses, extend it, develop it, and own it. This is the ray of hope [in] looking at how literacy is changing" (7).

The Troop dance program, founded in the 1980s, has gained recognition as a program that helps African American students to excel. Troop is a chamber modern dance company composed of about fifteen girls at any one time who have demonstrated outstanding talent and who show good potential for succeeding in college. The program offers intensive dance training with professional dancers, monthly performances, workshops, and lecture demonstrations with guest artists from professional touring companies. This community-based organization provides young African American women numerous opportunities for talk and reading and writing skills development—all centering around dance.

Philip, the program's European American group leader, tries to instill discipline, self-esteem, and commitment by focusing on artistic endeavors that help to bind the young people together as members of a distinctive, community-valued group. Having high expectations, contextual predictability, and an atmosphere of support are key elements in instilling focused discipline, self-esteem, and commitment in these youths. The staff has high expectations and provides models of excellence for the group: "I work with them tight, " says Philip, "and I get to know them. On the one side, they like it. On the other side, they don't. You see, they have to be accountable." Philip remarks, "I know it's not easy to work with me because I am disciplined and I know exactly what I want."

Familiar with the students' capabilities and convinced of their potential, Philip monitors the students' progress and demands excellence at every turn. He does not allow any straying from the task. He constantly directs the students' attention to the project at hand and provides encouragement and supportive language that comes at a rate that is far more frequent than that reported in most classroom language studies (Cazden; Ball and Heath). As they practice each dance, the focus is on mastery of one dance at a time: "One good dance, instead of two or three that we don't know well. And I want it clean!" And finally, Philip does not fail to celebrate individual and group accomplishments on a regular basis.

Throughout dance practice activities, Philip uses a "coaching register" in his interaction with program participants. This register is the oral accompaniment to activities of practice and demonstrations that prepare members of the group to work together toward a series of culminating events (Heath and Langman). The Troop dance program instills a sense of group accomplishment through frequent uses of inclusive directives, such as "let's" and "we," calling for joint effort to accomplish goals and a sense of support of the group's own potential outside or apart from the coach. Although the cultural background of the group leader is European American, Philip spends an enormous amount of time listening to African American forms of music and has studied African American forms of dance. His ongoing interactions with African Americans have provided him with many linguistic resources that he uses authentically and effectively to relate to the program participants and build bridges that link their cultural experiences, his own cultural experiences and mainstream American cultural practices and expectations. He is often heard using African American youth idioms, slang terms, and AAVE grammatical forms in verbal interactions with the program participants.

Lessons Learned from Troop

There is much here that we can learn from Philip concerning initial steps we can follow when holding high standards for our students and communicating these standards to our students. The notion of high expectations for behavior, performance, and academics is a constant theme that runs throughout program language. High predictability and the practice of placing models of what they can become are characteristic features of the program. Past successes of students like Ayana, who have completed the program and gone on to become accomplished dancers and successful college students, were shared with the current students through oral and written narratives and newspaper clippings. Because the high expectations the group leader holds for each student are guided by knowledge of the students' capabilities coupled with a strong belief in their potential, students meet those expectations time and time again. Building on their successes, the youngsters themselves are given roles of responsibility and placed in front of the classroom to act as teachers or peer models for other students in the class. Repeated calls to learn from their own errors and misjudgments are also common occurrences. Within the confines of the program's goals for excellence, strict discipline routines of practice and homework are implemented and negotiation and collaboration occur frequently.

Efficacy acknowledges affect as an essential element in teachers' constructs of knowledge. Efficacy therefore pushes us to theorize unspoken dimensions of teaching practice, for example, its felt reality, and to trace them to their sources. Efficacy refers not just to what teachers know about linguistically and culturally diverse students but what teachers believe about their ability to teach students from various cultural and linguistic backgrounds. Reflective optimism as the correlate perception of those students' ability to achieve is reflected in the expectations teachers hold for their students' achievement. Efficacy speaks to the cumulative impact of teachers' knowledge and experience on their feelings about their students and their ability to teach them. Affect in the classroom can influence students' motivations for learning. Affect carries the evaluative overtones that contour the social relationships in the classroom in a way that is comparable to (and, often, observable in) intonation in speech. Like intonation, when affect comes across in action, it embodies evaluation. When teachers lack experience and knowledge of students' diverse cultural backgrounds, they may unconsciously withhold, draw back from, or simply fail to recognize opportunities to fully engage and motivate, to communicate the high expectations of these students that is the hallmark of teacher efficacy and reflective optimism.

In *Teaching to Transgress: Education as the Practice of Freedom,* bell hooks examines concepts of well-being and self-actualization as terms teachers may use to articulate our inner connection to our work. Focusing on education as a process of engaging and negotiating relationships—between teacher and student, student and student, and with the material at hand—hooks names and challenges many of the dualistic separations that are currently inscribed in normal educational discourse and that "denigrate notions of wholeness" (16). In far-reaching terms, hooks names some of these binaries: the mind-body split, the separation of public and private, and the separation of "the will to know" from "the will to become" (18–19). Along with other feminist and critical theorists of education, hooks challenges teachers to incorporate more holistic terms as ways to frame the meanings of our work, the acts of teaching and learning. Rejecting the normal terms furnished by professional discourse and institutional routine, hooks and other theorists of teacher-education challenge us to reimagine the ways we occupy and negotiate the role of writing teacher.

Conclusion

This chapter opened with an analysis of a student paper and teachers' responses to it. We then examined Mary Ann, a European American student who evinces knowledge about AAVE but expresses frustration about how to move forward to a changed practice in which her knowledge of AAVE would be incorporated into her pedagogical repertoire. We suggested that teachers like Mary Ann learn to recognize the uses of AAVE-based discourse modes and patterns in their students' academic writing. But they are perplexed by what to do after that recognition occurs. In essence, she is asking how to move beyond the internalization of knowledge about AAVE-based rhetorical preferences to make that knowledge useful to her students as developing writers. We then described Philip as an example of a teacher who has high efficacy and reflective optimism, and in his example we pointed to characteristics of the relationship he established with his students. He has moved beyond "knowledge about" AAVE and established a productive relationship with his students. His authority for communicating his high expectations is related to his familiarity both with his students' abilities and with the course material.

By believing in their students' abilities to succeed and providing support for this to occur, by reassessing their strategies for assessing students' abilities, by doing so in the context of confronting and using their own emerging knowledge of AAVE, teachers can provide support for AAVE-speaking students (and all students) to develop their literate possibilities. In addition, teachers can learn from the example of Philip, who is eager to press the Troop dancers to their highest limit and who indeed takes on himself as their teacher the challenge to push them. In the texts our students compose, we love to see demonstrations of ever-more-sophisticated proficiency. But we must remember the classroom context in which those texts are produced. Students' participation in the interactive discourse of the classroom is a significant factor. In the next chapter, we turn to examine patterns of participation in the interactive discourse of community-based organizations where AAVE-speaking students do well, and we become consciously aware of the critical link between participation in interactive discourse and the production of successful literate behavior on the part of African American students.

3 / The Pedagogies of Others: Community-Based Organizations as Models for Participatory Literacy

It is early in the semester in Composition Theory. In class we have begun a discussion of George Hillocks's *Teaching Writing as Reflective Practice.* Noticing Hillocks's treatment of the impact of language variation in the classroom, we consider one passage in which Hillocks refers to a story told by Shirley Brice Heath in her landmark ethnography of literacy, *Ways with Words.* The story concerns the case of a boy who tried to explain that a fellow student had not ridden the bus to school on a particular day as she ordinarily did.

> TEACHER: Where is Susan? Isn't she here today?
> LEM: She ain't ride the bus.
> TEACHER: She *doesn't* ride the bus, Lem.
> LEM: She DO be ridin the bus.
>
> According to Heath, the teacher "frowned at Lem and turned away." In Lem's system of Black English, *ain't* is equivalent to *didn't,* thus indicating that on this particular day, Susan did not ride the bus. (Hillocks 17)

Two of the course participants—one white and one black teacher from the area's largest urban district—speak up, saying they do not let their students talk "that way" in their classrooms. Then one goes on, quickly explaining the method of intervention: "I look at them and say, 'What did you say? What did you say?' until they say it the right way."

"It always bothers me," the other adds. "The people who say we shouldn't teach grammar are the ones who already know it."

"I *have* to teach them correct grammar," the first teacher concludes. "I have to. It's my job."

While both of the teachers show concern for helping their students develop a mastery of academic English, from our point of view, the sentiments portrayed in this brief narrative represent much that we find regrettable in the ways teachers think about language, students, and their own role as professionals in a system regulating access to literacy. That these sentiments may be voiced by administrators, legislators, or parents does not persuade us that such responses tend to be educationally productive. To paraphrase "Students' Right to Their Own Language," such responses constitute bad advice for writers.

We believe similar problematic teacher beliefs and actions toward students' uses of AAVE may be found in college writing classrooms (Smitherman and Villanueva). It may be unusual to find college-writing teachers overtly correcting their students' spoken language in this peremptory way. But in other respects, the university writing classroom is not so different. For example, we have often heard college writing teachers express their conviction that it is their job to teach students to use correct English. These teachers seem sometimes to find a certain kind of professional validation in the labor they invest in red-penning what they believe to be dialect-interference errors, or laboriously explaining what is "wrong" with the expository patterns or oral-based idioms students sometimes prefer in their written discourse. (What is "wrong," it is usually explained, is that the language is "inappropriate." And, unfortunately, the discussion too often ends there because it is the teacher's prerogative to define "appropriate.")

Extant research suggests contrary conclusions (Labov; Smitherman, "Blacker"; Michaels; Ball). We think it is well and good to teach students about the written discourses they will need for much of the work they will do in the university and in other domains. We think it is even more important to teach students some things about "doing" writing, about writing as an activity to engage; to tell and show students what we know tacitly and explicitly about how written discourse comes together in the interaction of evolving intentions, apparent effects, and the materials at hand—information, our sense of audience, a feeling about the ideas and our expression of them. Correcting/policing nonstandard negation patterns, tense markers, or "inappropriate" rhetorical choices seems to be the easiest way to enact the writing-teacher function, and the least productive. But what to do about that?

Before leaving this story, we need to underline two significant points. First, we must remember we are interpreting these teachers' representations; the conclusions we draw must be qualified as such. As representations made in the context of a specific discussion, these teachers' statements should probably not be read as perfectly transparent descriptions of what they actually do in their classrooms. As the comment about "people who say we shouldn't teach grammar" reveals, these assertions may be aimed at establishing a particular stance toward membership in a profession. In this particular classroom conversation, part of the implicit message was directed at the university teacher, in a kind of "tales from the urban classroom" gesture meant to convey that a university professor could not know what teaching in city schools really involved. Second, what they say is true. It is their job: it's written into the curriculum that students are to gain fluency in Standard English. We do not disagree with that as a desirable goal. We are interested in methods of achieving it that are as empowering as this goal (ostensibly) is. We are interested that Lem's teacher does not seem even to suspect a misunderstanding, or, if she does, that it is worth trying to sort it out with Lem, that sorting it out might be useful to her own purpose of figuring out Susan's situation. For Lem, her ear is tuned only to what she construes as "wrong" about his speech. How empowering is that? And how understandable, that she does not think to, or does not bother with trying to learn what Lem is actually saying, that would help her to gain a general, overall understanding of Lem's language of communication. And, really, it ain't that hard:

TEACHER: Where is Susan? Isn't she here today?
LEM: She ain't ride the bus. [SHE DIDN'T RIDE THE BUS.]
TEACHER: She doesn't ride the bus, Lem.
LEM: She DO be ridin the bus. [YES, SHE GENERALLY DOES RIDE

THE BUS, BUT WHAT I SAID EARLIER WAS THAT SHE DIDN'T RIDE THE
BUS TODAY.]

We also find it problematic that in our own classrooms, the writing
teachers with whom we have shared this reading rarely think to
wonder whether they know better than Lem's teacher what Lem is
actually saying. In their rush, they do not hear Lem, either.

In contrast to the secondary-school teachers, college composition teachers may have fewer occasions to correct the nonstandard
English of their AAVE-speaking students. In the first-year writing
programs we are familiar with, competence in spoken Standard
English may be named as a curriculum goal. But teachers are virtually on their own to decide whether or how to make direct instruction a matter for their lesson plans. Composition teachers who want
to increase opportunities for students must wonder, are there other
ways? Yes, there are. The sections that follow show some of these
ways. We did not find these examples in first-year writing classrooms, though certainly individual classrooms could be found—we
believe that they do exist. However, where we readily observed examples of how classrooms can structure maximum participation are
community-based organizations.

Participation Patterns in Community-Based Organizations

*From the front of the classroom, Mr. Williams addresses his
students:*

INSTRUCTOR: If you're forced into having no choices, then . . .
STUDENT #1: Then you take whatever you get.
INSTRUCTOR: Sure, you're right! Your situation can force
you to take a job . . . any job. But that's only a dead
end—$9.00 an hour is tops. . . . You max out. Then
you cain't make no more money . . . and those attitudes start kickin' in. . . . Now . . . we talked about ice
cream. . . . You're at the counter. You have to make a
choice. What do you want?

STUDENT #1: [A student calls out.] I want a milk shake!

INSTRUCTOR: [Williams fires back in rapid, inquiring tone.] What kind?

STUDENT #2: Vanilla.

INSTRUCTOR: Well, then! Tell the man!

STUDENT #2: [With hands on hips she assertively says] Two scoops of pralines and cream. On a waffle cone.

INSTRUCTOR: Wow! On a waffle cone?! But . . . What happens to the person who gets to the front of the line and don't know what they want?

STUDENS: [Group responds in unison] Jus' step aside!!!

INSTRUCTOR: And, when do they come back to that person?

STUDENT #3: When they get to the end of the line. After they serve everyone who know what they want to do.

INSTRUCTOR: So . . . at the counter of life . . . as long as you keep livin'. . . and you get to the counter and don't know what you want or you're indecisive because of fear or not being ready to take advantage of the opportunity . . . then I'm sorry for you. Now . . . if you get a second chance . . . and you get back up to the counter again, and still don't know what you want . . . then what?

STUDENT #4: Mus' don't want no job!

INSTRUCTOR: You mus' don't want no job. Then, on the other hand, maybe tha's jus' what you want . . . a *j-o-b*. Seems like you sayin' "Just give me anything!" If you ask for a single scoop of vanilla versus a banana split . . . 'cuz it's gonna cost you more . . . Hum? . . . Are you willing to pay more? More time? More work? Well? [There is a reflective pause here. The room is silent. Then Mr. Williams continues.] Then remember . . . as long as you keep livin'. . . life is gonna present you with opportunity. And you have to be ready . . . ready to take advantage of it.

As Mr. Williams wraps up this discussion, he switches back to academic English and admonishes the students to heed his

advice: "Now, just because you have choices, doesn't make it
easier. Weigh your options. Having choices requires you to be
analytical and to break it down. Any questions?" There are
none. Students gather their books, pens, and notes and leave
the class in a reflective silence.

What can composition teachers learn from these community-
based organizations that can assist them in their efforts to improve
the educational odds of success for AAVE-speaking students? In looking at these organizations, the focus shifts from the written prod-
uct to interactive discourse in the classroom. Alongside the powerful, dynamic, wide-ranging uses of code switching and style shifting
found in this interactive discourse as effective precursors to effective writing activities, we contrast the well-intended but poorly
chosen behavior of correcting students' use of AAVE in the classroom.
In the community-based organization we present, participants were
given abundant opportunities to develop broad capacities to function within their local communities: to talk, write, and develop their
abilities to learn and adapt to new information and changes in their
lives. For the literacies sponsored by the programs we discuss, the
participants themselves and their culturally influenced language
patterns are viewed as resources. Racial solidarity forms the core
identity and meaning of these community-based organizations as
specifically African American sites of the extracurriculum.

Following Bandura's discussion of vicarious experiences ("Self-
Efficacy," *Self-Efficacy*), community examples show teachers' knowledge being appropriately used, and they show the influence of their
positive attitudes and high efficacy in the transformed pedagogies
in these community-based organizations. These examples further
illustrate what writing teachers can learn from community-based
organizations that can enhance their own sense of efficacy and reflective optimism in their work with AAVE-speaking students. Examining patterns of participation in community-based organizations,
we find models of interactive language use that scaffold students'
literacy learning. We propose that these models can be applied in
the composition classroom. Interactive discourse, the classroom talk

engaged in by students and teachers, has gained recognition in composition as a significant factor in student learning. For example,
Joseph Harris notes the linkage of "the cultural politics of the classroom" to the "micropolitics of teaching," that is, "how teachers set
up courses to encourage some kinds of talk and discourage others"
(95). Referring to political issues such as race, class, and gender as
topics for discussion, Harris poses an alternate focus for teachers'
reflections on power relations in the classroom: "How do writers
negotiate among and respond to the voices of others? How do they
forge a sense of self among the languages available to them? Such
an approach shifts attention from politics as a set of issues one writes
about to the politics of writing itself—to questions of style, authority, autonomy, stance. It also suggests that one measure of the politics of a teacher might be the range of voices and perspectives that
she helps students take on" (96). Seeing politics enacted in the style
and authority of the texts students produce, we add that student
texts are produced in a context that includes the interactive discourse of the writing classroom. The moves students make during
class discussions, peer-group interactions, and conferencing all provide scaffolding for many of the rhetorical moves they make in their
written texts (Greenleaf and Freedman; Stock and Robinson). We
propose teachers take note of the rich, diverse interactive discourses
observed in community-based organizations, with an eye to enriching the oral interactions available to their students and thereby the
possibilities for their students to make commensurate gains by "using rhetorical concepts on a microlevel germane to the specific context of conversation but equally applicable to the writing context"
(Gray-Rosendale 24).

In contrast to the classrooms discussed in several recent studies of interactive discourse in writing and composition classrooms
(for example, Gray-Rosendale; Greenleaf and Freedman; Stock and
Robinson), we find in the community-based organizations presented
here that students are expected to play a range of roles in which they
need to employ different styles and registers as they participate in
activities. Additionally, a consistent feature of these community-
based organizations is the prominent place the teacher-leader takes

in the group's interactions. This too stands in some contrast to the examples of self-sponsored writing groups which have been the focus of other scholarship on composition's "extracurriculum" (Gere). While clearly peer-to-peer interactions form a significant portion of interactive discourse evident in the community-based organizations that we present here, interactions involving the teacher-leader are as important, if not more important, to the overall successful communicative dynamic that takes place in these classrooms. The relatively prominent role played by the teacher-leaders is similar to the prominent role played by the teacher in Michele Foster's analysis of performance elements employed by an African American teacher in an urban community college.

Looking closely at participation patterns in community-based organizations can help us consider innovative ways to approach pedagogy in writing and composition classrooms. Through these organizations, we show how teachers may respect, value, and integrate into classroom practices our students' diverse cultural and linguistic backgrounds. Such methodologies must be seen as a dynamic part of a continually evolving process of personal and professional identity development. Observing the participatory pedagogies in community-based organizations can also help us reflectively analyze where the moment-to-moment verbal exchanges that constitute the interactive discourse of our classrooms position our students in relation to each other, the course material, and the communities of their nurture.

The examples of the community-based organizations given here provide writing and composition teachers four avenues for broadening and enriching the participation patterns in their classrooms. The teachers in these community-based organizations create opportunities for students to play multiple roles; the teachers have found compelling ways to integrate performance into the literacy activities of these community-based learning centers; the teachers make optimum use of students' oral and vernacular resources, including AAVE, in the composing processes students engage in; and, finally, the learning activities in these organizations encourage students to make maximum advantage of their community knowledge by positioning students as informers/interpreters. These four principles can be found operating in the interactive discourse of these organizations. Students' engagement in interactive discourse serves as "an essential and dynamic social process for accomplishing complex conceptual and communication goals" (Cazden 31). Practically speaking, there is much to be learned from examining the interconnection between the literacy learning events taking place in these organizations and their related social and community contexts, since the two are crucially intertwined.

We must first and foremost take into account the *mindset of the teachers* whose work we portray in this chapter. Where are these teachers coming from? What shapes their vision of their students? What empowers their faith in their capability to be a meaningful force for positive change in their students' lives? It is important to avoid, however, as Ladson-Billings rightly suggests, reducing the explanation of success to personality or personal characteristics to the exclusion of specific actions these teachers choose to take to better support the literacy learning of their students. The difference in the case of teachers in the community-based organizations we consider here seems to be in the source of these teachers' sense of efficacy—confidence in their own ability to make a difference in their students' lives—and in the reflective optimism these teachers hold regarding their students' capabilities.

Second, we need to recognize that in every dimension of literacy and language learning found here, the material for learning is immediately present in the students' experiences and related to the circumstances of their lives. From the use of AAVE as one of many language codes put to constructive use in classroom exchanges to the substance of family histories and African American cultural traditions that are used to inform the writing in community-based organizations, we find that students are being engaged as they participate in literacy events. It should be noted that this engagement is not forced or strained but rather seems to flow naturally from the relationships between students and teachers and from the teachers' knowledge of the students' community and their lives. This dimension is well illustrated in this chapter's opening exchange between Mr. Williams and his students.

A third dimension that comes into play is the racial solidarity that forms a central part of the core identity of these community-based organizations as specifically African American sites of the extracurriculum. It may be misleading to isolate this dimension of the literacy work evident in the sites studied here. However, in the presence of a dominant white discourse that has preferred to remain silent about race, it is essential to state plainly that these community-based organizations' reason for being in the first place is to fill a need to educate, to prepare, and to strengthen the participants who will be the leaders and hope for the community's future. These student and teacher participants engage meaningfully in the creation of a better future for everyone.

We will illustrate these principles and the practices that support them in the sections that follow through examples from community-based organizations and the teaching and learning that goes on inside them, and we invite readers to contrast these examples in their own minds with writing classrooms to which they may be more accustomed. It is often the case that a composition teacher's sense of efficacy is linked to professional identity, location in an institution, and membership as a credentialed participant in professional organizations. A strong sense of efficacy is evident in the professional lives of each of the teachers who were subjects of the ethnographies drawn on in this chapter. We share the examples of Mr. Williams and Ms. Gabrielle, both career instructors in job-training programs, to highlight how this sense of efficacy is expressed in their classrooms. The theme of racial solidarity is also illustrated in Ms. Gabrielle's classroom. The Ujima program provides another illustration of this theme of racial solidarity.

Why Look at Community-Based Organizations?

The term "community-based organization" encompasses a variety of formal and informal, voluntary and nonprofit groups and organizations relevant to young people. According to Milofsky and Heath and McLaughlin, these organizations are identified with a particular neighborhood or community, provide activities and support for community youths, and are nonprofit voluntary organizations that exist primarily for the targeted population. Community-based organizations exist in most urban areas as sites of the extracurriculum. These organizations, however, are generally overlooked as literacy-related resource sites for African American students and as potential partners in collaborative efforts on behalf of students and their families. The activities that take place at these sites are often mistakenly regarded as simply leisure, peripheral, or recreational resources.

However, many community-based organizations that participants judge to be effective make important contributions in the form of experiences and involvements that help prepare AAVE speakers express their ideas more effectively. Many community-based programs provide opportunities for African American participants to see themselves as responsible, capable, confident, contributing members of a valued community and can serve as models for those who are seeking to improve their teaching practices.

Anne Ruggles Gere challenged writing professionals to look beyond our classroom walls to acknowledge sites of the extracurriculum as environments of learning. We need to draw from them insights on how to work together to create enabling environments that enhance learning for AAVE-speaking students. If we take Gere's challenges seriously, we can *look* at community-based environments in ways that help us actually *see* the literacy-related learning that takes place there and to apply what we *see* to improve our writing and composition classrooms.

Sites of the Extracurriculum

Anne Gere's invitation to investigate present-day contexts where practitioners separate pedagogy from the traditional pedagogue also asked us to consider routes of influence and instruction where learning, reading, and writing take place in worlds outside school. The portrayals that follow explore such alternative routes of influence and instruction that take place in sites designed to serve inner-city AAVE-speaking young people. They are provided in an effort to help writing professionals better understand the many complicated forms of language and literacy that take place across contexts and cultures for African Americans who participate in such programs. The portrayals here will be of three different classrooms: Operation "Together We Can Succeed," a job training program located in an urban metropolitan community in a midwestern city; Upward Bound, another job training program in an urban metropolitan midwestern community; and Ujima, an Afrocentric rites-of-passage program. Participants in these groups represent a small portion of the many African American youths and young adults who meet in inner-city community-based organizations to take part in language exchanges, literate practices, and learning activities outside classrooms. These individuals bear testimony to the fact that engaged writing and complex problem-solving activities occur in many places outside our formal classrooms. The discussion that follows these vignettes explores how observed language use and literacy practices actually fit into a broader theory of language maintenance for AAVE speakers, which contributes to their development as writers.

Operation "Together We Can Succeed"
Having started this chapter with a dialogue from Mr. Williams's classroom, we return to a description of that community-based program here.

The city, state, and national flags fly over Workplace Mall, the building that houses the Operation "Together We Can Succeed" job training program. Operation "Together We Can Succeed" is a metropolitan civil and human rights organization. It is a nonprofit corporation and a public foundation. Founded in 1968 as an interracial movement of volunteers, Operation Together seeks to unite white and black people in a common effort to engage the widest possible range of personal talents and community resources to resolve the effects of discrimination and to build an integrated society. Today, Operation Together employs 450 people and involves forty thousand volunteers. They administer food distribution, child care, job training, and employment programs.

An inclined walkway leads a visitor into the supercomputer cluster where several students receive individualized reading, writing, and math instruction on the computer. Row upon row of other students work independently on self-paced computer programs. Proceeding down the corridor, one observes a smaller classroom where a group of eight participants are attending a careers class. In another classroom, students listen attentively to their communications teacher. The fast-paced dialogue that characterizes these classrooms commands all of the students' attention. Daily, from 7:30 A.M. to 4 P.M., these predominantly African American participants can be found voluntarily taking notes on their teachers' lectures, intently composing and revising autobiographies, poetry, essays, and resumes, and willingly expanding their existing literacy skills in a different place, at a different pace, and for a different purpose than they did just a short time before when they were *required* to attend classes in their local neighborhood high schools. Currently, each of the participants in this program is a potential candidate for our freshman composition classes. They are high school graduates or high school drop-outs who have, or are working towards, their GED. The initial level of instruction at Operation Together consists of a six-week series of classes that prepares students for the job market or for further study at nearby colleges. Our team of ethnographers has come to visit the program near the beginning of the six-week series.

Through their fast-paced, direct style of interaction, teachers lead students to confront their current realities, to think and talk about their life situations, to write about them and about what it means to now be a part of this program. Although most of the students in Operation Together are AAVE speakers of varying degrees, Mr. Williams and all of the instructors in the program are both academic English and AAVE speakers. Most instructors hold graduate degrees or other advanced degrees plus advanced, specialized training in math, science, or engineering. Their effective use of AAVE is intertwined with mainstream and academic English. This intertwining of language registers is one variable that contributes to their success in keeping all students engaged in the flow and content of the classroom instruction.

The instructional delivery in this program that is judged successful by the students is characterized by a fast-paced, direct style of communication in which students are challenged to confront the realities of their everyday lives. This style is observed in the students' communications class where students are asked not only to think and talk about their life situations, but to write about them and about what it means for them to be a part of this "second chance" program. Several students respond in poetic form. The following student includes direct references from prior class discussions:

My life is like that of a diver
Drowning in the deep waters of evil
Backstroking down the deep lanes of life
Trying to make it to the shallow end
Without scuba-gear, I feel I can't make it
Now thinking negatively, I'm rapidly sinking
But, in a blink of an eye
A school of sharks lifts me
Out of these life-threatening waters
And puts me on the Fastest Track of Hope
I have ever experienced
Diving into the waters of second chances
I have overpowered the current
I can now focus my life
On tranquil waters

Like Mr. Williams, this student relies heavily on a range of literary devices that make connections between poetic images and everyday life experiences. Through the use of simile, he likens his life to that of a diver. His poetic descriptions of life in the inner city include images of "drowning in the deep waters of evil," of "trying to make it to the shallow end without scuba-gear," and of being in "life-threatening waters." Like Mr. Williams, this student and many other students in the group make skillful use of analogy. The assignment asked what it meant for them to be a part of this program. In response, this writer refers to this experience as "diving into the waters of second chances." The program has allowed him to focus his life on what he hopes will become "tranquil waters."

The writing instruction in the program takes place at formal and informal levels and is supplemented by individualized lessons on the computers. No explicit grammar instruction takes place, despite the fact that most of the instructors are mainstream or academic English speakers. Mr. Williams and other instructors teach indirect lessons on oral and written language use by modeling a variety of discourse alternatives and through modest penciled corrections on students' written assignments.

The program encourages students to express themselves orally and in written forms. As instructors converse in AAVE, make effective use of style shifting, and make unobtrusive corrections on students' written assignments, they are simultaneously (a) stressing the importance of being able to express their ideas in different ways and (b) modeling the ease and effectiveness with which that can be done without "selling out" one's cultural heritage. This informal stressing appears to be value free. That is, instructors do not appear to look down on students who are strong AAVE speakers. One instructor, who later told me he was from the projects of Harlem, is socially and culturally tuned in to the students. However, he is a mainstream and academic English speaker during most of his verbal interactions with them. Because he is from what he refers to as "the hood" and, thus, culturally literate from the students' perspective, his modeling of transitional uses of mainstream and academic American English, computerese, technical job-related jargon, and AAVE are not adversely received by the students. In every classroom, this shifting among language varieties is coupled with high standards for completing oral and written assignments and a no-nonsense atmosphere where hard work, conservative dress, focus on acquiring the prescribed skills, regular and prompt attendance, and remaining drug-free are rewarded by a good probability of job placement or college placement at the end of the six-week program.

Ms. Gabrielle's Upward Bound Classroom
During each weekday, the participants in the program called Upward Bound can be found coconstructing knowledge as students talk collaboratively among themselves, take notes on their teachers' lectures, and compose and revise resumes, autobiographies and even poems. As they work on and plan drafts, they expand their existing

repertoires of literacy skills. Here, in addition to the individualized instruction on self-paced computer programs, students aged sixteen and above receive small-group attention in career planning and communication arts classrooms. The quick dialogue that characterizes this classroom commands all of the students' attention and varies in registers used by both the students and teacher alike. At times they use a standard academic variety of English to express their ideas, but at other times they shift to AAVE or liberally interspersed technical specialized varieties of workplace English or computerese as appropriate.

In Ms. Gabrielle's careers classroom, all of the students are encouraged to think about the limits of their own life possibilities in very broad terms. A poem hangs on the wall. It reads:

LINCOLN'S ROAD TO THE WHITE HOUSE

Failed in Business in 1831.
Defeated for Legislature in 1832.
Second failure in Business in 1833.
Suffered nervous breakdown in 1836.
Defeated for Speaker in 1838.
Defeated for Elector in 1840.
Defeated for Congress in 1843.
Defeated again for Congress in 1848.
Defeated for Senate in 1855.
Defeated for Vice President in 1856.
Defeated for Senate in 1858.
ELECTED PRESIDENT IN 1860.

—AUTHOR UNKNOWN

Commenting on this poem, Ms. Gabrielle says,

> I always tell my students, "Keep this one in your mind. He never succeeded at anything, and then he became President! Now can you imagine what your future holds?" Another thing I do on the first day of my class, is give them my speech about how, as an American, it's already been

ordained that "I can do anything I want" because the last
four letter of Ameri*can* is "I can." . . . And if my class is all
African American, I tell them, "I'm not buying any excuses,
because you have been doubly blessed. . . . Simply by the
way you're addressed (as an Afri*can* Ameri*can*), you've said,
'I can, I can.' So, don't come in here tellin' me about 'I plan
to,' 'I hope to,' or 'I'm fixin' to.'" I say, "Don't come in here
with that. Cause the 'plan to's' and the 'fixin' to's'—that's a
cop out. Because first of all, just by virtue of your birth
you're already saying, 'I can.'" I stand up there and I write
it on the board so they can visualize it. And I continue to
emphasize this with them. If a student comes up to me and
says: "Mrs. Gabrielle, I want to—" I simply ask them the
question, "Who you talkin' to?" They generally reply, "I'm
talkin' to you," and I say, "Well, I don't speak that language." I laugh and they remember what I've been saying
all along. Then they respond, "Oh! Oh, you're right. I mean
'I will— and I can—.'" I say, "ok, fine. Now, tell me what it
is that you're *going to do.*" And they tell me. So I make them
do positive reinforcement for themselves. And to me that's
the only real way. You see, I can stand up and I can tell them
all about, "yeah, I went through a lot of the things that you
went through and things like that," but I must make them
more productive and start to think "I can." In fact, one student came into my office this morning and she said, "Ms.
Gabrielle, I just wanted to thank you. Thank you, because
I know I can do this now! Now that I've been here in this
program," she said, "not only have you taught me some
techniques for job interviewing and things like that, but the
most important thing that I've gained out of it is that I am
in control of my life."

In addition to developing her students' capacities to read, write, and
use oral language, Ms. Gabrielle is clearly also challenging them to
develop the capacities to set goals, to accomplish those goals, and
to reconsider matters of how they perceive themselves in the world.

Ms. Gabrielle shows us something here: she presumes, dares, and makes the students take responsibility for their actions and their decisions. Ms. Gabrielle participates in a kind of relationship that is beyond the "curriculum"—beyond developing her students' capacities to read, write, and speak effectively. Ms. Gabrielle takes it upon herself to do the work of being *that person* who will challenge her students to new heights.

Throughout the program, Ms. Gabrielle is known by both students and fellow colleagues as a teacher who has the ability to engage students in learning exchanges that challenge them to assess their current situation and to execute proactive plans for changing those situations. I observed one of Ms. Gabrielle's classes that had twenty-five students, 98 percent of whom were African American. One-fifth of the students in this class were women, and all of the students had earned a high school diploma or the equivalent prior to entering the program. Throughout the lesson, Ms. Gabrielle's instructional style revealed a skillful use of a broad range of discourse tools. She draws on her students' "local literacies," that is, she draws on the students' experiences—in their everyday lives and within their communities—as resources and as useful forms of literacy to build upon. She draws on the students' local literacies as the content of the lesson, particularly role play and drama, and uses them to scaffold the students' learning. In her careers class, Ms. Gabrielle creates opportunities for her students to play multiple roles, and she integrates role play and performance into the literacy activities that take place in her class. In addition, she allows her students to make optimum use of their oral and vernacular resources, including AAVE where appropriate, in their writing and job-interview activities. She encourages her students to take maximum advantage of their community knowledge, and she recognizes, accepts, and incorporates their varied oral and written discourse patterns. When we look at community-based organizations as a model for pedagogical reform, we realize that teachers need to understand the patterns of discourse that influence their students' oral language and their writing. In community-based organizations, students are not penalized for using a range of language varieties and registers.

Ms. Gabrielle uses code switching regularly as she moves her students from one register to another with ease to demonstrate the use of the language that is most appropriate for a particular situation.

Analysis of Ms. Gabrielle's classroom language revealed a diverse range of discourse strategies and registers—more than would be indicated by the conventional construct of code switching between AAVE and Standard English. Ms Gabrielle used the following discourse strategies to teach: accepting language, praise and encouragement to link the information being discussed to the student's experience, transactional language to expand upon the ideas of the students, questioning to confirm understanding, invocation of collaboration and symbolic solidarity on the part of the students, and descriptive language to convey new information. Through shifts in her discourse, she consciously encouraged students to consider their perceptions of the world, to become creative thinkers, risk takers, decision makers, and reflective thinkers. She also frequently questioned the language that students used to represent their own positioning in their worlds, created opportunities for her students to play multiple roles in the classroom, and integrated performance in her curriculum. Ms. Gabrielle was able to integrate these practices into her teaching because she had gained knowledge of patterns of AAVE discourse patterns, and she was willing to use this knowledge to its best advantage in working with her students. Writing and composition teachers will also need to make overt efforts to learn more about students' individual patterns and needs.

Those Who View Me as Kirabo: *The Flower That Will Bloom*
Traveling off a busy interstate exit ramp and across a wide boulevard, drivers enter an urban neighborhood in a busy midwestern metropolis. Looming overhead, a large billboard reads "96.3 JAMS—UNITED WE JAM." Further down the road stands a large yellow brick building. It stands out like an oasis in the midst of the busy city life that surrounds it. Many blocks before pulling into the church parking lot, one can see the crucifix suspended above the rooftops, looming over the skyline. The soft pastel facade of this church building stands in stark contrast to other deserted and boarded-up buildings in the area.

The architectural design of the Christian Community Church resembles a converted supermarket. The entrance is modest and a guard shack stands in the parking lot, just adjacent to the only entrance on this side of the building. Inside the premises, a large meeting room serves as a community child care center during the week. On two to three Saturdays each month, however, a program called Ujima (a Swahili word meaning "collective work and responsibility") meets here to provide African American girls with language, literacy, and learning activities designed to "provide them with the training and extended family experiences necessary to deal with and to excel in today's fast paced society." Sharifa, a member of the Pan African Congress during the 1960s and the 1970s, spends much of her free time volunteering as the program's director when she is not working hard at her own professional career as director of a county health services program during the week. As participants enter the program each week, they receive an agenda of the day's planned activities:

Saturday, January 30, 1993

GENERAL MEETING FORMAT

Starting Time: 2:45 p.m.

Set-Up Coordinator: Sangoma Circle

Call to Order at 3:00 pm: All Members Stand

Leader's Swahili Greeting, Habari Gani

Group's Swahili Response, Njema, Asante

Opening Prayer: One prayer is led by a mentor and one is led by a mentee.

Call and Response and Sisterhood Affirmation Recited by Entire Group in Unison

A Welcome Is Extended to All Visitors and New Members

Updates and Announcements

LARGE GROUP TEACHING/LEARNING MODULE: *"Family History"*

1. Why Family History Is Important: Participants write a one page essay.

2. *Turn In Your Completed Family Tree from Last Meeting*

Sisterhood Circle Workshops and Small Group Planned Activities: 3:30–4:30 p.m.

This Week's Homework Assignments Given: "Herstory Collage"

All members should bring in a picture of a black woman in your immediate family or from our history who you feel has had an impact on the history of your family or our people. Write a brief bio on that person (no more than 1/2 page). We will Xerox the bio and pictures and return originals. A collage exhibit will be developed for display during Black History Month—February.

Discussion and Feedback

Announcements—Clean-Up—Closing 5:00 p.m.

These and other weekly activities, including impromptu oral performances, memorized recitations, reading, writing, literature, drama, art, music, and dance, are designed to foster a comfortable mentor/mentee relationship, open lines of communication, and develop local literacies as capacities to function within local and global communities. Here at Ujima, the participants have numerous opportunities to play multiple roles inside and outside their classrooms, and lessons are frequently planned that integrate performances into their classes. As in African society past and present, Ujima passes on traditions that develop the "total young woman who is able to responsibly think and act in adulthood." The seven principles of the *Nguzo Saba—Umoja* (unity), *Kujichagulia* (self-determination), *Ujima* (collective work and determination), *Ujamaa* (cooperative economics), *Nia* (purpose), *Kuumba* (creativity), and *Imani* (faith)—are interwoven throughout the oral and written activities to provide a basic Afrocentric value system upon which to build life experiences.

The Ujima program, along with its male counterpart program Umoja (meaning "unity"), represents a collaborative effort to provide a rites-of-passage program for both girls and boys as they come into young woman- and manhood. The programs adhere to the tradition and uniqueness both in concept and context of the initiation into adulthood ceremonies of the Xhosa people of Azania, South Africa. The Ujima program, with an average weekly attendance of approximately sixty to seventy-five girls, was borne of the philosophy that "Our youth are the Vanguard of the future." Ujima's emphasis is on a handing down of tradition, rather than being a social group. This handing down of tradition is typified by the mentorship roles that the adult women volunteers provide for the adolescent and youth participants, ages six to eighteen years. Additionally, the Candice Council (meaning "queen mother": the title "Candice" is derived from a line of fierce ruling queens from the Meroitic Sudan) is comprised of a group of women fifty-five years and older who serve as models of wisdom and knowledge. The membership is comprised of three cohort circles or groups of girls. They include:

Circle Name	Ages (y)	Meaning and Membership
Kirabo	6–10	"The flower that will bloom"
		46 youth enrolled, 14 registered adult mentors
Sangoma	11–13	"One who is aware of her cultural heritage"
		14 youth enrolled, 8 registered adult mentors
Nya Akoma	14–18	"The heart of patience and endurance"
		11 youth enrolled, 10 registered adult mentors

According to L. C. Mahdi, S. Foster, and M. Little, the lack of formal rites-of-passage ceremonies in Western culture leads to an inadequate growth and learning atmosphere for adolescents. As the purpose of rites-of-passage ceremonies is to guarantee that members of society are ready to pass from one life stage to another, this lack leaves Western adolescents and young adults socially and spiritually unprepared for the next life stage. They are not only unprepared to assume their adult responsibilities, but they are exposed to few adequate role models who are willing to teach these responsibilities to them. "More and more people are saying the health of our culture depends on our ability to provide a 'growth context' in which our young people can mature and find meaning and purpose" (Mahdi, Foster, and Little 80). Young people in our times find themselves entering a complex, technical society that lacks a clearly defined set of beliefs or ideals.

No cohesive forms of instruction or initiation into the adult world exist in our culture except certain academic expectations and the development of work skills. The deep, natural instinctive and spiritual changes which give meaning to the passage of our lives are generally ignored. (Mahdi, Foster, and Little 116)

This is not the case for the participants of Ujima. Mentors go to great lengths to provide these participants with language, literacy, and learning activities designed to provide them with the training and experiences they will need to prepare them to deal with situations they may encounter in today's fast-paced society. Activities planned for the girls here at Ujima focus on community service, effective communication, physical development, Swahili, job preparedness, and Christian values. The girls keep a year's worth of work in their own large three-ring binder. Weekly, the students read, write, and memorize rules of conduct, poems, and activities from this book and reflect on the goals and values of personal pride, cultural knowledge, and Christian character development in oral and written forms. The meetings take place the first, fourth, and fifth Saturdays of the month from three to five p.m. Participants must master the work covered during each meeting to meet periodic evaluations. Language use and literacy practices during the meetings focus on sending participants a message that is consistent with the church's teachings, lessons of their past, and realities of the present. The program philosophy states, "We must be in a slow hurry to transform our girls into positive young women."

To accomplish this, mentors share their life experiences with mentees and encourage them to express their thoughts and ideas in many forms. An entry from one Kirabo student's journal chronicles the day's activities. Wanika, a ten-year-old participant in the program, writes:

What Happened Yesterday at Ujima

At Ujima yesterday we listened to Opera, jazz, [and] rap. One lady had Opera, Ms. Jones had jazz and Mrs. Smith had rap. The lady who had Opera was saying that when you go to an Opera you can't sneeze, cough, yawn, go to sleep and snore you [are] to [be] absolutely quiet you [can't] say anything. Ms. Jones had jazz and she said jazz is nice and soft and it some times says massages about love and stuff. Ms. Smith had rap and was saying some rap is good because it sends messages like Queen Latifah her song U.n.i.t.y. she sended a message in that so[ng]. She said she used to like MC. Hammer but she doesn't any more because of his new song Pumps & Bumps. Then after that we sang Ex-scape, James brown.

Journal writing gives the students an opportunity to ponder the values that are being passed on and to reflect on the experiences they have not yet lived but heard about from their mentors. Some of the weekly activities focus on job-preparedness skills, including how to fill out job applications, job interviews, resume writing, writing follow-up letters after an interview, and selecting careers. During one group meeting, mentors focus on the sharing of knowledge and the affirmation of creative ideas as they discuss the job application process:

MENTOR #1: Now remember to fill in your complete name, address, and telephone number neatly on this practice job application.

STUDENT #1: Can I put a beeper number down as my alternate telephone number? [Group laughter.]

MENTOR #2: Girls! Don't laugh at her. Think seriously about her question and tell me what you think. Remember, all questions are good questions. Feel free to ask them. This is the place to have them answered . . .

STUDENT #2: I don't think putting down a beeper number is a good idea.

MENTOR #3: You're right. Putting down a beeper number isn't recommended. Why do you think that is?

STUDENT #2: Hm, maybe because of the image that a beeper carries. You could leave an image of a "call girl" behind.

MENTOR #2: That's great! Remember that you *are* presenting an image here and a beeper carries an image. This is your first presentation of yourself to your potential employer. So be aware of that. [The writing assignment that follows this discussion requires that the girls secure their social security numbers and remember to bring them to the next meeting. They then elaborate on the types of job experiences they are seeking.]

MENTOR #1: OK, let's go on to the question about what job you would like to apply for.

STUDENT #3: Manager! [Group laughter. The laughter comes to an abrupt halt, however, when a fellow student gives her interpretation of the idea.]

STUDENT #4: Well? It *is* good to aim high because if you think you have nothing to offer, then they [the employer] will probably think you have nothing to offer either.

MENTOR #1: That's a good point. And remember, it's always good to do some research on what's available and the necessary qualifications before applying for a job. If you qualify for the manager's job, then you shouldn't hesitate to apply for it.

This exchange helps students consider perceptions of their own self-worth. Placing students in positions as interpreters about what their fellow participants might be thinking is one way that community-based organizations position students as resources to help teachers and other students to understand practices and patterns that will help them to succeed. In Ujima, group leaders constantly draw on the students' everyday practices and experiences to demonstrate new concepts, skills, or ideas as a bridging device and to demonstrate how these resources might be used as participants adapted to new experiences. By helping to interpret what others might do or might be thinking allows students to actively participate in the meaning-making process as teachers provide appropriate direction and support. This entire process reflects the program's goal of teaching the participants the principle of *Kujichagulia:* self-determination in defining themselves, naming themselves, creating for themselves, and speaking for themselves instead of being defined, named, created, or spoken for by others. Mentors attend periodic workshops sponsored by Ujima that gives them pointers about how to create an atmosphere that facilitates the mentoring and communication process. In this workshop, mentors are encouraged to consider how to be alert observers, good listeners, constructive criticizers, and promoters of an atmosphere of trust and dependability. Most important, they are challenged to monitor what they say and how they say it. Their motto is: "You have got to walk it like you talk it."

Entering the church each week, we see people who hug and talk to each other as if they had not spoken in years. Beyond the lobby is a large meeting room/classroom. Its walls are adorned with pages of work completed by the program participants, hung like fine pieces of valuable art. Announcements cover the door from top to bottom. Several girls wear long braids and red sweatshirts that advertise the organization's name and motto: *Ujima*—Coming into Womanhood. An adult mentor comes into the room and motions to the girls to start setting up the chairs for the meeting. Other girls arrive and work collectively to set the chairs in rows of four and five, all facing the front wall. A bustling sense of group cooperation and unity of purpose fill the room. The billboard's slogan is recalled: 96.3 JAMS—UNITED WE JAM. The women and girls of this rites-of-passage program for African American girls form a united community in which they provide emotional support for one another and address common interests that bind the group together. All of the participants take their seats and the meeting continues with prayer, a welcome to new members and visitors, and updates and announcements. One of the day's lessons begins as Mama Olivia stands and directs everyone's attention to a long table situated in the main aisle. On the table the youngest members of the organization have displayed several items that were invented by African Americans. A label next to each item contains its inventor's name, date of invention, and U.S. patent number. In completing this project, the young girls have been engaged with reading, writing, numeracy, and technology as forms of literacy. Mama Olivia describes each item on exhibit and then adds, "We've made a lot of contributions to this country. . . . In fact, we *built* this country." A voice from the right side of the room calls out, "Amen! That's right. . . . With our sweat we *built* this country." Mama Olivia continues, "We've made many, many, many contributions to this country. We are contributors, and when someone says, 'Go back to Africa if you don't like what's going on here . . . , that's not valid. We can go back to Africa if we choose to. But this is our country." These women, united in sisterhood, clap in affirmation and appreciation of Mama Olivia's words and the girls' work. Another mentor, Mama Sunika, then says to the girls, "I want you all to think carefully about the things Mama Olivia has said, and remember that . . ." she pauses and the girls join her in completing the phrase, "Black history occurs three hundred and sixty five days of the year." The combined voices of these African Americans are indeed powerful!

In addition to the reading and writing activities needed for the preparation and delivery of this lesson, participants have been engaged with other types of literacy practices that do not generally take place in more traditional self-contained classrooms. Through choral repetitions of their affirmation of sisterhood at the opening of each meeting, through oratory and dramatic activities, and through the interactive discourse and spontaneous call-and-response messages echoed while others are speaking, are seen examples of the African American traditions of oral literacy working together to help create a culturally and educationally responsive environment. For us, this is the core lesson to be learned by composition teachers from this example. This distills the phenomenon of creating a "we" in a classroom—a sense of identifying positively with the group. The learning that takes place here is both relevant and enjoyable as the girls are shown and taught traditions of their own culture. The call-and-response patterns, the hand claps, and the head nods symbolize agreement, and they result in interactive, participatory communication.

Mama Olivia reminds the participants that one of the most important objectives of her interactions with them is to bring about the development of the total person, spiritually, mentally, physically, and morally. One poem she shares with the girls in the day's program appears on a poster on the wall of Mama Olivia's classroom. It focuses on choices, a theme that runs through all four community-based programs that we observed.

THE CHOICE IS MINE

I choose to live by choice, not by chance.
I choose to make changes, not excuses.
I choose to be motivated, not manipulated.
I choose to be useful, not used.
I choose self-esteem, not self-pity.
I choose to excel, not compete.
I choose to listen to my inner voice, not to the random opinions of crowds.

—ALEXANDER STARR

Through the lessons taught and through the demonstration of commitment and discipline, mentors like Mama Olivia guide their initiates to recognize the following:

> That empowerment is a central concept to be understood and operationalized. . . . Achieving a new sense of empowerment is the key reward for the students. In this case, empowerment means having more responsibility and capability to have the learning environment meet the students' needs . . . and having the ability to make things happen and the confidence in their ability to create their own destiny. Thus, the student is empowered to be successful in school. (Ujima Student Handbook 1996)

As with rites-of-passage practices performed in other cultures and societies, Ujima encourages the participants to learn about themselves and their cultural traditions through organized activities, field trips, and special projects focusing on African and African American history and culture. Mama Olivia taught a lesson on African American inventions to thirty-five students and seven mentors, all of whom were African American girls and women. Throughout the lesson, Mama Olivia's instructional style included language that was accepting, filled with praise and encouragement that linked the information being discussed to the students' experiences, and used strategies to invoke collaboration and symbolic solidarity. As Mama Olivia presented her lesson that focused on self-esteem, the audience involvement was infused with call-and-response patterns that elaborated on what Mama Olivia was saying. For example, when Mama Olivia said, "We *built* this country," someone from the audience responded, "With our sweat we *built* this country." Analysis of a four-minute segment of this lesson revealed that Mama Olivia contributed twenty utterances while the audience contributed twenty utterances as well, most in an interactive, call-and-response style.

Conclusion

As we have looked through the lens of ethnography at community-based organizations, we are able to *see* some new possibilities for African American students in composition classrooms. Four avenues for broadening and enriching the participation patterns in writing and composition classrooms emerged. The teachers in these community-based organizations create opportunities for students to play multiple roles. The teachers have found compelling ways to integrate performance into the literacy activities of these community-based learning centers. The teachers make optimum use of students' oral and vernacular resources, including AAVE, in the composing processes in which students engage. And, finally, the learning activities in these community-based organizations encourage students to make maximum advantage of their community knowledge by positioning students as informers/interpreters. These four principles can be found operating in the interactive discourse of these organizations.

In addition, the organizations gave their participants abundant opportunities to develop broad capacities to function within their local communities—to talk, write, and develop their abilities to learn and adapt to new information and changes in their lives. An organization's ability to facilitate the development of participants' capacities was rooted in the powerful sense of teacher efficacy that program leaders possessed. We conclude that one critical aspect of the teaching and learning evident in community-based organizations is located in the teachers' sense of efficacy, their faith in their own ability to make a difference in their students' lives, and their reflective (informed) optimism about their students' capabilities. As we have noted, this sense of efficacy was the fuel that empowered their faith in their students' capability to become meaningful forces in the world. This faith allowed the organizations to give participants abundant opportunities to develop broad capacities to function within their local communities.

In these community-based organizations, African American youths and young adults were given numerous opportunities to develop local literacies. Through lessons of the past, drama, dance, and portrayals of present realities, the participants in organizations like Ujima see themselves as positive young people. These participants are ensured access to adult role models that support them with opportunities to experiment with language and literacy interaction models that not only reflect standards of the dominant society but also standards of the students' cultures. Mentors help learners to interpret appropriate communicative behavior in different contexts and create successful contexts for learning. In community-based organizations like Operation "Together We Can Succeed," participants see themselves as members of structured environments in which vibrant discourse and written texts can interact. Through fast-paced, direct styles of communication, participants were led to confront the realities of their life situations. Through analogies, effective uses of a broad range of English varieties, and through writing about real-life experiences that are "like that of a diver," participants not only shared those realities with others, but they also took dives into "the waters of second chances."

Furthermore, because of the teachers' sense of self-efficacy, these organizations were able to stress collaboration, commitment, and high expectations and make available shifting types of activities that allowed youths to develop and practice language and literacy behaviors that work most effectively for them. They also provided the participants with opportunities to see themselves as responsible contributors in a dynamic, communication-filled environment that allowed them to question the status quo, give answers in areas in which they felt a sense of accomplishment and achievement, respond without censure, absorb new knowledge through experience, and disseminate knowledge among accepting adults and peers using a range of forms and mediums.

In these community-based organizations, community-based resources, including the participants' themselves and their culturally influenced language patterns, were viewed as assets. Because AAVE is the first dialect learned by many African Americans throughout the United States, a high level of emotional involvement often accompanies many discussions on the topic. Some people argue that AAVE is an essential part of African American cultural identity, while others see AAVE as an impediment to success. For many African American youths who grow up surrounded by peers who value the dialect, a linguistic paradox ensues when they give thought to language and literacy demands placed on African Americans in composition classrooms and in the professional working world. Geneva Smitherman summarized the double linguistic standards required of AAVE speakers.

> The language of Black people should be recognized and accepted, particularly when you consider, if you're talking about corporate America, you consider that you have people who have already proven their talent and their skills. They've negotiated life; they've gotten college degrees, MBA's. They've managed to pass whatever criteria the corporations required for them to get in, because they don't be gettin' people off the street, right? You have to do an interview, you have some type of assessment to get in these corporations. They've managed to do all this. They've managed to perform well on the job, and suddenly someone says, "Oh, you have one more little hurdle to go. You have to get rid of *aks* or *dis* or *I be*." And I'm opposed to that. (*The Oprah Winfrey Show*, November 19, 1987)

Because of the glaring instances of double standards they have experienced, many aspiring African American students who come to our writing classes are often steering a collision course between the colloquial vernacular and classroom or employer's linguistic requirements. On the one hand, many youths, regardless of ethnic background, have a desire to maintain a language of difference as a symbol of identity and solidarity (Fordham; Richardson, *African American*). Many African American youths persist in the use of AAVE because they want to maintain an allegiance to African American culture. In African American street speech, especially among males, masculinity and prestige are reinforced by the eloquence of one's rap. Active resistance to acquiring the dialect of the socially excluding elites may help to explain the survival of AAVE.

On the other hand, the majority of these same students are acutely aware of requirements for academic success in composition classrooms and employers' demands that mainstream or academic American English be used in the workplace. The fact is that most African American college students want to master the use of academic English. Interviews with African Americans from all walks of life reveal that it is clear that most acknowledge that mainstream or academic English is necessary if one expects to excel in the academy and in today's workplace culture (Baugh, *Street Speech*). The fact remains, however, that AAVE continues to survive even in the face of active opposition to its use in most classrooms and workplaces and there is an increased recognition that African Americans are expected to master the use of mainstream or academic English as part of their professional training. Pressures for group loyalty on the one side and pressures to stop using AAVE on the other, result in a linguistic schizophrenia or tug-of-war for many African American young writers. What we have observed in community-based organizations is a pedagogy that helps us to realize that this linguistic schizophrenia or tug-of-war does not have to exist.

And finally, each of these community-based organizations had a focus on racial solidarity as a part of their core identity as an African American site of the extracurriculum. This racial solidarity occurs among program participants as a result of the reality that the program leaders engage with diverse cultural practices in their professional and in their private lives. Some may think it misleading to isolate this dimension as an important theme in the literacy work that is evident in the sites studies here. Yet it is critical that in every organization that we observed as *successful* learning environments for African American students, all four of the themes we have discussed were present and working together in complex ways. Never did we find only one of these factors working in isolation in those sites where we found vibrant and engaging learning taking place. We have concluded that unless these fundamental themes come together and work together in synergistic ways, meaningful change will not take place in the learning environment for African American students. Rather than arguing that African American students must be in African American schools exclusively, we are saying this is the challenge all teachers need to take up.

Some people might say that what we present in these community-based organizations has nothing to do with writing. However, we propose that what these organizations confirm instead is the critical link between oral and written language in the African American community. The bond that exists between oral and written language is strong due to the historical tendency to utilize multiple literacies when completing literacy-related tasks. (In *Ways with Words*, Shirley Brice Heath describes residents of Trackton who oftentimes use multiple literacies within a communal context.) They also see value in the use of alternative literacies: literacies that resist the academic practice of artificially separating writing from the other literacies and presenting it in isolated, sterile ways. Gaining an understanding of the dynamic interplay between oral and written literacies calls for the education of the whole individual—and not attempting to present writing outside of a literacies context. What we observe in these community based organizations illustrates the possibilities for successfully teaching to African American students when oral language is effectively used as a precursor to a successful writing activity.

We focused this chapter on stories that highlight the participatory-literacy practices in community-based organizations, asking teachers to consider the interactive discourse and participation patterns in their own classrooms alongside these models in order to open up possibilities for change. Teachers' hearts may be in the right place. However, when their methods end up silencing students, as in the case of Lem, we can safely conclude that they are making poor instructional choices in relation to the education of African American students. They are effectively shutting down the education process for African American students when they shut out their participation in the interactive discourse processes in their classrooms.

In this chapter we have presented stories of community-based organizations as a model of vicarious experience for teachers who are seeking more inclusive, culturally informed pedagogies. In the next chapter, we offer a different model in the form of our own stories, offering the particularity of our own experience as we go through the process of moving beyond internalization. This transformation involves a process of analyzing and reanalyzing our own journeys toward efficacy, analyzing and reanalyzing our personal beliefs and assumptions, and negotiating and renegotiating our professional and extraprofessional selves.

4 / Self-Efficacy and Reflective Optimism: Moving Beyond Internalization

Having examined the practice of highly effective teachers in community based organizations, consulted much of the extant literature in composition studies, and contemplated our own growth experiences, we believe the nature of the change we are describing cannot be readily portrayed in the normal discourse of our disciplines, nor can it be easily mapped on a developmental curriculum. The writing teacher who is cultivating self-efficacy and reflective optimism toward his or her AAVE-speaking students is renegotiating disciplinary and personal knowledge and values. Needless to say, this process is complex and wide-ranging. At its psychological and affective core, this process of change occurs as the unfolding of a multivocal dialogue (in a Bakhtinian sense) involving a teacher's "sub-identities" (Mishler).

In this chapter, we identify the personal applications of arguments we have been making throughout this book. Our purpose is to model and organize our personal stories to indicate .

- The cognitive internalization of information is not enough to increase teacher efficacy because there is a difference between knowing about and knowing how, between knowing and feeling and between knowing and transforming knowledge in practice.
- As we have discussed it here, teacher efficacy is rooted in teachers' dispositions toward themselves, their work environment, and their culturally diverse students.
- By changing their affective stances toward their work and their students, teachers' encounters with high-powered theory can transform their dispositions toward literacy. In our own experiences and in experiences of our

students, we have seen this occur. In our experiences, the qualitative context of these encounters is intertwined with the cognitive aspect of discovering new knowledge. In other words, the social context of the people (classmates, peer teachers, others) with whom we negotiated the meaning(s) of theories that were formative to us proved significant.

- This transformation involves a process of self-analysis, studying one's own journey toward efficacy, reanalyzing personal beliefs and assumptions, and recentering one's sense of oneself in professional and extraprofessional dimensions.

The Journey Toward Efficacy in Composing Narratives

For many teachers, this process of change means pushing beyond their comfort zone, to commit the intellectual, emotional, and spiritual energy needed to become better teachers to all students, to locate in their teaching practice the sources of what is living and affective in their public and private lives. Learning to teach with commitment is a lifelong engagement, a labor of capacious love: passion for the work we do with literacy, honor for ourselves in doing it, and respect for our students whose faith in their own potential deserves nothing short of our full good-faith effort.

We believe it is necessary to recognize teacher narratives as vital tools for specifying the intertwining threads and dimensions of these changes. We metaphorically reidentify the construct of composition's extracurriculum, applying it to the cognitive and affective processes of self-reflection as teachers move toward transformed attitudes. Recognizing the social dimensions of the social-psychological perspective of learning, we want to underline the function performed by authoritative others to whom teachers turn in this process, be they other experienced teachers, role models inside or outside of school, or the texts of high-powered theory that provoke and inspire our journey.

In *Teaching Writing as Reflective Practice*, George Hillocks suggests that writing teachers draw on knowledge from three sources.

Sets of theories about written discourse, the composing process, teaching and learning form one source. A second source is reflective practice, that is, the attentive use of observation and interpretation that allows teachers to progress beyond trial-and-error in refining their pedagogy. The third source refers to values, attitudes, and beliefs teachers accumulate through life experiences. Knowledge of this sort, Hillocks suggests, is difficult to track to its origins. As we approach this narrative, we take Hillocks's formulation as a starting point, framing our exploration in terms of our accumulated life experiences through which we have formed values, attitudes, and beliefs.

Arnetha

I have come to realize that my life has been a journey—a journey that has brought me to the place and time where I find myself today. Time and time again, as I have traveled this journey, I have found myself situated in positions of advocacy for persons who have a history of denied access to quality education—and I have wondered why. Taking the time to reflect on my own journey has been one of my motivations for writing this book. I share the narrative of my own experience in an effort to move others toward positions of efficacy and advocacy; I write to those who have the potential to become agents of change in our schools. Through reflection, I have come to realize that two interconnected concerns have shaped my own professional development: one has to do with a desire to link issues of language and literacy with improved teaching and learning for those who have been disinherited and dispossessed; the second has to do with a desire to prepare other teachers to work effectively with culturally and linguistically diverse students who are underserved in our current educational system. My hope is to play some part in reconfiguring the school experiences of individuals with a history of denied access to quality education. Much of the work I do centers specifically on using writing and improved writing instruction as a vehicle for addressing these concerns. Throughout my career, I have explored these issues through my teaching of writing in underresourced schools and in teacher education programs in the United States and South Africa.

As I contemplate my own journey toward teacher efficacy—my own process of moving beyond internalization—I realize that I have known that I wanted to be a teacher since I was eight years old. As I search deeply to identify the heart and soul of the inspirations that contribute to my teaching practices and my sense of myself as a teacher, I realize that I cannot locate the traditional "stories of personal struggle" to share concerning my development of identity during my early years as a teacher of African American students. Having grown up in an African American community, I had a great deal of exposure to African American church folks, teachers, and ministers as role models. I was strongly influenced by our community's valuation of a good teacher and its historic belief that education is one of our most powerful allies in the African American's struggle for equal access and upward mobility.

Ted

Next to the computer on this writing desk, an arm's reach over the manila folder that holds my poems, the *College English* issue on personal writing, *The Structure of Scientific Revolutions,* and two books on narrative theory, lie the bedraggled remains of a legal pad. In faded ballpoint, top of the page: *6/7/93.* A journal entry in faded ink, begun during the final exam period for ENG 102:

> *About 24 hours after a phone call from M. who said, "It's the end of the year, a jagged time." I was thinking about an article I failed to finish, about "revulsion" and "vulnerability" in teachers' stories about the classroom, and I noticed as I sit here watching the time slip by in the exam hour, with the portfolios piling up in front of me, how much tension I feel at the prospect of opening these up and reading them. A knot in my stomach. Why? Does anyone else feel this? What's logical is the student should feel vulnerable here. It's the student's writing being evaluated. ("Revulsion" and "vulnerable" share a common root which translates as "plucked.") Meanwhile, the graduate students whose journals I'm reading express, again and again, anxiety, a sense of vulnerability in reference to their teaching ability. I feel it, too.*

Intellectual revolution is not the term needed. It is a start. I have five things to say to make that start.

1. The racial matrix. "You are white; / that's true." It is likely that the teacher so addressed in Langston Hughes's poem, "Theme for English B," had not thought of himself as "white," per se. As recent theorists have discussed, whiteness has often functioned silently; such silence is a manifestation of power, serving to protect the hierarchical status quo. So what are the difficulties and possibilities present when composition as a discipline confronts race, and when that confrontation is particularized in the efforts of specific teachers who wish to actualize the potentials for literacy present in their students' experiences negotiating the codes of race in our society?

Dear Langston Hughes: When we meet on this page, as we do, again and again, do we ever meet each other outside the frame of you and me: "older and white and somewhat more free?" Of course, I'm asking this by proxy for my real question, which is: once we put race on the table, can we, do we, must we wish to ever have it off the table, at least for a while? Could race go out for a smoke, let us talk on this page?

That is a dumb question, I feel you critical educators saying; hopeless nostalgia for color-blind universalism, the "You know, I don't see color here, I only see children," which is what the Ann Arbor King School teachers said in testimony in the Black English case.

You can rationally argue, but only up to a point, for example, that teachers should respect and even learn enough themselves to respond usefully to AAVE. It is rational because you will be a more effective teacher as a result. But there are other results that are not necessarily reducible to means-ends rationality. It is valuable in itself.

The tag line of "Theme for English B": "Older and white and somewhat more free." Each of these is a relative term. Older. White. Is white relative not categorical? Somewhat more free. Teachers want to be professionals constructed by their command of disciplinary knowledge. When race is recognized, when they want to respond to it, the responses echo throughout their whole being, all the nodes of interaction (Mishler) through which their sense of identity is constructed.

2. The ideological matrix.

- Race is an element in individual identity and a dimension of social organization.
- Preservice teachers showed greater confidence in their ability to teach African American students than inservice teachers did, according to research by Pang and Sablan.
- I'm interested in how amazingly limited my verbal-cultural repertoire is—as one student helpfully pointed out after I woefully mispronounced her name: "That is so white. Just like my husband. He listen to Rush Limbaugh all day!"
- Nearly four in ten whites, but only 9 percent of blacks say that blacks are treated the same as whites in the nation. A majority of blacks express pessimism about whether a solution to the problems of black/white relations in the United States will ever be worked out. Indeed, black Americans are as pessimistic as they have been since the question was first asked in 1993, with 66 percent claiming that race relations will always be a problem in this country. At the same time, white Americans express less pessimism about the future of black/white relations than at any time since 1993. Currently, 45 percent of whites say that race relations will always be a problem, and the 21 point gap between white and black Americans' expectations for the future of race relations is the largest that Gallup has recorded. ("Black and White Relations in the United States: 2001 Update")

Remarking the ignorance that results from "the silence surrounding the demands of teaching outside one's immediate cultural frame" (248), McCracken states, "It has not been easy to find a discourse to address the ways that unexamined attitudes about race, class, language and gender perpetuate failure in schools, in spite of the urgent need to do so" (247).

Exploring the ways personal and professional identities may become more integrated, David Wilson and Joy Ritchie invite us to see teacher narratives as embodying such a discourse. Referring to the concept of ideology, Ritchie and Wilson point to the aim of teacher narrative as a tool to investigate existing systems of belief, including unspoken assumptions that inform institutional practices as well as teachers' internalized role definitions. Examining how the ideology of race structures our self-understanding outside the classroom, teacher narratives can thus become a catalyst for transformation inside the classroom. Voicing the boundaries of what we have believed to be possible about teaching and students, we can begin redefining what we value about our work as writing and composition professionals.

3. The language matrix. I want to complicate "code switching" by pointing out that it is a metaphor. Likening "code switching" to "translation" provides a jump-off for high theory, for example, "incommensurability" and "abnormal discourse" (Kuhn).

I wish to convey how strange this epistemology feels, coming from where I come from, a beige space with orange plastic chairs, windows looking out at the campus police and parking offices. From inside, trying to understand what "abnormal discourse" sounds like in my writing classroom. From inside simultaneously, this sense that the real work in the field is going on in the pages of big theory. (I thus give my Cleveland version of an issue recently raised by Lynn Worsham questioning the circulation of theory in our field, a field I don't even know what to call anymore: rhetoric? composition? theory?)

It is not the deep structure of the code, only; it is the deep structure of the switch. The community-based teachers code switch. And why shouldn't we (if the opportunity or felt need is there) learn and do the same, not only out of need, but from wanting to, because we might actually enjoy our greater communicative repertoire?

It is not that we need the ability to switch flawlessly into another code or register. We signal instead that we understand and identify with the move you make and can emulate your move in some ways through some degree of code switching; we do not have to say it in words or grammar: we shift registers, shift modes of interaction. A picture is worth a thousand words and an instance of code switching is like a picture. Philip, along with the other teachers, does not explain it, he models it. When Ms. Gabrielle starts insisting, "You're African Americans, you have a double opportunity"; "I can, not I wish. I can," she is preaching to them. Philip puts his hands on his hips and says, using that language, something to the point, "I don't know what you think you coming from but while you here this is what you gon do this way while you here." It is part of him working them tight, taking a stance: I care about you, I know you, and I know you hear me talking to you.

4. The narrative matrix. What is the story we construct for ourselves about who we are as writing teachers, what we are doing with the work of the writing course, and who we imagine, or interpret, students to be?

We tell our stories to make sense of our professional lives. Yet we do not make sense—interpret—our experience as writing teachers in isolation. We compose our interpretations, in professional forums such as conference papers or journal articles, in versions made coherent by disciplinary conventions.

In *Storied Lives: The Cultural Politics of Self-Understanding*, George C. Rosenwald and Richard L. Ochberg point out that "the stories people tell about themselves are interesting not only for the events and characters they describe but also for something in the construction of the stories themselves" (5).

To think about the effect of recentering my perspective, I have learned the need, the heuristic possibility, to ask: from a student's perspective, from an African American student's perspective, what would be the story of this ENG 102 section, "my" composition course?

Thinking of lessons composition teachers can take from community-based organizations, I'm led to ask: what explains the success of these programs? What sustains such motivated participation by students and teachers? What activities and structures of activity characterize these groups? What shared assumptions, values, and expectations shape the participants' actions? In particular, what role does expressing, affirming, and performing African American identity play in guiding the flow of activities in these sites, giving meaning to them for the participants?

Pondering these questions, let us recall our premises.

Most writing teachers, being white (need we say "with all that this means in our imperfectly integrated society"?) have little, if any, sustained interaction with African Americans in informal settings. As a result, most composition teachers have not been "socialized" into the "ways of behaving, interacting, valuing, thinking, believing, speaking, and often reading and writing that are," according to James Gee, "accepted as instantiations of particular roles by specific groups of people" (xix)—in this case, the group constituted of people identifying themselves with African American language and culture. As Dr. G. said—telling a story to me, sort of, signifyin'—"He tryin. He don't have the deep structure.".

5. The agency matrix. So does this make me not like you? I think about Langston Hughes coming to Columbia, and first of all they want him to sleep in the boiler room, not up in the dorms with the white students, and when he is not in class, he is going downtown, to a reading room, a site of his extracurricular education.

Once, when Composition Theory met for the first time, I elected to introduce the students to the substance of the class with a short homework assignment. At the end of our first meeting, I handed out copies of a column by Patricia Williams ("Aren't We Happy Yet?") in which she comments on survey data that show black people and white people hold different perceptions of racism in our society. This writing has designs on us as readers. It presents evidence and inferences. At the same time, as a column written for a general publication, it dispenses with the academic convention of reference notes. Since literacy today includes at least in part the capability of using information technology, "your task," I told the class, "is to read the column, identify points in it where Williams is referring to or drawing on sources for evidence, then try to track down the sources on the Internet." I consider Williams's writing exemplary, in many ways embodying rhetorical strategies I prize, and I said as much to the class. I appreciate the textual politics Williams is engaged in, how she "negotiate[s] among and respond[s] to the voices of others" (Harris 96). I appreciate the cultural work her writing accomplishes, its force as an intervention against convention.

Race is at crucial times an element of the character of our interactions with students, and this quality of interaction is what we are talking about when we talk about "attitudes," "affect," the "atmosphere" in the classroom. My students struggled to get past how *angry* Williams seemed.

Noticing that teacher narratives are authorized by the first person "I," we want to remain alert to the narrative and cultural imperatives activated by that rhetorical choice. If the work of teacher narrative is guided by the impulse to construct a meaningful teaching-life story, we should think about how these stories are also constructed with an audience in mind, a context that gives flow and feeling to the utterance.

I realize for example that one of the barriers to teacher change in response to taking racial difference into account is that, after white teachers recognize the need to respond to (not ignore, under "universalism") racial difference, it is my experience personally and with other preservice teachers that one can get stuck in a moral hang-up: I'm condemned by my whiteness to have already been found guilty of benefiting from privilege, especially the privilege of never having the need to question my deep assumptions (about writing and literacy, about schooling, about the content of the meaning we make) as a teacher about the way I teach. It is a way of getting positioned by the heavy moral burden of racial discourse in the United States, positioned as stuck, culpable, irredeemably white, trapped by a sense of disempowerment-by-moral-failing where even the label "white liberal educator" can seem like a slap in the face.

What I need is not redemption I can never get but tactical know-how. And once I make that shift in perspective, the question of my ability to change shifts from morality, which seems far bigger than my individual capacity to transform, to tactical efficacy to overcome the lack of procedural knowledge (Hillocks) to make racial difference pay in the writing classroom. Concretely, I'm talking about agency as a kind of relationship that might be forged between, let us imagine, a white teacher and an African American student that, neither denying altogether nor dwelling solely on racial difference as its defining feature, holds that difference as a valued element in the relationship.

Personal Beliefs and Assumptions: Early Contexts for Efficacy

We have noted examples in community-based organizations of how literacy learning events can be structured as highly participatory, energetic, and culturally informed engagement with personal growth in the context of community and communal involvement. The evidence is clear that in these sites, AAVE-speaking students, who in the routines of traditional school may feel shut out, cut off, disaffected, or neglected, come alive and thrive. In these community-based sites, vibrant engagement is the norm rather than the exception. Viewing these examples with an eye to how we can use them in the university writing class may cause writing and composition teachers to wonder how they can come to foster similarly vibrant learning relationships. Aside from pedagogical technique, something complex is going on in the learning transactions in these community-based sites. We have found that the exemplary practices of teachers in community-based organizations stem from a combined synergistic interplay of teachers' sense of commitment to their teaching, a powerful sense of teacher efficacy and reflective optimism that is grounded in their belief in their students' capabilities, culturally informed knowledge about their students, and engagement with issues of race in their private and professional lives.

We have also found that the teachers in these community-based organizations interact with their students in ways that are informed by the emphasis on racial solidarity that is evident in these institutional settings. That is, their identity as "teacher" is not readily equated to the "professional," "accredited," "licensed" teacher with whom we in the academy are familiar. Rather, these teachers took on an extraprofessional identification in their interaction with their students that played a critical role in their success as teachers. So critical was the evidence of this extraprofessional identification in these teachers' display of self-efficacy that we have concluded that in order to become effective teachers of AAVE-speaking students, most of today's composition teachers will need to undergo a process of change that reaches to the very depths of their professional beliefs—that is, to emulate the extra-professional identity these teachers have with their students.

Arnetha

Our gazes were fixed to the TV screen as my family and I watched the nightly news broadcast. We gasped in horror as the Los Angles police SWAT team fired round after merciless round of bullets into the wood-framed house located near the corner of 53rd Street and Compton Ave. Before our very eyes, the house burst into flames, sentencing the gang members who were trapped inside to death by incineration. I had spent the night in the old neighborhood and arose early the next morning to escort my nephew to school. As we walked past the charred remains of the building on our way to school the next morning, I was enraged by the fact that the evidence of last evening's violence had been left on public display as a warning to the children passing by on their way to school. *Note . . . this is what will happen to those who persist in resistant and noncompliant behavior.* I overheard the excitement and noisy chatter coming from the crowds of black and brown students. As they walked along, they gave blow-by-blow accounts of the previous night's events. Not one detail was omitted. These elaborate accounts were coming from the mouths of the same students whose academic cume folders bore the stamp "underachiever." These students could be overheard giving richly embellished, colorful descriptions and cohesive accounts of the previous night's neighborhood activities. In addition, they delivered well-developed, logic-driven arguments "for" or "against" the actions that had been taken by the police. The schoolyard was buzzing with enthusiastic improvisations and hypothetical arguments about how the matter could have or should have been handled differently. The thought crossed my mind: "What an opportunity for an exciting writing assignment." Yet, as the bell rang, these enthusiastic schoolyard debates and lively conversations reduced to quiet murmurs. The kids all fell into regimented lines, and, like little robots, they entered the classroom. As they did so, those once energetic voices fell silent—they became lifeless and suspicious and guarded—and one by one the students settled in to the school's daily routine of activities—teacher centered, choral responses, rote memorization, fill-in-the-blank worksheets. They proceeded—without the lively improvised debates, without the embellished stories, without the colorful descriptions—as they commenced with the school day with business-as-usual. Their first assignment: turn in your books to chapter 7, read pages 79 to 84, and answer the question at the end of the chapter. Find the right answers in the pages assigned and write a paragraph that summarizes what the author has said. It occurred to me that the linguistic and intellectual resources these young students brought to school were not being fully utilized.

I grew up in an inner-city, African American community in South Central Los Angeles, and I can recall the family stories that touch on issues of denied access to quality education. My mother and father shared brief sketches about their childhood and early adult experiences in rural, segregated, Natchez, Mississippi. My mother was the fourteenth child born to Hattie and Pharo Hayes. Although the family was poor, my mother's early memories of growing up on a farm were actually quite pleasant. She was constantly surrounded by brothers and sisters who gained great pride in knowing that they were one of the few black families in their community to hold a deeded claim to their forty acres and a mule, even though times were lean and their land was coveted by the nearby white land owners. The income of her father, Pharo Hayes—a highly respected, itinerant Baptist preacher—was supplemented by earnings from the older siblings. My mother spent her early elementary school years in a one-room country school, which was expanded to two rooms in her later elementary years. There, she taught many lessons to the younger students when the school budget could not be stretched to pay the salary of a second teacher. In order to receive a secondary education, she traveled to town, lived with kin, and worked after school in their store. She was a gifted and articulate student who did exceptionally well in elementary and high school, and could easily have fulfilled her dreams of becoming a nurse early in life had she not been born to poor parents in the segregated South. Many years later, while I was a student in junior high school, my mother returned to college, working many long nights into the wee hours, to graduate with a nursing diploma. After graduation, she practiced in the neonatal intensive care unit and ophthalmology clinic for over twenty years. The most important lesson I learned here from my mom was about determination, persistence, and personal efficacy as I watched her achieve a lifelong goal despite the early frustrations of denied access to quality education.

My father was the eldest child born to Mary and James Mathews. He recalls needing to leave school early in life to work the land of white farmers in order to help support his seven younger brothers and sisters. This practice of working long hours for little pay continued until he was able to escape the bonds of poverty by entering the army during World War II. He has told the story many times of serving his country faithfully and valiantly as a medic on the front lines in Germany, knowing that he would not be allowed to live with dignity if he returned to the segregated South. My father vividly recounted how he had been denied access to quality education growing up in segregated Mississippi, and he wanted better for his own children—a better education, a better life. For him, this meant that his children should be raised in another part of the country. His intuitions were confirmed when he later found out that the first year after the war ended, southern bigots had lynched over seventy African Americans, including veterans still in uniform who returned from the war with what white folks referred to as "an uppity attitude" and "a taste for freedom in their mouths." Having heard these reports, my father knew that he would not be returning to his family's hometown of Natchez, Mississippi, after his discharge from military service. And so, as the story goes, after two years, nine months, and twenty days of service, when asked his city of demarcation upon discharge from the army, he replied without hesitation, "San Francisco, California." There, he eventually forged the opportunity—through much opposition from a white work supervisor—to return to school. After working all day and attending school late into the night, he completed the mathematics requirements and went on to graduate from the International Correspondence School with a diploma and specialized training in radio, TV, and communications and later as a medical mechanical technician. Through much tenacity and long hours of work, my father eventually rose to the highest levels in his field and also found the time to own and operate his own small business on the side, "Mathews Radio and TV Service."

As he often puts it, "this was no small accomplishment for a country boy from the sticks of Mississippi."

And indeed, it was no small accomplishment because during the early years when he first arrived in California, things were far from easy. Immediately following the end of the war, he sent for his wife and infant daughter to join him in San Francisco. There, they began a new life in what they believed would be the "land of opportunity." They were woefully unprepared, however, for what they found. Life was a struggle for the family as four more children were added to the family unit. Job mobility and decent housing were hard to come by for a young black family in the city by the bay, and so they moved to Los Angeles when I, the youngest child, was three years old. There, my mom and dad found better opportunities and steady employment—my father as a medical repairman at the Veteran's Administration Hospital and my mom first as a line worker in a large paint manufacturing company and much later as a nurse. Our family of two adults and five children was more fortunate and perhaps more frugal than most. After several moves, the family purchased a small two-bedroom home in a transitioning black neighborhood in South Central Los Angeles. I can vividly recall climbing the avocado tree in the front yard of the home and wondering what those strange fruit could be; I remember falling out of the apple tree in the back yard and being treated by my dad because we hardly ever went to the hospital; and I remember our adventurous treks with our new friends who lived just down the alley at the rear end of our property line—friends we walked to school with on many occasions. The public school conditions where we lived were typical of those found in most inner-city black neighborhoods in the 1950s, and the community life was sometimes unpredictable. The experiences I had there were at times nurturing and at times challenging. Both the good and the bad experiences provided the context that contributed to my development of a sense of efficacy. I share the vignettes that follow to illustrate the context within which the embryos of my feelings of efficacy as a teacher emerged and later thrived.

The event so passionately discussed on the school yard that I described above may be remembered by many readers as one of the episodes involving the Symbionese Liberation Army and Patty Hearst from the headlines of the 1970s. Reflecting on this experience caused me to think about my own early school experiences, to question my own beliefs about how teachers should build on their students' lived experiences through writing that captures and extends teachable moments. It caused me to reflect on Mrs. Edwards and Mrs. Earl, memorable teachers from my childhood, and I have faint recollections of the lively student voices on my own school yard, particularly during the tether ball competitions and rivalries that took place before we were summoned into the classroom. As I search to understand the development of my own stance toward advocacy and my belief that teachers must be agents of change in the lives of students who are struggling or not achieving at their maximum levels of capabilities, then I realize that this stance emerged at a very early age. Reflecting on my inner-city school experiences brought back memories of my many classmates who never realized their full potential. It brought back memories of my early decision to become a teacher because I perceived this as a career through which I could dare to be different—behind the closed doors of my own classroom, I could dare to make a difference in the lives of my students and in my community.

I can vividly recall Mrs. Edwards, my third grade teacher. She was rigid and very controlling. She patrolled the isles of our classroom like a drill sergeant and would not tolerate students speaking in class without first raising their hands. Her desk was located at the rear of the classroom where she kept a watchful eye on seatwork that was to be completed silently and independently—there was no cooperative learning or peer support. When she was teaching, she stood at the front of the class—disseminating knowledge to the empty vessels that sat silently before her. Her lessons were uninteresting and, as far as I can recall, she never smiled. I remember getting scolded in front of the class and even slapped for doing something I had not done. I wanted to march right home and tell my parents about this injustice. However, I was afraid to do so because I knew that getting in trouble at school was something that was not tolerated in our household. If I had been unsuccessful in pleading my case, the consequences could be quite serious. Although I decided to suffer this injustice in silence, I firmly concluded that Mrs. Edwards was like a black widow spider because she was slowly, meticulously, killing our inner spirits.

But then there was Mrs. Earl. Mrs. Earl was really something. She was a breath of fresh air for my soul. She was smart and bold, articulate and self-confident. She was what some folks today describe as an efficacious teacher. When she was teaching, she was "in her element," and in this way, Mrs. Earl became my idol—just the kind of teacher I wanted to be. She selected interesting topics to teach about and kept us hanging on her every word with the use of multiple registers in her speech and a quick and exciting pace. While holding high standards, she gave us hard work that made us feel smart, but she was always there to explain and to relate the work to our immediate world. And she liked me. She saw something in me that was worth nurturing, and, as Mike Rose says, she made me feel special for using my mind. Not only was she a skilled teacher of African American students, but she believed that we could learn. She was what Gloria Ladson-Billings refers to as a *dreamkeeper* in every sense of the word. I felt smart in her class and I felt confident in her presence. She was upbeat and fun loving, and if something interesting happened unexpectedly in class, she was not tied to her lesson plan. She was one of those teachers who could capitalize on a "teachable moment." And, I think, most important, she had a knack for making every student feel like they were her favorite. Under her tutorage, we thrived as a community of learners. I admired her and wanted to be like her. It was in her class that I determined that this is what I wanted to do with my life: be a ray of sunshine in the lives of students whose educational and life experiences were sometimes very, very gray. And I knew then that I would someday have a class of my own in which I could see the joy of learning in the eyes of my students. I'm still working toward achieving that goal in every class that I teach.

As an elementary school student, I developed an appreciation for the power of language as my peers established positions of prestige, mostly in non-school settings, through skillful uses of "the word" in the African American rhetorical tradition. On numerous occasions, I was outwitted or outperformed by neighborhood friends and schoolmates who demonstrated intellectual and linguistic skills that were far superior to mine. On more than one occasion, I was left standing speechless after a verbal encounter with Cynthia. She was blessed with a gift of words and had the ability to silence any adversary, to cut right to the core of any debate or verbal duel with a clever cut delivered through words. Once I tried to signify on Cynthia by asking, in front of a small group of friends, her intent in wearing a dress that had a low-cut neckline. Her response was succinct and to the point: "Cleavage, honey. It's called cleavage. And, as we all know, that's something you'd know little about." Totally defenseless and embarrassed, I prayed that someone would fill the silence with words that would quickly change the subject. I envied those who had this gift for words and marveled at their oral and written skills outside of school, even though I was the one who always got the good grades in school. Sadly, most of these students never realized their full academic potential, and most found their high school diploma to be the last degree they would ever receive. Following graduation, many secured jobs in service industries or government agencies and worked in unfulfilling jobs for the next twenty or thirty years. A few of my contemporaries returned to college programs ten or twenty years later and received associate degrees in criminal justice, bachelors degrees in interdisciplinary studies, or masters degrees in business administration. The success of these few individuals caused me to realize the extent of the wasted potential that occurred, and I imagined the enormous contributions so many of these students could have made had they been taught by excellent teachers like Mrs. Earl, had they been nurtured by teachers who truly believed they could succeed, and had they had equal access to high-quality educational experiences at critical turning points in their lives.

Unlike many of my peers, I excelled in all my academic subjects. In addition, my oratory skills were strong. While there were few occasions to use these skills in the school environment, I was mentored and nurtured in this area by the members of my church family. I never missed a week going to church because there I received numerous opportunities to develop my oral literacy skills. There I was encouraged with warm hugs, hand claps, and frequent "amens" as I studied the scriptures, composed short talks, and spoke like a little preacher on numerous programs. It was there, in church, that I learned to think independently, developed leadership skills, and gained the confidence to speak before large groups. In this extracurricular learning environment, I was mentored by my role models. There, I gained great pleasure in learning and in demonstrating what I had learned. Thus supported, I finished high school well equipped with higher-order thinking skills. Thus prepared, I did not wrestle with issues of identity when I became a teacher, for, as I have told you earlier, I have known that I wanted to be a teacher since I was eight years old, and I believed that one day I'd be providing the mentorship to others that had been provided for me. I'd needed the help of others along my way and assumed that I would take a stance of advocacy on behalf of my students someday as well. I did, however, wrestle with how best to realize this goal, how to operationalize my vision of having a positive impact on the day-to-day educational lives of students who were oppressed by our educational system simply because they were young, simply because they were poor, or simply because they were students of color. Inspired by the community role models from my past, I became more and more committed to challenging the legacy of academic failure that plagued so many of the African American classmates I'd known as a child—classmates that I had known to possess multiple intelligences that were not being tapped in the classroom. It was about this time when it dawned on me that if I was going to fulfill my lifelong dream of becoming a teacher, I would need to go to college. But I had no idea about the procedures of getting into college.

While I had no idea about how to get into college—I was never called into the counselor's office at my predominantly white high school to discuss these things—I was fortunate to have one older cousin who had attended a predominantly black high school where she was nurtured and tutored through the college admissions process. I admired her accomplishment and asked her about getting my hands on a college application. She shared her materials with me, and I subsequently enrolled in a nearby state college. It was my cousin who secured the application for me and advised me on filling it out. I mailed it to only one institution of higher education. This is something I would not recommend to any student because had I not been admitted, my life would be very different today. As it turned out, I was accepted and had rich experiences beyond my imagination as the sixties came to a close and the seventies brought a new set of social challenges that resulted in my development of personal and professional commitment to issues of equity and social justice. After completing an undergraduate degree in three years and a masters degree in one year, I began my teaching career as an ethnic studies resource teacher in an inner-city elementary school in Richmond, California, determined to challenge the legacy of academic failure that plagued so many of my neighborhood friends and schoolmates. I brought to my teaching beliefs and assumptions about the responsibilities of good teachers of culturally and linguistically diverse students, which stemmed from my own early experiences as a bidialectal African American female.

Ted

I did not learn to write essays in my Freshman Comp class. Professor L was a pretty good teacher. I was a pretty distracted student.

Except for one assignment. It must have been a process analysis paper: write an essay explaining how something is done. "Pick an audience," I thought I heard Professor L say. I'd been working in the dishroom of my dorm, Edwards Hall, earning spending money. I worked with about a half-dozen other guys plus a full-timer, Juan, whose last name we were never told. We took the trays at "the window," slid them along a stainless steel counter to "the pit" where we rinsed then loaded the bowls, plates, and desert cups, the glass racks and baskets of flatware on the conveyor that carried them through the dishwashing machine. My paper was titled (approximately), "Working in the Dishroom: Procedure, Technique, and Style."

I was really into this paper, excited by the concept that you could distinguish procedure, technique, and style. "Procedure" was what we employees were given as general instructions. "Technique" included our informal alterations to procedures, for example, how you might load bowls a certain way. "Style" referred to an individual's characteristic approach to the work. For example, on the crew we had a guy who liked to sing and wear funny hats. We had a guy who liked to mess with the leftover food. One guy liked to work at the window so he could hurl dishes with maximum force toward the pit, trying to break them. I wrote the whole thing in pretty high heat. Due date comes. Dr. L says, "Under your name, write the audience to whom your paper is addressed." I thought I was developing an extended metaphor for applied rhetoric, so I wrote, "THIS ESSAY IS ADDRESSED TO YOU." (I underlined the "you" in case Dr. L didn't know who I meant.) When I got the paper back, the feedback began and, as far as I was concerned, ended, with the note Dr. L wrote on the first page: "I specifically told you NOT to address me." She underlined "not" in case I didn't know what she meant.

I learned to write essays from my roommate, John, who also taught me how to hitchhike. What is no joke is the social relationship (our friendship) that sponsored my learning. The knowledge of essay writing he shared with me was inflected by the knowledge he shared about hitchhiking, skimping by in the wilderness, and playing guitar. In each of these areas, his pedagogy was consistent: Show, don't tell. Sophomore year, we took Environmental Economics, the professor nonstop explaining the economic rationale for the sprawl development that already in the late 1970s was burning open space on Colorado's front range. There were economic principles. "Marginal benefit," "opportunity cost," "externality": it could all be explained. That was our assignment for the midterm paper. I disliked the sprawl and I was puzzled by the language of economics. Forces of the market, blah blah blah. We've got to stop this! was my attitude. Denver sank heavily in the brown fog. Everywhere, grazing land, crop land, rabbit brush, zoned for P.U.D.

John finished his paper. I showed him mine—a paean to cornfields. It relied on implication, connotation, and unspecified value assumptions rooted in my visceral negative attitude toward the topic, the prof, and the discipline. To the call of Econ 240, my draft responded with weak poetry, meaningful description, and sincere lamentation.

"This is all wrong," John said. "You can't do it this way."

I do not remember exactly what he did after that. It involved a blank sheet of paper, a pencil, and my draft. With an emerging outline on the blank sheet of paper and circles and lines on my draft, he showed me how to reassemble an essay with three points, an intro, and a conclusion. I was floored. I could see this was the way to do it. I turned in the resulting paper and saved myself from what would have been a C, or, likely, worse, in the class.

I could have used John's peer tutoring back in Freshman Comp. I learned more in that one-on-one session than in my sixteen weeks with Dr. L. That one-on-one session stands as the critical learning experience that later in my own teaching I continually sought to emulate. And still do. I never feel like I'm working more effectively than when I'm working one-on-one. "Uses class time well" is usually one of the low marks on students' evaluations of my courses, and by the pang of guilt I feel when I see that, I know they are right.

I grew up in a family that assumed higher education would be part of our futures. Parents and grandparents on both sides of the family were college-educated folk. My mother and father both returned as adults to complete postgraduate programs. There were teachers in my family and a pattern of civic involvement in education-related activity. My mother taught kindergarten twenty-three years in a racially and economically mixed public school. She says she kept paint in her car. She says Sunday mornings she would sometimes drive to the strip mall across from her school. She would paint over the Vice Lords graffiti, so her school children would not see it. With the Black Hawk State Historical Site, she developed a cross-curriculum, cross-grade study guide, began taking her own students on field trips there. Later, she led teachers from other school districts. With others, she persuaded the parks department to plow up a softball field in a prairie restoration project. In 1989, she was named Science Teacher of the Year in Illinois. My father labored on the boards of the local chapter of Project NOW (a community action agency funded by the Office of Economic Opportunity), as well as on the board of a local community college and one of the state boards of Illinois higher education. He recounts being locked in a campus room when student protesters occupied an administration building.

When I want to understand my identity as a writing teacher, I have to think about innumerable conversations about teaching, education, and writing that took place in my home. And when did I start thinking about race? (Grade school, about age seven.) When did I start thinking about "whiteness"? (Not so long after. There was this book, John Howard Griffin's *Black Like Me*. My sister read it, then gave it to me.) In the 1960s and 1970s, my neighborhood was all "white." But whereas some of us espoused overtly bigoted opinion to whomever cared to listen, others were committed to the idea of civil rights, such as we understood it. "We believe in equal opportunity," my dad explained.

Teachers interested in cultivating a sense of efficacy and reflective optimism about the literacies, and learning potential, of AAVE-speaking students need to learn some basic information about African American English and AAVE discourse patterns. My course of study in African American vernacular culture began with blues music. My roommate, John, used to shop for records by diving the cutout bin. He'd go for the cheapest LPs. More than two dollars was too much. After one visit to the West Elizabeth Street record store, he came back all smiles, a double-album LP under his arm: *Memphis Swamp Jam*. (You can get it now on two CDs, *Mississippi Delta Blues Jam in Memphis*, volumes 1 and 2.) To the mix of stereos blaring Doobie Brothers, Fleetwood Mac, and Steve Miller, we added Napoleon Strickland, Memphis Piano Red. We listened to Bukka White's "Christmas Eve Blues." The full-on intensity of the guitar, the ferocity of his vocal attack and playing, scrubbing huge volumes of chords, squeezing them to yelping cries, knocked us out. This was a new feeling we sensed. We dug the bittersweetness, the pervading sorry humor of the blues. "Ain't nothing under that tree for poor old me." Plus we thought the white-bread, blond rock favored by floormates was, well, *not enough* anymore. Ignorant as we were to larger landscapes of racial history and the Gordian knot of race, literacy, and power relations, we could still understand the dialectic of Furry Lewis: "Arrested me for murder, I ain't killed no man. / Arrested me for murder, I ain't killed no one. / Arrested me for forgery, can't even sign my name" ("Judge Bushay's Blues").

The self-sponsored blues seminar continued later on in the writing program. Word came around about a bar in Old Town. The Bear and Whale was a biker-meets-grad student-meets-drug dealer place. We started dropping by for "Blue Mondays" when the house band, Jumpin Johnny and the Blues Survivors, would do a couple of sets, occasionally letting patrons sit in. (You can get Jumpin Johnny's *Crescent City Moon* from Bullseye Blues, a label owned by Rounder Records.) This extracurricular study filled the background when Etheridge Knight came to read poetry on campus. By then, another friend, Jack, had wangled his way to a position of responsibility, taping readings by visiting writers for future broadcast on the campus radio station. After Etheridge Knight's reading, he kept a copy of the tape. We listened to it. When we read the poems again, we could hear Etheridge Knight's voice in every line, the way he spoke-sang through the enjambed rhythm and clustered consonants in "The Idea of Ancestry," or "He Sees Through Stone."

I recently visited Fort Collins to give a poetry reading with Jack. Introduced by our former teacher, Jack and I were amused at the picture he painted. He said, "Books were like Frisbees to them. I would say 'go home and read a page out of Pablo Neruda' and off they would dash." Off we dashed, indeed, though not to the library as our teacher supposed. It was not that simple. We did read to each other. In the living room, after the Bear and Whale closed, we would open Russell Edson, or James Wright, or Robert Bly's translations of Neruda and Lorca. With these poets, we engaged in our own abnormal discourse processes of translation, reorganizing our taxonomies of thinking. And we'd listen to that tape of Etheridge Knight reading poems, and shivers would go through us, and we'd want to write poems that did that, too.

We were students, of course. But we were not, in our own minds, acting as students. One primary sense of myself as a writing teacher I locate here. My involvement with poetry writing continually bumped into my comp-teacher consciousness, disrupting its narrative of monocultural texts with a felt sense of pleasure in the effects produced by colliding discourses and a sense of felt urgency in the need to respond. To respond, that is, to the poet whose survival (in the case of Knight) seemed so much to depend on someone hearing everything he was saying in the way he said it.

Professional and Extraprofessional Contexts for Continued Efficacy Development

For teachers who otherwise lack socialization in African American communities, this means renegotiating their sense of themselves in relation to their work and in relation to culturally diverse students. Rooting out the sources of our sense of efficacy as writing teachers asks us to think about our classrooms from the perspective of affect. Efficacy locates affect as an essential element in teachers' constructs of knowledge. Efficacy speaks to the cumulative impact of our knowledge and experiences on our feelings about our students' ability and our ability to teach them. Efficacy therefore pushes us to theorize dimensions of personal and classroom experience that often remain unspoken in the discourse of formalized professional conversation.

Affect in the classroom influences our students' motivations for learning because it carries the evaluative overtones that animate the interactive discourse—the conversational back-and-forth, the dialogue of learning in the classroom. This was obvious in the community-based organizations we observed. But the salient point with reference to white teachers in multicultural classrooms, and in particular with reference here to AAVE-speaking students, is the lack of contact many white teachers have with diverse people of color outside the teaching setting, and the roles and relationships of the classroom as an institutional context. Teachers who are not connected to the students and are disconnected with their communities are susceptible to entering the classroom with reduced expectations— of their own ability to teach all students well as well as of their students' potential to achieve at the highest levels.

Arnetha

Over the next twenty-five years following high school, my academic and professional career encompassed a broad range of experiences, including classroom teaching at preschool through university levels, school administration, diagnostic and therapeutic work in speech pathology and audiology, and the ownership and directorship of a private early educational center—Children's Creative Workshop—that served the families of preschool and elementary school students in an inner-city West Coast community. Opening Children's Creative Workshop was certainly another milestone in my lifelong journey toward efficacy. I made the decision to open a school when our own first child was born. I simply could not imagine going elsewhere to share my professional passion for teaching with other people's children while leaving my own daughter in the custodial care of others. As I contemplated the senselessness of such a move, I wrestled with the thought that, while I was working tirelessly to create a learning environment in which students were being prepared to soar to unimagined heights as future intellectual and community leaders, my own child could possibly be spending her day in an environment where she was not being stimulated to achieve to her own fullest potential. I began to imagine that there could be a scenario in which I could blend my professional and extraprofessional identities in a context where I could provide an enriched learning experience for other people's children and provide a nurturing and stimulating learning experience for my own child. With the encouragement and support of my husband, Children's Creative Workshop was founded as a grassroots, community-based, early education center, eventually serving students from preschool through third grades.

I opened this early education center after working for several years in an all black public school in Northern California. While the students in this public school were generally well behaved and interested in learning, the majority of them were not achieving at their highest level of potential—and never were they expected to write texts longer than a paragraph. When I arrived at the school, class sizes were large, daily lessons were regimented, and the curriculum was generally uninteresting and lacking any semblance of cultural relevance. The educational center that I subsequently opened specialized in its ability to provide small class sizes, a culturally rich curriculum that integrated Montessori theory with writing process methodology in every content area, requiring the students to demonstrate critical and analytical thinking through their writing. A large majority of the teaching staff were persons of color who lived in the immediate or nearby community, and we had a great deal of parental and community involvement. Each of the teachers possessed a high degree of teacher efficacy—they were creative, loving, intellectual, talented, and they also possessed reflective optimism, that is, they held very high academic standards and strongly believed in their students' capacity to achieve to the highest levels—and they wasted no time in letting the students and their parents know it. Each teacher's daily lesson plans included Montessori practical life activities, reading, math, science, creative arts, large motor activities, computer technology, and lots of writing. Each evening, students completed homework assignments with their parents. Field trips, regular open houses, and our annual graduation ceremony were major programs in our community that allowed the students to demonstrate their oral and written skills. The school was in existence for over eleven years and many years after its closing, I received messages from parents and graduates from the school who were now attending law school or graduating cum laude from various institutions of higher education.

My early teaching experiences with the Creative Children's Workshop teachers provided me with countless professional encounters with teachers who had a passion and a love for teaching our students—mostly African American students. These teachers were strong and articulate, firm, yet warm and compassionate, demanding, yet confident that their students could meet the high standards they set, and they saw their students in extraprofessional contexts every day in the community where we all lived, learned, and worked. While working with these teachers, I observed firsthand countless examples of the linguistic resources diverse students brought to the classroom and had numerous encounters with teachers who developed rich, productive learning environments for these diverse students. While working with these excellent teachers at Children's Creative Workshop, I kept in touch with promising pedagogical trends affecting the education of African American students by taking continuing education courses and working as an itinerant speech pathologist in the local school system. Through these fulfilling experiences with predominantly African American students and with these successful teachers, my sense of professionalism and efficacy grew and my philosophy of teaching evolved as I came to regard students as active, capable learners and teachers as agents of community and educational change. To sustain this growing sense of efficacy over the development of my career into the professoriate, it was important that I nurture it through professional collaborations. If I wanted to continue to grow, I needed to seek out collaborations with colleagues and professional organizations. I needed to observe models of efficacious teaching beyond my own professional setting. I needed to establish collaborative relationships with professional organizations. Through these organizations, I was able to make contact with other individuals with like interests, individuals I could talk with and learn from, places where I could find role models as inspirations, like the Conference on College Composition and Communication (cccc), the American Education Research Association Writing Special Interest Group, the Black Caucus of the National Council of Teachers of English/cccc, and the assembly for research at ncte. Making such contacts several times each year helped me to stay up with the current research, recent innovations, and best practices for generative application in my own classroom teaching.

During my early years as a teacher, I gained great pleasure from helping my students to open up their capacities as writers, whether I was working with my preschoolers, elementary, middle, or high school students. Regardless of the grade level, the challenge for me has always been to value the learning styles of my students as diverse learners, to understand how to build on the lived experiences that my students brought to the classroom, and to use that information to enhance the teaching and learning environment for these very capable students. Throughout my early years as a teacher, I harbored both a fascination and a curiosity about the contradictory reports that African American students possessed great agility with the spoken word in the tradition of the African American *griot,* yet they were generally considered to be "poor writers" in most academic settings. Sadly, they also began to see themselves as "poor writers" at an early age. My internalization of the principles demonstrated by the community role models of my early years was further demonstrated through my belief that the students in my classroom could have a very different experience. The students in my classes were constantly challenged to communicate their ideas in writing. I hoped they were aware of my desire to be one of those teachers who acted as a catalyst, who opened the door for students to the untamed and liberating possibilities that writing can offer. Who opened the door to all of the potential of these African American writers and the passions that the freedom of writing can bring.

I eventually decided to return to graduate school and to teacher education to broaden and refine my sense of self as a competent professional. I was seeking answers to complex questions concerning teaching and learning and the challenges of preparing teachers who worked effectively with culturally and linguistically diverse students. One of my primary goals in becoming a teacher educator was to work toward empowering classroom teachers with a vision of the powerful roles they could play in reforming education for poor, marginalized, and underachieving students. I seek constantly to encourage a strong sense of efficacy in these teachers.

Ted

Before returning to graduate school to pursue doctoral studies, I worked as a part-time writing instructor. For two years, I commuted between the university campus in Ann Arbor and the urban campus of Wayne State University in Detroit. At the margins of the course schedule, I taught 8 A.M. sections or evening sections. When there were no sections to teach, I temped for ManPower, cleaning doctor's offices from 3 to 11 P.M. During summers, a solidly middle-class man employed me to tend the family's gardens and yard. On a cul-de-sac in a nice neighborhood in Ann Arbor, I crept through the weeks, accompanied by the clang of the flagpole pulleys at Martin Luther King Jr. Elementary School. Wages I earned here I supplemented with stipends earned reading placement tests of incoming students for the English Composition Board at UM.

From the juxtaposition of these labors, some of my core dispositions as a writing teacher developed. I loved writing. I loved certain aspects of teaching, such as connecting with students, helping them to succeed. But I was uncomfortable in the role of writing teacher. I thought then, and think still, that being a teacher is a noble and fine vocation. But I was then, and still am, a little embarrassed to be an English teacher. I was and still am disposed to regard the formal registers of academic discourse as pretentious language not worth aspiring to master. Yet verbal niceties, an outward neatness of thought and expression, seemed to be what we were supposed to teach. Revisiting their landmark essay, "Audience Addressed/ Audience Invoked," Andrea Lunsford and Lisa Ede note, "The subject of discourse invoked in AA/AI is a subject who feels both agency and authority—that subject is also implicitly stable, unified, and autonomous" (170). Rethinking this assumption, they go on: "That a student might find herself full of contradiction and conflict, might find the choices available to her as a writer confusing and even crippling—might in fact find it difficult, even undesirable, to claim the identity of 'writer'—did not occur to us" (171). In my own early teaching experiences, my sense of professional self, this anxious teacher identity, was formed in conflict out of a rough accommodation between my poet heart and the choices available in the composition classroom.

For better or worse, this ambivalence put me, I suspect, on the same page with many students, which was fine, except I did not know how to teach from this mixed-up position, how to make writing pedagogy translate into opportunities for powerful learning. Course evaluations typically showed students found me approachable, "nice." On the other hand, I did not expect very much of myself as a teacher, nor extend myself to probe the givens of my working milieu. My attitude was, "Here are the required textbooks. Here is the syllabus. This is the assignment. Get to work." It was on the students to feel agency, find authority, motivate themselves, do good work fitting into the curricular groove. If they came to me, I was happy to help them out, truly. But I did not initiate the effort, even for students I could see floundering. And I did not think long or hard about the whys and wherefores of the writing I was hoping students would learn. Eager to establish and protect my authority as a teacher, particularly since it felt so hollow, I was reasonably content to identify with the current traditional rhetoric being offered, and let the students fend for themselves.

I am not sure exactly when that changed, or if there was a single, transforming moment. Maybe there was an accumulating sense of dissonance that created a need to break with the givens of this early version of my professional identity. For example, there was the problematic way in which I effaced myself as a functionary in an institutional regime of literacy I continued to accept, even though deep down, outside the classroom, I really had doubts about it. Race, or racism, hardly entered the picture, at least not explicitly. I did not see myself as intending to discriminate against students who spoke or wrote with the influence of African American English. Flagging nonstandard negation patterns, incorrect tense markers, coaching against the use of "inappropriate" or "disorganized" discourse patterns seemed the easiest way to enact the writing-teacher function.

Still, increasingly, this approach seemed actively stupid. I kept bumping into my extracurricular commitment to poetry writing. My passion for how written discourse comes together from deep sources in our lives, from passionate commitments, from intense interests, from a love for a word like "buoy," kept intruding. I *knew* about writing as an activity to engage, about the interaction of evolving intentions, apparent effects, and the material at hand—including information, sense of audience (how far can we go together?), the feeling of an idea, the multiple resources of our plural languages as embodiment of that feeling. I wanted to get that through in my teaching.

Of the courses I taught then as a part-timer, I now remember little of the students, the lessons, the classrooms. Most of what I remember consists of surroundings—empty offices, rain sheen slicking the summer streets. The story I compose, these memory fragments arranged by the impulse to understand them, is the narrative inverse of other, authoritative teaching stories. For example, I imagine Mina Shaughnessy writing *Errors and Expectations*. I picture the scene she constructs, "sitting alone in the worn urban classroom," "reading and re-reading the alien papers, wondering what had gone wrong and trying to understand what I at this eleventh hour of my students' academic lives could do about it" (*Errors* vii). So much the center, that "I" at the eleventh hour. Not my story; I was the alien. Down memory's long corridor, where streaks of light paint a window, a figure hustles past outside. "See?" I'm saying. "He was walking from the car one evening. He was on his way here, to teach his class. He didn't know it then, but he was on his way here, to this page, too." Rolled up in that green pack on my back I carried my students' narratives like a map to a future I could not imagine. In my training as a TA prior to this point, I'd been given nothing with which to understand how race might play a part in anything related to teaching composition. I was teaching as I had been taught, though not happily.

That was a night I stayed late on that downtown campus to see Gwendolyn Brooks give a poetry reading. I wrote a letter describing it. My mother taped it to the refrigerator. Years later, she mailed it back. Sitting here, I study the artifact: slightly yellowed flyer. "You are invited to an evening of Poetry Reading with GWENDOLYN BROOKS. Thursday, May 29, 1986, at 8 P.M. in the McGregor Memorial Conference Center." On the back, I'd written,

> Among the hundred or so who all finally trickled into the space, another white guy, beard and beret, and other earnest young students conversing—grad school, the big "D" to get done, etc. etc., with tape recorders, and an older white couple near the very front. Then the V.P. for P.R. introduced the mayor's P.R. liaison who awarded Ms. Brooks the key to the city, then the Department Chair introduced Ms. Brooks, then the reading began, each poem followed by enthusiastic applause. Ms. Brooks was steady as a rock and filled that room and all those people with her presence and her voice and her poems no problem. She really almost

sings them with a voice that goes pretty deep and also real high like a sing-song schoolgirl's voice too, and cadences in the presentation, repetitions in the lines of the poems that swing, and most were about identity, she said—"love, life, light, laughter, longing and laceration." . . . She growled, chuckled, sneered, jeered, teased and praised. She answered questions at the end. She liked rap music and reggae. I left for home at nine-thirty.

That was the night of the umbrella collision. "Umbrella collision" was what the woman said, who brought her beautiful ten-month-old to class. Three weeks into summer term, she dropped out. We bumped umbrellas on the steps of the classroom building. Rain falling, the air, Cass Corridor almost glowed. When seven ring-neck pheasants strutted, copper from the sumac fringing the east commuter lot, I saw them as talismans, arcs of memory sparking home from a dog-crowded Illinois cornfield.

When I reached the fourth floor, I knew the adjuncts' space would be empty. Where I kept office hour would be dreamlike, silent. Under my umbrella, this was all I foresaw as I started up the steps. Bump. Startled, I looked up. Under her umbrella she looked at me. "Umbrella collision," she said stepping by, disappearing, disappearing, disappearing.

Perhaps for a moment, in that thin instant, I imagined I could be in love with her. An instant later, I knew I could not. But for that one second, she stopped being a student, a number on the grade sheet, a field of errors coming across in an "unsatisfactory" draft. Right then, she appeared complete: a person. She left the class and I regretted it. I believe this was the first time I actually felt bad— culpable and genuinely sad—about someone not making it (not taking it) in my class. I was bummed. I figured out, right then, it would be fun to talk to her, because I could learn something from her. Because of what she said, out of nowhere: Umbrella collision. Umbrella collision? Wasn't that the truth! A two-word poem. Her caption for the figure of our failure to connect. At least, I see I could have taken, as her teacher, the modest step of learning a bit more—

about her and all my students. Scheduling conferences would not have killed me.

If my teaching changed after that, I started changing, too. I can't explain the cause-effect in a rational, straightforward way. The rational analysis angle doesn't feel complete or real. It leaves out the radical particularity, the grainy textures of the idiom that reaches across professional/public and personal/private spheres of interaction where teaching lives. What feels real is what happens in chapter 15, the pivotal chapter in *Adventures of Huckleberry Finn*. In chapter 15, Huck recounts a long night of separation and a long search of his own soul on the "monstrous big river" (96). In a heavy fog, separated from Jim and the raft, Huck sets out, paddling furiously in the canoe to catch up, then simply floating while the current carries him on, whooping for Jim and listening for Jim in return. "It was the still places between the whoops that was making the trouble for me," he says (96).

> I was floating along, of course, four or five miles an hour;
> but you don't even think of that. No, you feel like you are
> laying dead still on the water; and if a little glimpse of a snag
> slips by, you don't think to yourself how fast you're going,
> but you catch your breath and think, my! how that snag's
> tearing along. (97)

This reversal, this inside-out turn of perception, anticipates the core moment in the narrative during which Huck's outlook toward Jim is uprooted, if not dispensed with entirely. The transformation in Huck comes to fruition in the final action of the chapter. Having embarrassed Jim by playing a trick on him, Huck feels the sting in Jim's rebuke: "trash is what people are who put dirt on the heads of their friends and makes them ashamed" (100). Hard as it is, Huck finally apologizes. In doing so, he acknowledges his own part in the reciprocity of friendship, of *Jim's* friendship, the mutuality Jim asserts across the racial divide.

It is not enough to reflect on changes in our teaching practice as technicians. Our observations of teachers in community-based organizations, along with our positive experiences as students working with memorable teachers who had a big impact on our own development, lead us to recognize the possibilities for composition teachers who create a space for affect in the classroom. Partly this refers to taking note of the modes and norms that characterize interaction. Partly this includes becoming aware of and drawing on students' affective responses to the writing class. It also means taking care to keep track of our own affective responses vis-à-vis participation and vis-à-vis communicating passionate involvement with the work of the class: high regard for the students, high regard for writing and the intellectual work that can be done with it. It is not enough to be an economist. The dictionary gives this definition:

> *externality* n. An incidental condition that may affect a course of action. "Our economic system treats environmental degradation as an externality—a cost that does not enter into the conventional arithmetic that determines how we use our resources" (Barry Commoner).

My students' low achievement was a cost they paid. It did not enter the conventional calculation of my pedagogy, except as their depressed grades counted as credit for my supposedly high standards. Eventually, I realized my complacency and resulting failure to appreciate the insights my students could offer ("umbrella collision") *were* costs I paid—in loss of joy in my work. That is what was in it for me, really, deep down, under the part about being someone else's idea of a "good teacher."

Analyzing One's Own Journey Toward Efficacy

Through these narratives, we are sharing some of the formative events in our processes of self-reflection and transforming attitudes. For Ted, a primary source of extraprofessional inspiration has been poetry and the community of friendship around poetry writing. For Arnetha, primary sources have been family and spiritual inspiration. Overlooked to some degree in the scholarship are the extracurricular sources of efficacy that sustain us. Whereas Ashton and Webb's "ecology" of efficacy offers a snapshot of influences affecting teachers' sense of efficacy, we are still in need of a model of adult identity formation that lets us consider longitudinally how teachers' self-understanding grows and changes over time. Such a model invites us to notice how teachers' professional identities are negotiated in relation to other extraprofessional identities.

In a study of life histories of craft artists, Elliot Mishler found that the movement toward claiming the work identity of craft artist is mediated by other interchange points, for example, family roles or other job and career obligations. Over time, the intersecting relationships among these axes shift alignment. Mishler highlights the notion of a craft artist's work identity as "only one of several relatively distinct and autonomous axes of self-definition" (8). Mishler concludes that identity should "be defined as a collective term referring to the dynamic organization of sub-identities that might conflict with or align with each other"; that the study of identity should focus on formation over time; and that "the formation and achievement of work- and other sub-identities" is significantly associated with "life-course disjunctions, discontinuities, and transitions" (9). As we consider the notion of a model of adult identity formation that will be useful to writing and composition teachers who wish to imagine new possibilities for African American students, we add to Mishler's definition the notion of internally persuasive discourses put forward by Bakhtin in his discussion of ideological becoming. According to Bakhtin,

> it happens more frequently that an individual's becoming, an ideological process, is characterized precisely by a sharp gap between these two categories: in one, the authoritative word . . . , in the other, [the] internally persuasive word that is denied all privilege, backed by no authority at all, and is frequently not even acknowledged in society . . . not even in the legal code. The struggle and dialogic interrelationship of these categories of ideological discourse are what usually determine the history of an individual's ideological consciousness. . . .

Such discourse is of decisive significance in the evolution of an individual consciousness: [in this way] consciousness awakens to independent ideological life. (243, 345)

When Bakhtin describes the way in which our consciousness awakens to independent ideological life, he is describing what we are referring to as extraprofessional identify formation. When teachers begin to respond to the call to revise the way we teach and, moreover, to revise who we are as teachers (how we present ourselves in the classroom, how we make ourselves available to all students, how we envision our roles publicly and institutionally), then we have begun to engage in the process of identify transformation that is needed to reimagine the possibilities for African American students in our writing and composition classrooms (Ball and Freedman).

In *Mind in Society,* Vygotsky's discussions on internalization help us to further understand how teachers develop a positive stance toward working effectively with AAVE-speaking students. The development of this positive stance can be viewed as internal activity that can become observable through the change in teachers' discourse and classroom practices over time. As writing teachers engage with theories and pedagogical approaches for working effectively with African American students, their considerations about this topic arise out of external, practical activities—such as their professional and private engagement with diverse populations, readings on theory and research on African American students, interactive discussions with informed colleagues, reflective writing, and practical teaching experiences. Vygotsky argued that there is an inherent relationship between this external activity and the internal activity, that is, when developing commitment and self-efficacy, but that it is a developmental relationship in which the major issue is how external processes are transformed to create internal processes.

Arnetha

As I mentioned, I entered the research community at a time when linguistic research on the systematic nature of AAVE and its impact on literacy learning was flourishing.

At about this time in my career, it also occurred to me that if AAVE-speaking students' writing experiences were to change, then writing and composition teachers would need to play an active role in this transformation. I became more determined than ever to carry out my research in authentic learning environments that were faced with the challenge of improving writing instruction for underachieving, poor, marginalized, and inner-city students. These environments include traditional schools in which students of color are underachieving; community-based organizations that have become an integral part of an alternative education system that offers a range of choices to individuals who seek "second chance" or "last chance" opportunities on the road to personal, academic, or economic success; and teacher education programs that prepare teachers to teach in the urban and inner-city context. My investigations in these three intersecting contexts ask the following questions: (a) How can we apply what we are learning about the oral and written practices of African American students in extracurricular settings to improve the academic experiences of a broad range of underachieving students? (b) How can we apply what we are learning about the organization and implementation of instruction in successful community-based organizations to enhance the teaching and learning of students in more traditional classroom settings? and (c) How can we apply what we are learning about the development of teachers who are sensitive to linguistic issues to facilitate the development of reflective practitioners who are committed to becoming agents of change in writing and composition classrooms? Embarking on this research became another milestone, not only in my own development of a sense of efficacy and determination to influence change in this area for students, but also in my commitment to help other teachers to realize the critical role of teacher efficacy in their teaching.

Ted

Composing these narratives offers us a way to further explore the contention that the "teaching life and the lived life are . . . finally the same thing" (Bishop, "What We Don't Like" 119). George Hillocks refers to beliefs, attitudes, and values as a source of teacher knowledge; the emotional, intellectual, perhaps spiritual residues of our life histories shape our approach to teaching, students, writing. But the teaching shapes the life, too.

In *Storylines,* Elliot Mishler delves the topic of adult identity formation, using life-story interviews with craft artists as his data. Mishler finds that career trajectory was marked by an "erratic" path, and that work identity "appeared to be . . . one of several relatively distinct and autonomous axes of self-definition" (8). Reading Mishler tells me to recognize teacher identity formation in more comprehensive way. The literature on teacher narratives frames its dialogic in the interaction of the personal and professional dimensions of identity. In the construct of efficacy, the personal-professional dichotomy becomes less clear. Following Mishler, each term is an aggregate of different kinds of social interactions involving different groups of people. These interactions continually rearticulate our identities, including work or professional identities. Second, as much as my narrative shows the serendipitously conjoined influences of disparate life experiences, I acknowledge that we are not destined by our life histories to be one kind of teacher. Anyway, we cannot depend on life circumstances to produce the attitude and approach to teaching needed.

I vision it this way: There is a moment, entering the classroom (the space of teaching) when our lives hail us. Yet, from our vantage within the intellectual, social, and moral space of teaching, we choose how to respond to students whose expectations, whose promise, hail us as well. When I think about race as an element crucially involved in our work in the writing classroom and crucially involved in our lives beyond the classroom, in terms of our racially informed dispositions toward language, literacy, and diverse students, we may be products of our upbringing. However, we are not by definition submerged in them. If fact, the premise of teacher efficacy as we articulate it here is that teachers reexamine and renegotiate preconceptions and prejudices.

Do I have sustaining confidence in my ability to teach all students and in particular to work effectively with students whose home language is AAVE? The trajectory of this chapter rushes toward a predictable "Yes!"

Yet, alongside the self-satisfied glow from that long-ago summer in Cass Corridor, I should like to present a more recent counterperspective. When I measure my teaching practice against the models we present of teachers in community-based organizations, when I think of the fine poets, actors, and teachers I have joined in workshops and staff-development programs, I know it isn't true. I am not the exemplary teacher. I'm pretty average. If I'm different enough to make a difference for some students, okay. But my narrative isn't "Wow!" I'm not "Wow!" And my teaching isn't "Wow." On the other hand, I think it will be a good day when teachers are no longer viewed as "Wow" when they work truly and well with all their students.

Partly my story concerns motive. What felt need propelled me in this inquiry, this journey of self-reflection? What I thought I knew, I began to suspect, became a barrier to learning. I have wanted to write, think about, transform what I don't know about what I know. My journey began confounded, dumbfounded, with a recognition of what I did not know. The shape and size of my ignorance, perched across from my credentials, my inherited culture, my comfortable position in a racialized hierarchy. How could something so heavy be so invisible?

Conclusion

In this chapter, we have presented and examined narratives of our own processes of claiming efficacy as teachers. A unifying theme that runs through both of our stories is a desire to be that teacher who acted as a catalyst, who opened the door for students to the liberatory possibilities that writing can offer. Of course, through the narratives we compose, we, in a sense, discover the process we describe. Telling our stories, we come back to the formative events in our journeys toward efficacy, articulating their meanings from a new angle. In the telling, our lives become something else again, a series of new meanings harvested from the seeds of actual events.

Reflecting on our own processes of moving beyond internalization, we have foregrounded the ways in which, as teachers, our professional growth has occurred in relation to other parts of our lives. We have also sought to demonstrate that this movement beyond internalization is ongoing, a continuing project; it means we grow and change as teachers alongside our students.

Exploring how teachers at different stages of their careers and from different backgrounds mediate their dispositions toward literacy, we have concluded that teacher efficacy in these matters is rooted in teachers' dispositions toward themselves, their work environment, and their culturally diverse students. In the curriculum, teachers' encounters with high-powered theory may transform their dispositions toward literacy by changing their affective stances toward their work and their students. This transformation appears to involve a process of self-reflection, analyzing one's own journey toward efficacy, reanalyzing personal beliefs and assumptions, and renegotiating one's sense of oneself not only in professional but also in extraprofessional dimensions. Building on lessons learned from the participatory literacy practices found in community-based organizations, as well on as the stories we have shared, we examine next key principles, practices, and policies that open up the possibilities for reenvisioning composition classes for African American students.

5 / Playin' the Dozens: Unleashing Students' Literate Possibilities

So how can a first-year writing teacher who perhaps has little formal training in writing pedagogy nor formal knowledge of AAVE take concrete steps toward improving the opportunity for success of AAVE-speaking students in his or her classroom? What we have shown up to this point in every positive example of successful teaching are people who have extensive knowledge of AAVE.

In *The Dream Keepers*, Gloria Ladson-Billings reviews research on programs that are effective with African American students. These programs fall into three types:

> those designed to remediate or accelerate without attending to the students' social or cultural needs; those designed to resocialize African American students to mainstream behaviors, values, and attitudes at the same time that they teach basic skills; and those designed to facilitate student learning by capitalizing on the students' own social and cultural backgrounds. (10)

Arguing for the "culturally relevant" approach, Ladson-Billings helps us envision a first-year writing course that takes account of students' individual, group, and cultural differences, seeing the latter "as strengths to base academic achievement on" (11).

To break down how this can be done, we take our text from Steven Zemelman and Harvey Daniels. We restate (with changes) part of the quote we used as the epigraph to our article "Dispositions toward Language: Teachers' Constructs of Knowledge and the Ann Arbor 'Black English' Case." Discussing classroom atmosphere, Zemelman and Daniels state,

If the linguists are right that the social context is the driving force behind literacy acquisition, then *the social context of your [composition] classroom is the most powerful and important variable you can experiment with.* More important than what textbook or speller or dictionary [or handbook or software] to use; more important than what kinds of assignments to give; more important than how to set up cumulative writing folders; more important than the criteria by which you assign kids to peer response groups; more important than "teaching [Elbow]" versus teaching [Bartholomae and Petrosky]. More important than anything.

Zemelman and Daniels call this assertion their "hypothesis" (50). As a hypothesis, it remains open for testing, although reflections on our own experiences lead us to agree. A sly effect of this statement is its invitation to pass over meat-and-potatoes pedagogical issues (textbooks? assignments? writing folders? peer groups?) in an exclusive focus on atmosphere or social climate as the only variable that matters. Still, the emphasis on the "social context" of the writing classroom is well placed. When we want to tell teachers what to do to begin making changes, we couch our recommendations within the expectation that they be considered as parts of an overall whole: a change in any one variable may be a good step in the direction of promise, but no single change will likely lead a teacher very far on the path.

So, how can a first-year writing teacher take concrete steps toward improving the opportunity for success of AAVE-speaking students in his or her classroom? Teachers can start with their daily lesson planning, by making explicit for themselves their substantive goals, participation goals, and affective goals for each class session. Each of these aspects contribute substantially to classroom success for their students. Next, teachers must articulate for themselves their knowledge about their students' cultural practices and their thoughts about their own sense of efficacy and reflective optimism concerning their students. These categories are interlinked. When teachers demonstrate reflective optimism toward their students, believing that they can in fact succeed, they become reflective practitioners, contemplating ways on an ongoing basis in which they can capitalize on their students' everyday discourse patterns as a resource. This is the beginning of becoming a reflective practitioner who is willing to envision new practices and new possibilities.

The Dozens

When we called this section "The Dozens," we were building on the term *playin' the dozens* as a metaphor that we do not want our readers to miss. AAVE is a logical and systematic variety of English that has stylistic, phonological, lexical, and grammatical features that distinguish it from academic as well as mainstream American English. AAVE speakers use certain linguistic features that, although they appear in other American English varieties, occur in AAVE more frequently, systematically, and consistently than in mainstream American English. The black preaching tradition, signifyin', cappin', rappin', and playin' the dozens are all speech events that are grounded in the rhythmic, kinesthetic, climactic, and formulaic structure of AAVE's style of rhetoric.

One variation in style includes the use of a ritualized speech act called "playin' the dozens." This ritual insulting is highly stylized and is a competitive game in which players make up elaborate obscenities to describe one another's relatives, especially the opponent's mother. For example, "Yo mama so bowlegged, she look like the bite out of a donut." The dozens are well formed only if they remain impersonal. This is usually achieved by making claims so exaggerated that they are obviously false. When engaged in *playin' the dozens*, the verbal competitors can playfully engage in the game precisely because the insults that are being hurled around are so far from reality that everyone knows they are untrue. Therefore, no one really gets personally insulted and the player with the most stinging and creative humor is declared the winner. It is all done in fun. However, if one of the players hurls an insult that hits too close to home by saying something that resembles the truth, then the fun is over. The competitor who realizes that something true and embarrassing has been said about his mother can become highly offended and may move into attack mode. What had been taken lightly suddenly becomes fighting words.

We have used this title here, "The Dozens," because we want to tell our readers "the time has come for the writing and composition community to become highly offended because something true has been said that should move them into attack mode." If readers agree that what we have said so far in this book has any merit, if it hits close to home, if it is true, then we want them to become offended about the state of affairs concerning the experiences of AAVE-speaking students in their classrooms. We want them to become determined to become advocates for change—advocates for attacking this problem head on. Just as the verbal competitor who is playing the dozens suddenly comes to the realization that their mother has been insulted, today's writing and composition teachers must come to a realization that their attitudes may actually be acting as an unconscious barrier to their effectiveness as writing professionals. Only then will they reassess their dispositions toward language in their classrooms. Only then will they determine their readiness to advocate for change. Once inspired, teachers can begin that attack, using the dozens that follow as suggested points of departure.

Affect

1. Readjust Attitudes

WHAT: It all starts with attitude, this journey towards unleashing students' literacies. Reimagining the possibilities for AAVE-speaking students in composition classrooms begins with an attitude adjustment. We need, first, to adjust our attitudes toward nonstandard language and the unspoken, sometimes unconscious, prejudices we may possess. Teachers and students may hold negative language attitudes. They may not be aware of it, but they prejudge nonstandard pronunciation, usage, grammatical constructions, and discourse.

As we have noted, the Ann Arbor "Black English" case focused on the barrier to achievement created by teachers' unconscious negative attitudes toward AAVE. The language barrier resulting from negative attitudes was the focus of the Ann Arbor case, and for college writing classrooms, they remain to challenge successful practice and our students' educational progress today (Richardson, "Race"). In their article "Influencing Future Teachers' Attitudes toward Black English," Bowie and Bond found that teachers still continue to exhibit negative attitudes toward African American English, many stating that African American English has a faulty grammar system and that children who speak African American English are less capable than children who speak Standard English.

More than twenty years ago, in response to the Ann Arbor case, the Black Caucus of the NCTE and CCCC disseminated a carefully prepared statement regarding AAVE. They said that the language of black students is a strength on which teachers might draw in order to develop effective approaches to teaching. However, when asked about the status of this issue, Geneva Smitherman framed it this way:

> Nothing new of substance is known that we didn't know 15 years ago about sociolinguistics and education in the schools. However, what we did not realize 15 years ago is that negative attitudes concerning language are very deep seated. We, therefore, did not realize how difficult it would be to have an impact on those attitudes and to change them. Currently, information needed to change those attitudes is insufficient. People listen to the information about the competence of languages, they take it in and then—like cognitive dissonance—they exhibit language behaviors that are totally contrary to the information. There has to be something going on in the deep recesses of the minds of individuals such that the information that they have gained has no access to, or effect on, their behaviors. People have been given the information—the facts—but they still behave in the same old ways. (personal interview by Arnetha Ball, January 1995)

HOW: How do you change your attitude? For starters, we can contemplate the story below and hope that such encounters will act as a jump start that ignites a desire and a personal motivation to travel the sometimes painful road to attitude change.

When Judge Joiner ruled for the plaintiff children in the Ann Arbor "Black English" case, the Ann Arbor School Board had to decide whether to appeal. There were two meetings. In the first, four School Board members and the board president voted to appeal. The vote was taken in a closed meeting, and it therefore violated the state's recently enacted "sunshine" law. The board was required to meet and vote a second time.

Prior to the second meeting, the board president met with a group of linguists who explained the issue of negative language attitudes at the center of the court's ruling. Initially, the board president said she regarded the ruling as "bullshit law." Her conversation with one of the linguists changed her mind. She said the linguist explained it this way: "President Dannemiller, I don't know you, but I can guess this about you, that you think of yourself as a fair-minded and nonjudgmental person. Am I right?" She said yes. The linguist continued. "President Dannemiller, I don't know you, but I can guess this about you, that you are a well-educated person and you appreciate well-formed, correctly phrased speech. Is that true?" The president agreed it was true. The linguist went on: "President Dannemiller, I don't know you, but I can guess this about you, that even though you say you are not the judgmental sort and that another person's imperfect use of language doesn't trouble you or lessen your opinion of him or her, you still react negatively, don't you, if only for an instant?"

Describing her reaction, the former school board president leaned forward. "You know what?" she said. "He was right!" She paused. "He looked at me and said, 'That is what this lawsuit is all about.' And I got it!" She snapped her fingers. "Just like that. I finally understood what they'd talked about in court. And I changed my vote." (Personal interview with Kathleen Dannemiller, May 12, 1990)

Just as the Ann Arbor school board president came to a realization, today's composition teachers must come to a realization that their attitudes may be acting as an unconscious barrier to their effectiveness as writing professionals. Acknowledging that one has an attitude toward language is a first step toward changing one's vote.

2. Confront Racial Insecurities and Prejudices

WHAT: The sociolinguistic issue of negative language attitudes and their seeming imperviousness to change becomes understandable when framed in the sociohistorical context of race and racism in America. Teachers must confront the insecurities and prejudices we each hold as part of a move toward self-efficacy and reflective optimism.

In the service of developing a pedagogy that enfranchises rather than excludes African American students, we need to critically reflect on and analyze the ways our insecurities and prejudices may predetermine the relationships we extend to students as well as their relationships to the work of the writing course. What networks of connection might be activated, supporting us in our exchanges? What traditions might be accessed as a means to understand the cultural work literacy can do? We are thinking, for example, of a tradition at the core of African American culture, a discourse of inspiration that comes out of the black church and pervades the rhetoric of slave narratives such as Frederick Douglass's autobiography, or the political activism of the civil rights movement. This is a discourse of liberation realized in a language of hope that makes ample use of an ongoing activist spiritual tradition. We are suggesting that this tradition holds a vocabulary of potential, a potential teaching discourse that can be realized through reading and writing assignments, that can connect literacy to that sense of great purpose, of communal struggle in the expectation of success. One of the fullest theorizations of such an approach can be found in Elaine Richardson's *African American Literacies*.

Making an examination of race an explicit part of their course work invites teachers to construe "difference" as a strategic category of meaning that may be foregrounded or relegated to the background for purposes that are determined by the agents involved. Teachers who persist in their failure to acknowledge their own socially constructed racial identity are bound to sabotage this effort. As Clifford Geertz has written, "It is the asymmetries between what we believe or feel and what others do, that makes it possible to locate where we now are in the world, how it feels to be there, and where we might or might not want to go" (114).

HOW: How can we support teachers in their efforts to confront the insecurities and prejudices we each hold as part of a move toward self-efficacy and reflective optimism? By reimagining their professional growth as part of a project of self-actualization (hooks), teachers can begin to exercise the critical self-awareness that is part of lifelong learning. Tools like Peggy McIntosh's inventory of white privilege, or Beverly Tatum's excellent discussion of race privilege in *"Why Are All the Black Kids Sitting Together in the Cafeteria?"* offer starting places. In simplest terms, it becomes a matter of speaking up, if at first only to ourselves, about race and racism not only as a public/professional concern but as a lived reality that permeates our everyday lives.

3. Create a Space for Affect in the Classroom

WHAT: It is important for composition teachers to create a space for affect in the classroom—a place for feeling. The modes and norms of interaction found in the classrooms of successful teachers of AAVE-speaking students are often quite different from those observed in other, traditional classrooms. According to Kochman, the predominant mode—that of the middle and upper class—is relatively low-key: dispassionate, impersonal, nonchallenging, and characterized by a detachment that is cool, quiet, and without affect (18). Kochman further notes that "emotional expressiveness has considerably less force and effect in white cultural activities and events, because white norms for proper participation require that individuals exercise greater emotional self-restraint" (112). According to Kochman, whites sometimes become distressed or resentful when blacks let their feelings become too expressive or intense in disregard of established white norms or when blacks, as audience members, respond verbally to some action that is taking place. Therefore, the norms governing "proper" participation in many composition classrooms and the engagement of individuals in public discussion of an issue require that participants keep their emotions contained and relatively subdued and that turn taking be regulated by an empowered authority.

Many composition teachers may not think about consciously trying to create a certain persona for themselves nor the happy, serious vibe that characterizes a group working at optimum capacity. Normally when we talk about the affective dimension of our classrooms, we refer to "chemistry" and "atmosphere" and too quickly relinquish the possibility that we can take steps to bring about such a working environment. We realize there are far too many variable human factors for teachers to exercise complete control in creating the learning atmosphere in their classrooms. Yet teachers can take certain measures to improve the mood. When we speak of affect here, we refer to the emotional tone of classroom interactions. In our zeal and our fervor to fulfill our charge to transmit "acceptable" society norms—cultural as well as behavioral—to all students, the educational community has sacrificed some potential resources that reside in the cultural and linguistic heritage of some students. The successful teachers in community-based organizations were not conflicted by the presence of high-keyed, interactive cultural practices. They were able to use these resources to engage their students in the classroom activity, to challenge their students to think critically, and to use the cultural capital they brought with them into the classroom.

HOW: How do we help teachers create a space for affect in the classroom—a place for feeling? According to Kochman, African American modes of discussion are generally more high-keyed, interpersonal, and at times may even appear confrontational. Early research in linguistics found that when arguing to persuade,

blacks sometimes assume a challenging stance with respect to their opponents. But . . . blacks are not being antagonists

here. Rather, they are contenders . . . cooperatively engaged
in a process . . . that hopes to *test the situation through challenging the validity of opposing ideas.* (Kochman 18, emphasis added)

Another characteristic of the affective, interactive discourse patterns
observed in successful community-based classrooms was the presence of the African American discourse pattern of *call and response.*
Call and response embodies an interlocking and synergistic communicative dimension in which members of a group participate
interactively by adding their own voice—"can I get an amen?"—to
the voices of others to serve both as counterpoint and counterforce,
alternating, stimulating, and encouraging each other and receiving
the stimulus of others until a collective agreement or a regeneration
is achieved. In the successful community-based classrooms we have
observed, students use patterns of high interaction, personal engagement, and call and response to bring their own voices—and to invite others to do likewise—into a complementary or even challenging relationship with the discussion at hand so that all participants
might benefit from the power of those combined voices.

Today's writing and composition teachers need to realize that
in our zeal and our fervor to fulfill our charge to transmit so-called
acceptable norms to all students, the educational community has
failed to use potential resources that reside in the cultural and linguistic heritage of our African American students. We have attempted to
replace their stylized patterns of interaction with norms that are
more in keeping with white middle-class styles of communication,
even though the former patterns foster forms of communication in
which many African American students habitually assert themselves
within the group in critical and engaging ways. It is important that
writing and composition teachers realize that when AAVE-speaking
students bring affect in the classroom, they are doing what Roger
Abrahams refers to as

doing your thing, which in African American culture does
not mean, as it has come to be translated in white culture,

acting independently of the group. Rather, in the African American community, doing your thing means asserting yourself within the group, such as entering into a performance by adding your voice to the ensemble, by playing off against others—competitively and cooperatively at the same time—as each instrument does in jazz. (Abrahams 83)

The main function of interaction and call and response in the African American cultural style of discourse is to sustain the connection between the speakers and their audience and to provide ongoing feedback. Herein lies a sound principle that writing and composition teachers should welcome into their pedagogical reflections: How are they opening spaces in the interactive discourse of their classroom for speakers to sustain connections with one another and to provide ongoing feedback? That every teacher ultimately becomes adept at the use of call-and-response-style interaction is not the ultimate goal. The positive, participatory environment that can be engendered through call-response—that is the key.

4. Hold High Expectations and Communicate Them
WHAT: We are striving to become teachers who do not miss opportunities to establish vibrant relationships with all of our students. When we think of contexts in which teachers hold high standards for their students, we can revisit examples seen in the community-based organizations we have discussed. Philip, for instance, the Troop dance program director, is explicit in reflecting on the expectations he has for program participants. "I work with them tight," says Philip. "On the one side, they like it. On the other side, they don't. You see, they have to be accountable."
HOW: Philip also says, "I get to know them."
If you are not finding ways to be continually surprised by your students—what they know and do, what they love and care passionately about, what articulated traditions inform their best sense of themselves, then, as a teacher, you are missing the chance to continually revise upward your estimation of your students' capabilities. So one aspect of forming high expectations is to get to know

your students beyond what you think you know of them from their writing. For example, we were recently surprised to learn that in a class of about twenty-five students, nearly half said they knew how to read music. We have been surprised to learn of students' extracurricular achievements, such as being in charge of organizing an annual family gathering drawing cousins, aunts, uncles, in-laws, grandparents, godparents, and significant others from across the country. We were surprised to learn of another student's armed services training in foreign languages. We were surprised by a student's involvement in Toastmasters, and more so by the fact that she had earned a trip to England through her success in Toastmasters competitions.

As a model for holding and communicating high expectations, Philip is instructive for the discipline that is required of the students. He remarks, "I know it's not easy to work with me because I am disciplined and I know exactly what I want." But Philip holds high expectations of himself as a teacher, to know what individual students are capable of achieving and to work with them closely at the growing edge of their ability. He monitors students' progress and demands excellence at every turn. As they practice each dance, the focus is to completely master one dance at a time: "One good dance, instead of two or three that we don't know well . . . And I want it clean!" Recalling Lisa, the student whose paper we discussed in chapter 2, one begins to consider the virtues of learning details of Lisa's own sense of her achievement in that draft. What does she know she has accomplished? What areas of thinking can she be helped to delve more fully? On what aspects of composing or revising her prose can she best be coached at this point? This is not to insist that Lisa necessarily "perfect" the paper she has begun. It is to find in the composing processes the rhetorical choices she has made, those "turns" where she can be best assisted—in revising this piece or in moving to another. This would also suggest that in addition to conversations about the procedures, technique, and style of her writing, some portion of a teacher's attention would be well invested in encouraging Lisa's continuing full participation in the work of expanding her literacy repertoire. Having at hand some exemplary texts representing the writing achievements of African American women would be a great starting place. With this knowledge, a teacher would be prepared to share access to a rhetorical and cultural tradition that could be a source of inspiration to Lisa. More immediately, approaching Lisa with the intent of showing appreciation of her abilities, offering time and attention to her, teachers would send a powerful signal that Lisa's potential to achieve really matters.

Participation

5. *Create Opportunities for Students to Play*
Multiple Roles in the Classroom

WHAT: I'm talking with a graduate student who is teaching composition for the first time. Five weeks into the semester, she is describing her students' participation in their class meetings. There have been some early rough spots. A couple of students have monopolized the discussions, talked over their classmates, and disrupted the class. Today, we are thinking about who talks and who does not, trying to get the picture of the pattern in relation to where the students place themselves in the space of the classroom, the students' gender, their apparent age (the average age of students at our university is twenty-seven), their racial or ethnic identity, their work and family obligations outside of school. "There's one guy," she says, "one of the ones who is really quiet. He's African American. He sits on the side of the room. He comes to class every day, he does all the homework. But he never talks."

In classrooms where oral participation is seen as an important scaffold for written composition, the persistent silence of any student should be grounds for careful reflection. In preparing lessons for their writing classrooms, teachers need to give attention not only to the content of the material but also to opportunities they create for students to actively participate. The European American TA involved in this case, like many teachers we have worked with, found herself unwilling at this point in the course to continue to let this student remain on the sidelines. At the same time, she was not sure how to break the silence. Would she embarrass him by directly asking a question he could not answer, thereby thwarting the larger goal of encouraging him to speak up? Would he resent her effort to draw him out? Would she be seen as complicit in exposing him to the focused attention of all his classmates? Stepping back from these questions, we can say first that they show the teacher does not know the student well enough yet: they need to talk outside of class. Second, the scenario proves the virtues of creating different kinds of ways for students to participate in classroom exchanges. The teacher-led, whole-class discussion is only one form, and it does not do an especially good job of giving lots of students the opportunity to take active roles in the class agenda.

In the community-based organizations we have described, participants learned to perform numerous functions of the program's operation. For example in the Troop community dance organization, students were often given roles of responsibility that placed them in the front of the class to act as teachers or peer models for other students in the class. With this in mind, composition teachers need to think about the dominant mode of interaction in their classrooms in order to create multiple roles for participation in the classroom. It is not enough to wait for quiet students to chime in and contribute to the conversation. The teacher has to be proactive in creating a structure for such students to contribute and participate.

HOW: How do we help teachers create opportunities for students to play multiple roles in the classroom? For example, in the story above, the teacher used the quiet student's paper as a model in the next workshop. In another case, a student who had missed several class meetings was given the opportunity to fill the function of recorder/respondent during her classmates' presentations of their final projects. Yet another technique finds students depending on one another for knowledge of course readings. By putting students in small groups of four or five individuals with each member having the responsibility to read and present the information contained in their assigned reading, all the students in the group can be held accountable for all of the knowledge in the reading. The emphasis here is on assuming roles of responsibility such that if a group member does not do an adequate job, the rest of the group suffers.

6. Integrate Performance in the Classroom

WHAT: We are reminded in the writing of Shirley Brice Heath of the prominent role of performance in the early socialization experiences of African American children. As teachers we can recognize this potential resource to draw on in real-time interactions in the classroom. Formally through presentations of work in progress and informally through modes of conversation in which knowledge is shared, performance is an underused mode within the context of the traditional composition classroom. So often it is the case of confusing performance for a lack of substance or artificiality rather than a resource.

There is a cultural misunderstanding to be aware of here. Just as we value authentic voice in student writing, we value as progressive teachers a kind of authentic relationship in the writing classroom. What we mean by this is a kind of lack of pretense or a leveling of the hierarchy between teacher and students. However, when we disparage the "sage on the stage" model of pedagogy, we may foreclose the potential benefits and power of performance as transformative experience (Gere). Michele Foster has shown the effective use made of performance by a teacher in an urban community college classroom. Foster's research raises interesting questions about the uses of performance by teachers who come to the classroom from different cultural frames of reference than their students. Certainly, the writing process movement and the writing workshop approach have posed delicate issues for teachers concerned not to position themselves in the middle of their students' writing progress. The effort among some compositionists to steer authority toward students, simultaneously playing down the authority and voice of the teacher as sage on a stage can be viewed as running counter to the high value placed on overt performance in African American culture. Other teachers have shown the effectiveness of incorporating student performance in the language arts classroom. Some of this work comes explicitly out of practices that are mainstream in creative writing classrooms (Weems, Sones, and Lardner). Some uses of performance come from theater arts. For example, Heather Dorsey and Mark Pedlety describe using a tableau-performance method to help developmental students articulate and reflect on anxieties and expectations they have as they make the transition from high school to college.

Performance is also an important dimension in the written texts students produce. This is evident in the following text written by a college-bound African American senior in a high school English class. A careful reading reveals that the composition has the quality of a performance, with the performer delivering his ideas directly to a specific audience. A. H. Dyson explains that a performer differs from a mere communicator in both the nature of the language produced and in the kind of stance taken toward an audience ("The Case"). Techniques used to create a performance vary across different sociocultural communities and, within the African American tradition, include such phenomena as the rhythmic use of language, patterns of repetition and variation, expressive sounds, and phenomena encouraging participatory sense making such as dialogue, tropes, hyperbole, and call and response. Although the first part of the essay is somewhat formal and detached, it becomes much more discursive when the writer talks about one of his personal heroes, Malcolm X. This student uses "we," "you're," and "you" to establish an atmosphere of direct interactive communication with an assumed familiar audience. After establishing this atmosphere, the student goes on to use school writing to perform rather than simply to communicate.

Emerson Composition

"There is a time in every man's life when he arrives at the conviction that envy is ignorance; that imitation is suicide; that he must take himself for better, for worse, as his portion."

These are the sentences I have chose in this composition. In this composition I will attempt to explain, analyze, and evaluate the sentences, as well as relate them to a contemporary, historical, social, or religious figure.

To explain and analyze what Emerson is saying is quite simple, his thoughts are man versus self-reliance. Emerson is saying that man is afraid to expand his horizons and succeed in society, because of the fact that he clings on to others for support. The true success of an individual comes from self-reliance, because you always know what you need and you'll always do yourself right. To achieve self-reliance would place you among the list of great human beings. Emerson says, "When private men shall act with original views, the luster will be transferred from the actions of kings to those of gentlemen."

To evaluate these sentences on a scale of one to ten, I'd give them a nine. The reason I wouldn't give them a ten is because they are to deep. These sentences are very complex, but lots of knowledge can be taken from them . . . Emerson says, "To be great is to be misunderstood."

I would like to relate what Emerson is saying to the great El-Hajj Malik El-Shabazz, or better known as Malcolm X . . . Malcolm felt that if *we* [emphasis added] the black race continued to envy . . . *we* [emphasis added] would become an ignorant race. . . . Malcolm took hisself for better or for worse when his father was brutally killed. . . . He did this by saving all of his hatred and vengeful ideas and focused [them] into something positive. . . . Malcolm X had no idea what power resided in him, but he used what he had and only to discover that he had many talents. His main one [was] his ability to earn trust and establish unity among brothers and sisters.

This concludes my composition and I hope *you've* [emphasis added] enjoyed my explanation, analysis, evaluation, and my comparison to a historical figure. In short, Emerson was a great man also, with the ability to write and give words new meaning. [Like Malcolm,] I'm sure he was also a misunderstood individual. I will leave *you* [emphasis added] with this little bit of information to conclude my report.

When reading this text, the alert reader becomes aware that the writer has successfully controlled and enticed the audience into his written world. This performative essay is characteristic of traditional

African American discourse patterns used in the black church's preaching tradition. It states its primary source text clearly at the outset to set the essay in motion. The black preacher can take the scrolls of the ancient Israelites and "bring it home" to the needs of his audience today, interpreting it and applying it to contemporary events. This young AAVE-speaking student has effectively employed these same techniques in his written essay.

While listening to the talk-aloud protocol that was recorded during this student's writing session, I was able to confirm his excitement and pleasure as well as his intentional use of colloquial phrases in his writing. He also used phrases like "Dang! That's great! I sure am good! . . . God, that was great!" throughout his talk-aloud protocol. Hand clapping could also be heard during the taping of his writing session. In all these ways, this student provides evidence of a strong sense of self-awareness, purposefulness, and performance in his personal engagement with the text he has produced.

HOW: How do we help teachers in their efforts to integrate performance in the classroom? As teachers who set the stage for classroom interaction, we can model and create spaces for performative exchanges to occur (Foster). "Teaching is a performative act," bell hooks writes:

> And it is that aspect of our work that offers the space for change, invention, spontaneous shifts, that can serve as a catalyst drawing out the unique elements in each classroom. To embrace the performative aspect of teaching we are compelled to engage "audiences," to consider issues of reciprocity. Teachers are not performers in the traditional sense of the word in that our work is not meant to be a spectacle. Yet it is meant to serve as a catalyst that calls everyone to become more and more engaged, to become active participants in learning. (11)

In addition, as readers of students' texts, seeing our students' compositions as performance gives us a new vocabulary to encourage students to expand metacognitive awareness of purpose in their writing. We can let the student have ownership of the text and of the pleasure and purposefulness of what he or she sets out to accomplish. By being alert to performance, we can help AAVE-speaking students—and all students—better achieve their desired effect in their writing.

7. Reconceptualize the Writing Conference

WHAT: A valuable source for gaining a better understanding of students' use of AAVE is through an expanded conceptualization of the writing conference. For teachers to gain the information they need about students' language, writing conferences must become centers for dynamic, free-flowing exchanges of ideas between students and teachers. Writing conferences should not only serve as places where skilled teachers provide students with guidance that is directed, encouraging, and validating. They should also serve as places where social and cultural perspectives are shared. "Writing to" students about what they have done in their papers is not enough. Diverse students must be conferenced "with" and told about what they have done, what features are influencing their cultural patterns of communication, and what new features teachers want them to incorporate into their ever-broadening range of resources.

Writing conferences may also become places where students can feel free to respond to teacher inquiries without censure, where they can express their intentions and purposes in creating a text, where they can absorb new knowledge through open-ended discourse, and where students can disseminate knowledge to receptive adults. During student-teacher writing conferences, patterns once unconscious to the AAVE-speaking writer, foreign to the average writing instructor and thus judged as incorrect, can be understood in light of shared social, cultural, and linguistic experiences that enhance evaluation and pedagogy.

Working with students on their uses of style and discourse conventions has been noted as a primary source of frustration for many writing teachers due to their lack of understanding of what the student is trying to accomplish. Often students will incorporate personal experiences in the written text in metaphorical ways that can be better understood if discussed in the context of a writing conference. This subtle referencing and indirectness can be discussed and shared between the student and teacher. Together they can investigate the relationships between the student's informal language patterns and the demands of academic discourse in schools, exploring ways to use a wider variety of discourse patterns to express ideas and experiences.

HOW: How can teachers reconceptualize the writing conference? When teachers observe oral patterns in their written texts, they can ask the student a few probing questions that will help the teacher arrive at a fuller understanding of the writer's intentions when using the oral code. The student then can be given strategies or tools that will assist him in producing a more detailed transcription of his message. For example, students might be encouraged to use ellipses to indicate a pause, italics to indicate emphasis, and bolding to indicate loudness or intensity. This coaching could most efficiently take place within the context of a writing conference but must take place on an individual basis; all students who are AAVE speakers will not have the same intentions for given usages in their writing. These kinds of concerns address craft issues in composing and revising. We need also to recognize the potential affective possibilities of the conference, since it affords the opportunity for teachers and students quickly to move between the curricular and the personal sides of academic work.

8. Position Students as Informed Interpreters
WHAT: In the community-based organizations we have described, students were positioned as resources to help teachers and other students to understand community-based literacy practices and discourse patterns. Leaders constantly drew on the students' practices and experiences to demonstrate new concepts or skills as a bridging device and to demonstrate how these resources might be used as participants adapt to changing life situations. The actions of many successful teachers of African American students testify to a belief that students develop composition skills and strategies most successfully through an interactive process approach that emphasizes the coconstruction

of the underlying cognitive and linguistic skills that are prerequisites for understanding and appreciating tasks at hand. In addition, the actions of these successful teachers attest to the belief that knowledge is actively created as opposed to passively received.

To be clear, we are not proposing that teachers single out African American students to serve as the representative black voice. We want to position all students as experts—or, if not experts, then on their way. Of course, in an anthropological sense and as commonly used in ethnographic research, members of the community are recruited to provide access to nuances of the norms, values, practices, and messages intended by members of the group. And if composition teachers truly seek an understanding of communication practices and intentions of African American students in our classrooms, we may find it quite productive and useful for those concerned to invite students to serve as informed interpreters to coconstruct this mutual understanding. At the same time, we see a principle here that can be applied across the board. Not only might AAVE-speaking students be positioned to capitalize on their special knowledge of community language and literacies, but a sound pedagogy would make way for all students to draw on community knowledge, local languages and literacies as potent material for investigation, interpretation, report, and reflection.

HOW: How can teachers begin to position students as informed interpreters in their classrooms? In the community-based classrooms we have described, students and teachers work together in the construction of meaning. Students are actively involved in the meaning-making process as teachers provide appropriate direction and support. Gerald Duffy and Laura Roehler explain that discussion is a critical part of this type of teaching and learning. They argue that through discussion, teachers structure classroom interaction in ways that the teacher can learn what is on the students' minds from the students' responses, and can restructure the learning situation in order to expand upon, clarify, or correct student responses. In composition classrooms, this principle can be applied first to reflecting on, "problematizing" or interrogating the course itself in terms of its institutional position and the language practices students are being asked to take up. Positioning students as informed interpreters of their experiences with school writing and academic literacy can open the door to a generative inquiry into the relationship between writing or literacy and its social-historical and personal contexts. Such a discussion can be labeled a "Critical Language Awareness" approach to teaching writing. The goal is to cultivate greater understanding of

> discourse choices and the way in which they position language users. In relation to writing, it means recognizing that writing in a particular way means appearing to be a certain type of person; that is, writers need to be aware that their discoursal choices construct an image of themselves and that they need to take control over this as much as they can, not so that they can deceive their readers but so that they do not betray themselves. (Clark and Ivanic 231)

As students reflect on writing this way, they are also already writing about something. And here, too, a huge opportunity exists for teachers to position all students as informed interpreters of the specifics of their experience. Writing projects or assignments set up to put students in between experiences with which they are immediately familiar and discussions or thematizations of those experiences by others allow strength and room for growth. For example, projects that ask students to construct neighborhood or family histories depend on students' taking the role of informed interpreter. To illustrate, here are directions from two such projects from Ted Lardner and Todd Lundberg's *Exchanges: Reading and Writing about Consumer Culture*:

> *Neighborhood*
> Take a walk through your neighborhood, and write a narrative of your experiences and observations. You will want to focus your narrative on some aspect of your response, on a theme of one sort or another, so that you can organize your impressions, showing the significance of the things you observe and describe. Look back at the reading as sources

for questions or themes with which you can frame your work. There are several directions in which to take this project, but perhaps the encompassing question is how the relationships among people who interact with each other and share this neighborhood are expressed by the buildings and streets and the "transition zones" where public and private spheres meet. You might look, for example, at how housing and yard landscaping seem to express certain values, or what kind of space is devoted to public gathering, such as park space, a town hall, or a library. You might pay attention to automobiles, noticing what concessions have been made to cars in the built landscape. With these examples, you can think about what ties a neighborhood together as a community, if anything, and what forces seem to work against the establishment of networks of interdependence.

Likely readings included with this project are excerpts from landscape design theorists, such as Yi-fu Tuan and John Brinckerhoff Jackson; urban historian Dolores Hayden; journalist David McLemore's story about Sandra Cisneros's purple house in San Antonio, TX; and journalist William Hamilton's report from Highlands Ranch, CO, concerning the isolating effects on adolescents of sprawl development. (620)

Family History
One way to see more clearly the meaning of our daily experience is through the lens of history. But history need not be conceived as ancient or distant events, involving people in far-off places. Indeed, discovering the historical traces in events in our day-to-day lives can illuminate them, showing the effects of large social and economic events on our neighborhoods, our families, and us. This project calls on you to begin a family history. The background readings suggested here introduce themes that can be helpful starting places. The case-in-point readings stand as sources of themes or as models for this project. Richard Rodriguez ["Pocho Pioneer"] traces his immediate family's history,

relating autobiographical details to larger historical trends. [David] McLemore's account shows how the history of a place can be controversial and relevant to how we live there today. [Robert] Kaplan's densely detailed descriptions show how a place can come alive in words. Your task in your family history is to link the details of your family's experience to the history of the place you live. How did your family get here, when did they come, and in the future does it appear your family will remain in this place? (621)

These are very compact descriptions of projects that potentially extend over several weeks, including reading, direct observations, rereading, drafting, revising, and reflection. The emerging projects, the stories each student would tell, would necessarily be supported through collaborations among peers and in conferences with the teacher. As that happens, students draw more and more out of their direct experience as informed interpreters, articulating their knowledge for others in new ways.

Substance

9. Develop a Knowledge Base of Discourse Patterns of AAVE

WHAT: According to Georgia Garcia and David Pearson, one of the keys to meeting the assessment needs of a diverse student population is a "dramatically improved teacher knowledge base" (254). In order to accomplish this, teachers need an understanding of what is already known about the characteristic patterns in the spoken linguistic systems of their students. This is a crucial first step toward improving evaluation and the instructional process. A close examination of the written text by an AAVE speaker reveals oral influences within four domains:

1. syntactic patterns that may exemplify themselves in the student's grammatical uses

2. semantic patterns that may exemplify themselves in the student's vocabulary or word choices

3. phonological patterns that may exemplify themselves as spelling variations

4. stylistic patterns that may exemplify themselves in the student's discourse styles and expressions (Ball, "Evaluating" 231)

Recognizing how the characteristic patterns of students' spoken language are reflected in their written texts is one key principle that underlies the successful evaluation of students' writing. Another key principle is the notion of expanding the role of writing conferences to include opportunities for teachers and students to better understand each other's intentions and visions for constructing a successful text. Using the writing conference to share basic assumptions and to develop common background knowledge is an important step when working with culturally and linguistically diverse students. Still further, key principles that underlie the successful evaluation of students' writing can be gained by observing the strategies of professionals that work with students in non-school contexts, for example, in community-based organizations.

HOW: How can we help writing professionals develop a knowledge base of basic discourse patterns of AAVE? And what can writing instructors do with their improved knowledge of the basic patterns of AAVE discourse in texts they receive from these students? First, we can begin by heeding the advice of John Baugh to develop attitudes of ethnosensitivity—viewing social topics and practices from the cultural perspectives of students who come from cohesive social groups ("Design"). A teacher's knowledge base can be improved through a review of literature developed over decades to provide a more complex, more complete linguistic profile of African American linguistic behavior and through analyses of students' writing to become aware of the systematic differences in AAVE and Standard English patterns present in their texts. Once this expanded knowledge base is established, teachers can situate student assessments using information gained from their expanded conceptualization of writing conferences. One teacher put it this way: in any classroom, two dictionaries should be visible and accessible for everyone's use: a Standard American English dictionary and a dictionary of African American English such as Geneva Smitherman's *Black Talk*. The implication is that the expansion of knowledge about AAVE can be and probably should be undertaken as a mutual inquiry between teachers and students. June Jordan's account of a writing class based on this investigation is compelling. Such a focus for a writing class serves many of the ends compositionists most desire, including the discovery of the tension between an audience's expectations and a writer's multiple purposes. (See Clark and Ivanic for a fuller discussion of "purpose" in written discourse.)

10. Recognize, Accept, and Incorporate Varied Oral and Written Discourse Patterns

WHAT: We do not advocate that all teachers need to learn to use and teach "Ebonics," though that would be a positive step if done well. We are saying teachers should develop a knowledge base so they will understand what patterns of discourse are influencing their students' writing. We ourselves have encouraged students to use many languages and registers as appropriate to the learning at hand. Like Toni Morrison, who uses colloquial speech to capture the culture of a community, or Geneva Smitherman, who uses colloquial speech to make an emphatic point in her academic writing, students can be encouraged to use colloquial speech in their writing to achieve particular purposes. All students should learn Standard English and academic discourse, but they should also all be exposed to a variety of ways of expressing their ideas. For example, a popular contemporary writing textbook includes exercises that ask students to interpret passages of colloquial speech from a wide range of groups represented in our culture and to produce texts that authentically represent the colloquial speech of a wide range of groups. Recognizing and accepting varied oral and written discourse patterns in our classrooms is all about expanding that range.

HOW: How can teachers come to recognize, accept, and incorporate varied oral and written discourse patterns in their classrooms? They can begin by becoming familiar with some of the culturally influenced patterns African American students include in their oral and written discourse and begin to view them as resources teachers can draw on to enrich their writing curriculum. They include

- using repetition to create formulaic patterning

- establishing a link or sense of rapport with the audience through the use of inclusive lexical terms like "we're"
- taking on a quality of performance in the style and delivery of the text
- using orally based organization patterns in addition to topic associations, compare-and-contrast patterns, and the traditional five-paragraph essay used in most classrooms (see Ball, "Cultural Preference")
- using dialogue that interacts with the audience with phrases like, "You know what I mean, man?"
- using common African American idioms that assume mutual understanding based on similar cultural experiences
- linking topics through the use of personal anecdotes and narratives interspersed within expository texts

Another important aspect of this task is recognizing the power of situational code switching. Although most participants in the community-based programs we have described were African American English speakers, the general consensus gained from their prior schooling experiences, the news media, and hiring trends for African Americans indicated that AAVE is not an acceptable form of communication in the workplace. Observations of the transitioning uses of discourse in community-based organizations, however, revealed that AAVE was not looked down upon and that code switching was the generally accepted solution to the problem of adaptation to the changing requirements in different communicative situations.

At first glance, the use of code switching may appear to be an obvious and simplistic solution in which the AAVE speaker assimilates to the linguistic demands of society and the employer. A closer examination, however, reveals that the code switching demonstrated in community-based organizations can be viewed more accurately as a transitioning use of discourse that actually fits into a broader theory of language maintenance and resistance for AAVE speakers. In keeping with the trickster tradition, code switching embodies a gesture of ideological independence and allows the AAVE speaker to control the terms of their own self-representation rather than the simple acceptance of the terms set forth by the dominant workplace culture. Situational code switching takes place when a single speaker uses different varieties of language at different times such that each switch corresponds to a change in the situation. This gesture of ideological independence allows AAVE speakers to maintain an element of control over their own destiny and a sense of unity among themselves as members of an identifiable group.

Once we have gained a knowledge base of discourse patterns of AAVE speakers, then teachers must make overt and aggressive efforts to learn more about students' language varieties. As teachers learn more about students' language varieties as well as their individual patterns and needs, they can begin to accept students' language variation in writing as evidence that students are experimenting with what they are learning: skills that can lead to effective code switching. Initially, teachers must focus not on word choice and surface-level features of students' writing as much as on larger strategies for improving students' writing abilities and broadening their range of writing experiences. Finally, in addition to analyzing students' texts to discover the oral features of students' cultural expressions that influence their written text, teachers can learn to broaden the region of validity for student text productions through an expanded conceptualization of the writing conference. Now the writing conference becomes a dynamic, free-flowing exchange of ideas where skilled teachers provide guidance that is directed, encouraging, and validating and where students unlock the power of their writing by sharing the "secrets" of their language.

11. Reassess Approaches to Assessment

WHAT: Teachers recognize the importance of teaching accuracy and mechanics to students of color because they realize that all students will be held accountable for demonstrating their abilities to use spelling, grammar, and punctuation in conventional ways. Teachers also state that African American students need to have the ability to write cohesive, organized, content-rich compositions that employ "standard" language practices and they need to be able to use the "right" language at the right time. These teachers even go so far as to say that we do our students a disservice if we do not provide them with access to conventional accuracy and provide them with an understanding that assessment is often defined in terms of conventions of accuracy. These teachers, however, go on to state that, although important, surface-level errors should not be the primary focus of writing assessment. Rather, the primary focus should be on the wonderful and profound ideas that the students are trying to express, their emerging skills in forming, shaping, and conceptualizing in writing, on using writing in realistic, functional, and practical ways, and on providing praise, encouragement, and sensitivity to the needs of the individual learner. Indeed, research has shown that student writing that employs African American style at the discourse level received higher evaluations. However, most teachers do not get to this level because they become distracted by what they assume is dialect interference in the surface-level errors in standard academic English, but which, according to extant research, are in reality common basic writing errors (Smitherman, "The Blacker the Berry"; Rickford; Farr).

HOW: How might teachers reassess their approaches to assessment? Knowledgeable about the difference between common, cross-cultural surface-level errors and AAVE-specific deeper discourse structures, teachers are empowered to accept and even celebrate the texts produced by their AAVE-speaking students that strongly reflect the oral characteristic features of their cultural language. This is especially appropriate in the early stages of the writing course and whenever the use of Standard or academic English is not a part of the particular assignment. As the course progresses, teachers should expect, and again celebrate, the presence of a mixture of AAVE and academic features in students' texts since this variation is an indication that students are experimenting with what they are learning.

In the early stages of a course, it is best that teachers refrain from focusing too heavily on word choice and surface-level features of students' writing but rather on larger strategies for improving students' writing abilities and broadening their range of writing experiences. Teachers should specify a limited number of goals or skills they are focusing on for each assignment and should evaluate students' ability to demonstrate mastery of those specific goals (recall Philip's strategy of requiring students to do one clean dance instead of two or three). At the more advanced levels of the writing course, teachers should hold students responsible for using a wide range of writing styles that have been taught and practiced in response to an array of specific, authentic assignments. These assignments should require controlled and intentional use of a wider range of discourses, including academic English, perhaps Shakespearean English, as well as the integration of AAVE or Spanglish or other ways of representing authentic styles of colloquial speech. These assignments should also reflect the teachers' recognition that linguistic systems should be evaluated by whether they are the most appropriate or most effective variety of English for the communicative situation at hand. From this perspective, another variety of English could be more appropriate in a particular context than academic or Standard English. It might also be valuable for teachers to inform students that, unfortunately, when some individuals who are unfamiliar or uncomfortable with diverse linguistic styles such as AAVE come in contact with these interactional styles, there is a tendency for them to evaluate the differences negatively. Therefore, it is empowering for students to learn the differences in speaking and writing varieties and gain the ability to employ them when desired.

Finally, three significant points remain foremost in teachers' minds when evaluating the writing of diverse students. First, many variations in the writing patterns of diverse students are not random but are influenced by the patterns of the students' spoken linguistic system in predictable ways. Second, students, although members of culturally and linguistically diverse communities, are individuals, and their individuality will also be reflected in their writing patterns. Third, some of the variation in students' writing will be attributable to cultural influences while others will not—it will be the teacher's responsibility to distinguish based on the teachers' knowledge of the student's cultural and linguistic practices and patterns.

*12. Seek Nurturing Professional Collaborations
That Model and Support Effective Teaching*

WHAT: We cannot do this alone. The models we were able to observe in community-based organizations show us the value of establishing coalitions with professionals in those communities. It is important that teachers seek out nurturing models of efficacious teaching that supports us in our development toward a similar stance. We can seek out collaborations within our departments, within our buildings, within our professional organizations. But it also means that we must establish collaborative relationships with professionals in community-based organizations. We must step outside the confines of our classroom walls. Also, we need to recognize the informal coalitions of allies we interact with in our personal lives who are addressing similar issues from different positions. We need to recognize and involve ourselves in the families and extended relationships that form an integral part of our students' identities and the fund of their cultural knowledge.

HOW: How can writing professionals begin to seek nurturing professional collaborations that model and support efficacious teaching? Making connection with any one of these groups of potential allies and collaborators would be a good start. Teachers are on a mission. We must make links as we move toward transformation; these collaborations will translate into generative practices over time. They occur at many levels. Collaborations may be spaces in which we find individuals we can talk to with like interests—individuals with whom we can talk about issues we are struggling with (Stenberg and Lee). That is one level. Another level is finding role models as inspirations for teachers, and a third level is finding models such as experts we can bring into our classrooms—in person or virtually via interactive computer technology. We recommend that our readers become a part of a community of learners (for example, become a part of a professional development school, teacher research group, CCCC SIG, caucus, or join the research assembly of NCTE) along with other passionate teachers who can help in efforts to harness current research, recent innovations, and best practices for generative use in classroom teaching.

Conclusion

At the classroom level, African American students' preferred modes of expression should be included in the curriculum, not only as building blocks for bridging African American students' experiences with academic-based writing but also as a rich resource of knowledge that all students should know as they broaden their abilities to express their ideas in a variety of forms. Including these devices in the writing curriculum is a strategy that is in keeping with other educational approaches that have successfully used the cultural resources of their students to enrich the learning experience. Rather than avoid the students' cultural experiences, identities, and interests, other successful programs in the academy and in the extracurriculum have consciously sought them out and used them as one of the major sources of the curriculum. The results are positive.

We understand that many writing professionals have come to the realization that their attitudes may be acting as an unconscious barrier to their effectiveness as writing professionals. They want to know how to become advocates for change, how they can begin to enact the themes we have shown in the examples of community-based organizations and in the lives of actual teachers. Many classroom teachers want to know some concrete steps they can take as they embark on the journey toward implementing the transformative changes we have proposed. As a *starting point,* what we provided in the prior section is a discussion of a dozen steps toward change. We present twelve changes teachers can initiate and monitor as they reflect on, analyze, and transform their classrooms and teaching practices. For those writing professionals who want to teach African American students in more powerful, effective, and sensitive ways but do not know where or how to begin, these twelve steps can be used as a starting point from which to implement the themes outlined earlier in this book. The suggestions provided here are only a beginning point. The challenge remains for individual teachers and for our profession as a whole to begin with the dozens but then to move forward in generative ways to implement a pedagogy that is well suited for the unique population of African American students we serve.

In the process of reflecting on students' activities in the writing classroom, teachers need to closely observe their students. At the same time, they need to reflect inwardly on their own actions and feelings as they assess affect, participation, and substance in their classrooms. This is why we have written our personal narratives into this book—to explore the interplay between personal and professional aspects of our teaching identities and to show the emotional and cognitive tensions that result from that interplay. These tensions shape our stances toward writing and teaching. They define our knowledge as teachers of African American students— and all students.

6 / Where We Go from Here

Race remains widely discussed in scholarly and public contexts. Academics deconstruct the "social fact" of race (Omi and Winant, "Theoretical"), defining an enforceable fiction the category of difference "race" signifies. Public discourse about race abounds as well, as citizens weigh in not only on affirmative action and racial profiling but also on education reform and school financing, access to health care, urban policy—the list goes on. On the popular front, the sociocultural meanings of hip-hop fashion, language, music, and dance remain to be unpacked as young people across a demographic spectrum embrace ethnic hybridity as normative (Chideya).

With these discourse exchanges continuing apace, we see room for material change in our institutions and classrooms. While race remains a topic of many intellectual conversations, racism remains a problematic experience in day-to-day life. As a system of advantage, racism is harder to talk about, much less do something to remedy, because it is built into institutional routines. Racism is hard for many to see; because the routines seem natural, their consequences appear inevitable. Notwithstanding our best intentions, many of us participate in practices that have discriminatory effects. So there's the rub. Day in and day out, teachers willing to be different *can* make a difference in improving the educational opportunities of AAVE-speaking students. But we have to be willing to be different, to do different, to make a difference.

In chapter 5, we sought to give teachers something to hold onto and do in their own classrooms. Here we wish to shift our perspective, to think about efficacy and reflective optimism from the perspective of writing program administrators (WPAS), teacher educators, and researchers. We offer suggestions for actions, as well as implications and questions for further research. We organize our remarks to disparate audiences, although we recognize the importance of avoiding the creation of false divisions, particularly between "practitioners" and "researchers." Classroom teachers, WPAS, and teacher educators do indeed act as "researchers," employing methodologies that range from informal observation and reflection in situ to narrowly defined, rigorously factored "objective" analyses of survey and other data. So, whether integrated in a teacher's own reflective practice, articulated in terms of a specific writing program, or disseminated as widely applicable findings, we see members of each group making significant contributions.

Writing Program Administrators

The dynamics of program administration and organization have been shown to influence a teacher's sense of efficacy. A number of researchers have demonstrated that teachers' sense of efficacy is positively influenced by faculty collegiality, teacher control over important working conditions, having a sense of ownership, and participation in staff development (Ashton and Webb; Little; Raudenbush, Rowan, and Cheong; Guskey).

Opportunities for participation in "extra-role" activities in school have also been associated with teachers' job satisfaction and collective efficacy (Somech and Drach-Zahavy). A message to those at the writing program administration level therefore calls for policies and program development that support these activities. We believe writing program administrators will improve the educational opportunities of AAVE-speaking students (and all students) by seeking to improve teacher efficacy by initiating and supporting collaborations within and across writing program and institutional boundaries, and by situating efforts aimed at broadening teachers' knowledge of AAVE-related pedagogical issues within collaborative staff-development activities.

Collaboration
Isolation is a recurring motif in research on efficacy. Teachers are isolated from one another, isolated from administrators, and, frequently,

isolated from students who come from different communities and cultures. Teachers' isolation emerges as a limitation to student achievement. It is a double logic that leads to this result. In reference to cultural discontinuity between school and home, for example, Ashton and Webb explain:

> When teachers are unable to cope with these cultural discontinuities, they feel less effective with these students and their parents. To protect themselves from this threat to their sense of efficacy, teachers may limit their contacts with these families, thereby increasing the likelihood of further discontinuity and, ultimately, alienation of these families from the school. (22)

Ashton and Webb are referring to K-12 teachers in this discussion. Nevertheless, we see similar tendencies at work in college writing programs. College writing teachers have not customarily sought community contacts with parents or families of their students, yet it is interesting to speculate about what might happen if they did.

Moreover, in the organizational culture of universities we are familiar with, teachers typically lack ready opportunities to interact with one another. While the emergence of "learning communities" represents a potential transformation of undergraduate education, purposefully sustained collaborative (and interdisciplinary) interactions focused on teaching are the exception rather than the norm. What one teacher does in his or her classroom has little impact beyond the closed classroom door. What is encouraging is that composition teachers seem to be at the forefront of making changes in ingrained university culture, showing interest in team teaching and interdisciplinary and interinstitutional collaborations. We see an important role for WPAs in leading and supporting these efforts because we see in these efforts the avenues to building teachers' sense of efficacy, and we can cite research that, at least indirectly, supports our claim.

In a study of teachers in thirteen elementary schools, Anit Somech and Anat Drach-Zahavy probed the involvement of teachers in "extra-role behavior" and sought to correlate extra-role behavior with job satisfaction and efficacy. The authors define "extra-role behavior" as "behaviors that go beyond specified role requirements, and are directed towards the individual, the group, or the organization as a unit, in order to promote organizational growth" (650). In the study, twenty-four items were identified as examples of extra-role behavior. Some were oriented toward benefiting other teachers. These included offering colleagues lesson material teachers had prepared for their own classrooms, or working with others to plan assignments or collaborative projects. Some activities were oriented toward benefiting the school overall as an organization, such as organizing social activities for the school, decorating the school, or organizing extra activities with parents. Finally, some behaviors were oriented toward benefiting students, including spending extra out-of-class time to help a student, arriving early for class, or acquiring expertise in new subjects that will improve teaching (654). In the study, teachers were surveyed to assess their job satisfaction, sense of self-efficacy, and sense of collective efficacy (that is, an individual's assessment of their organization or team's ability to do its job). The authors established correlation between extra-role behavior and job satisfaction, self-efficacy, and collective efficacy.

The authors worked from the premise that "behaviors that go beyond in-role duties become a fundamental component for achieving effectiveness in schools" (655). And they find that "job satisfaction, self-efficacy, and collective efficacy [are] key factors that were positively and distinctively related to teachers' extra-role behavior" (657). Discussing their results, the authors note

- strong positive relationship between job satisfaction and extra-role behavior toward students;
- both job satisfaction and self-efficacy were related to extra-role behavior towards the team;
- teachers with higher collective efficacy, compared with those with lower collective efficacy, engaged more frequently in extra-role behavior toward the team. (565, 657)

In their concluding discussions, Somech and Drach-Zahavy suggest
that teachers

> find themselves in a profession that isolates them from their
> colleagues. Strong collegial relations can counteract these
> feelings. Hence, reducing isolation from peers through joint
> planning and implementation of activities would be likely
> to foster extra-role behavior. (657)

We are interested in how university writing teachers may interact with each other and how WPAs can take a role in fostering these
collegial interactions that seem to benefit teachers' sense of satisfaction and efficacy in their work. Teachers can feel efficacious to the
extent that the professional space created for them by the intersection
of program goals and personal commitments is marked by expectations that reflect their voices as competent, well-trained educators.

Writing program administrators often are in a position to commit resources (if only of energy and time at first) to collaborative
initiatives involving teachers from a variety of disciplines who are
interested, in improving student achievement in their courses. Similarly, WPAs are often in a position to link university writing teachers
with K-12 teachers. Many state university systems have demonstrated interest, for example, in lowering costs of remedial programs
at the baccalaureate level by improving the articulation between high
school and college curricula. In Ohio, for example, the Ohio Board
of Regents sponsors a long-running program called the Early English Composition Assessment Program. For nearly two decades, it
has offered university writing professionals funding to establish
collaborations with high school English teachers to help bridge the
gap between high school writing instruction and the expectations
of university composition programs.

In addition, as administrators with constituencies around the
university, WPAs are in a position to broker collaborations between
mentoring programs that may be housed in student-support-service
programs. At South Seattle Community College, first-generation,
low-income, and/or disabled students find tutoring and other vital

resources in CLIC, the Collaborative Learning and Instruction Center. CLIC offers eligible students thirty hours per week of access to tutors, advisors, computers, and reference materials, staffed by four part-time tutors and two full-time advisors. According to Sash Woods, CLIC's approach is based on challenging the "false dichotomy between the rigorous and the nurturing":

> There are three aspects to creating this environment. One is broadly sowing resources in a variety of formats so that the conditions exist for truly informed choice. The second is designing an atmosphere of respect in which students are viewed as capable and gifted. Finally, there is planned structuring of diverse opportunities for connections in which learning is generated through relationships.

At Cleveland State University and fourteen other public and private universities in Ohio, the STARS (Student Achievement in Research and Scholarship) mentoring program serves undergraduate minority students of high academic achievement in their quest to pursue graduate degrees (http://www.regents.state.oh.us/stars/). Through four chapters in northeast Ohio, each year about thirty juniors and seniors participate in the STARS program. About fifteen students graduate each year, and virtually all the graduating students move on to graduate school. The STARS program recruits undergraduate minority students of high academic achievement and engages them in undergraduate research and mentoring activities. STARS students participate fully in three major activities: an undergraduate research project, culminating in a formal presentation of research at the annual STARS statewide conference; a mentoring relationship with a professor in the student's major; and a seminar to prepare for graduate school with a series of workshops to guide students through the application process and to orient them to the expectations of graduate study. Writing teachers and tutors have roles to play in each of these mentoring programs, and WPAS are often in the position to foster collaborations between teachers in first-year writing programs and staff and students involved in these support services.

Another site for collaboration that has recently gained attention is service learning. To cite an example, Dr. Mindy Wright, director of the Writing Workshop at Ohio State University, has created a service-learning course that links university students as tutors to children in nearby public elementary schools. One day each week, the university students travel to the partner schools to tutor elementary students in reading and writing. Tutoring work provides the university students opportunities to serve a specific need in the community. At the same time, the community service work gives the university students hands-on experience as a reference for reflection in their exploration of "literacy" in course texts and writing assignments.

As our discussion of extra-role behavior and collaboration would suggest, we think service learning/outreach scholarship benefits teachers' sense of efficacy, rounding their understanding of students' capabilities by seeing students acting in contexts outside the university classroom. Composition teachers acknowledge how service-learning courses offer students nonacademic in addition to academic contexts in which to read and write (Cushman and Emmons). We would add that service-learning or community-outreach projects offer similar opportunities for teachers to resituate their literacy teaching in contexts additional to the university/academic literacy context. Our proposal to wpas is to consider how service learning may benefit teachers in their programs by giving them the opportunity to enhance their sense of efficacy through these kinds of collaborations.

Staff Development

One of the most critical elements that writing program administrators can promote to help writing professionals become successful teachers of all students is the implementation of policies that support professional development programs that focus specifically on preparing writing and composition teachers to work effectively with diverse student populations. In order for writing classrooms to become places where hearing diverse voices becomes a natural and constant phenomenon, wpas need to be ready to initiate dialogues in which the presence of diverse voices is appreciated and rewarded. To sustain their efforts, WPAs must participate in continuing education workshops offered at places like CCCC and other professional conferences. We believe they must also engage personally in activities that make their own lives and communities more culturally sensitive and diverse.

The approach that WPAs choose is an important variable. In "Developing Pedagogies: Learning the Teaching of English," Stenberg and Lee describe their efforts to create a "teacher-learner community comprised of members with a range of experience" (340). Articulated as a project of critical inquiry, the "pedagogical inquiry" they describe entails "an ongoing process of discovering—and responding to—revisionary possibilities" (340). In their discussion, Stenberg and Lee draw on the context of TA mentoring to illustrate the need for accounts of pedagogy that "show the processes through which pedagogical development occurs" (341). They seek to "establish teaching as a critical process that parallel[s] writing as a critical process" (343). We believe WPAs can play a role in nurturing teachers' developing confidence in their abilities to teach all students well, particularly as they create a climate around the writing program along the lines Stenberg and Lee describe. Staff development forums where teachers and other stakeholders, including students and staff, can collaborate in reflecting on and rethinking pedagogy, seem more likely to produce the feelings of collegiality and participation that correlate with efficacy. Carmen Werder, P. J. Redmon, Jeff Purdue, and Kathryn Patrick describe such a program, the Teaching and Learning Academy at Western Washington University. The TLA involves fifty faculty from across the disciplines, along with about twenty students and staff members. In biweekly study groups, participants in the TLA meet informally to examine and discuss issues related to teaching and learning on the WWU campus. According to Werder et al., "the real motive for the TLA is not really any particular reform effort, but rather the revitalization of our whole institutional learning culture."

Scholarship in this area has begun to show the possibilities when writing program administrators position the writing curriculum as the object of practical inquiry and reflection for program staff (Phelps). Michael Apple documents a historic dilemma of American teachers in past decades who were systematically "deskilled" by reforms, program demands, or policies that increased external control over the curriculum and pedagogy. At the same time that these teachers were losing their professional autonomy, they were under increased pressure from students and parents in the community to deliver more effective and needs-responsive education. Today's accountability-driven society threatens a return to these trends, which have had a negative effect on teacher efficacy and on writing and composition classrooms populated by African American students. "Standards," Thomas Fox has argued, "often inhibit access" (*Defending* 2). In the ongoing work of a hypothetical writing program, we can imagine what he means. We recollect the litany of complaints, for example, that constitutes the usual feedback from faculty colleagues—within the English department and across the college. The gist is that students don't know how to write: What are they learning in those courses? Why can't they write a coherent sentence? We recollect our own experiences in TA-training programs, including instructions from writing program directors such as "If you turn in a grade sheet with all As and Bs, I will not accept it" (message: Be tough).

Fair enough. We have argued for a conception of reflective optimism—high regard for students' ability to meet standards—as a necessary complement (and corrective) to efficacy (when teachers purchase efficacy by discounting expectations). What too often seems to happen, however, is that appeals made to high standards give insufficient consideration to developing practices that make it more likely for students to meet them. No child left behind? To the extent that anyone can be "for" a slogan, we are for that. It is where policy hits program administration that hard work remains for WPAs. Writing program administrators have a world of burden to contend with, true. Workloads divide their institutional identity. They are half-time faculty on the publish-or-perish promotion track, half-time administrators, on top of which, saddled with high responsibility, they often have limited authority and even more limited budgets.

Acknowledging these built-in constraints, we believe administrators of writing across the curriculum programs, writing centers, and first-year writing programs including basic writing programs should come together with teachers to build consensus on exactly what the educational goal of the program should be and how should these goals differ given the increased numbers of culturally and linguistically diverse students entering the writing program at every level. Different groups may have different goals or expectations for what constitutes "good" teaching or different definitions of what "good" teaching is. These matters should be discussed with all of the stakeholders in the enterprise—including the students who are involved. If they choose to do so, if they are able to muster the resources (human and otherwise) necessary, writing program administrators have a role to play in sustaining reforms that foster efficacy and reflective optimism among writing teachers.

Teacher Educators

In our efforts to make a difference in the classroom experiences of AAVE-speaking students, we must also address the challenge at the teacher-training level. Here, professional development programs require radical changes so that composition teachers gain an appreciation for the role they must play in allowing African American students' voices to be heard, legitimized, and leveraged within the writing classroom. A radical shift of priorities in the use of time within teacher professional development programs would eventually have to occur if such perspectives are to take hold among future composition professionals. Teachers must be trained in the selection and allocation of instructional resources, materials, and methodologies that are representative of a wide variety of different ethnic and cultural group experiences.

In chapter 4, I (Arnetha) shared my own story of growing up in South Central Los Angeles and learning about the language prowess of African American students in my community. I told of the resources my fellow classmates brought to the classroom and of my teachers' inability to use the resources that these poor and underachieving students brought into the classroom to enrich their curriculum. I then shared my experiences as a teacher in schools that were labeled "multicultural" that had as their common denominator a predominant population of students of color who were socially and economically disenfranchised and who were viewed as a "problem." Finally, I shared my experiences as a teacher educator in one university-based teacher-education program, my eye-opening experiences while working in South Africa, and my subsequent application of the lessons I learned to my own reform-centered teaching in my own teacher-education classroom. It was my cross-national teacher-education experiences that served to crystallize the realization that the greatest challenge facing teacher education today is the need to prepare teachers who are interested in acquiring the attitudes, knowledge, skills, and dispositions necessary to work effectively with diverse student populations and with those who are socially and economically disenfranchised. With that realization, I have created an approach that facilitates the development of teachers who envision themselves as becoming excellent teachers of diverse student populations.

In my early experiences as a teacher educator, I observed numerous cases in which student teachers were able to produce seemingly appropriate answers to examination questions and class assignments without actually making differences in their teaching practices. The teachers were not integrating sound theoretical perspectives into their personal teaching styles in ways that would allow the power of those perspectives to transform their day-to-day teaching practice. I can still recall the look on the face of one student teacher who glibly stated,

> I can discuss topics of interest in my undergraduate teacher education course and never think about them again until another education class brings up the topic. . . . The knowledge in my brain is doing no good because I'm not using it. . . . Teacher education programs can't force any student to internalize the theories that they have "learned" in their class.

After sensing this same attitude from too many students over a period of several years, I knew I had to do something more proactive to address this phenomenon. I began to develop a teaching approach to help teachers develop the attitudes, skills, and dispositions necessary to become *change agents* in schools and to increase their feelings of efficacy and commitment to teaching diverse student populations.

My teaching approach was guided by a desire to discover the process through which teachers—who are engaged in a theory-driven teacher-education program—can move beyond positions of cognitive internalization of theory and best practices toward transformative positions of reflective commitment needed to guide them in their generative development as classroom teachers of diverse students. Vygotsky's discussion of internalization can help us to understand how this learning and development occurs—how the information presented to teachers in teacher-education programs moves from an interpsychological plane (as a social exchange in which teacher educators encourage students' conceptual considerations) to an intrapsychological plane (where these social classroom activities are embraced by student teachers to become an internal catalyst that generates teacher advocacy, efficacy, and commitment). In my teacher-education course, I found that as teachers were exposed to theoretical perspectives, challenging discussions, strategically designed curricular activities, and extensive thoughtful, reflective, introspective, critical writing, I was able to detect changes in their attitudes toward teaching diverse students. These changes were reflected in the teachers' changing discourses as they moved beyond the production of seemingly appropriate communication about theory and practice toward an internalization and synthesizing of ideas that led them to commitment that transformed their experiences as teachers.

Upon entering my course, students were confronted with the challenge of considering these issues through interpersonal and socially mediated forums, including individual and shared reflections on these issues, extensive written engagement with carefully designed prompts on various thought-provoking topics, and discussions that challenge their preconceived notions on these issues.

Exposure to theoretical readings and practical activities takes place during the course to serve as a catalyst to engage students in dialogic conversations that can impact their thoughts on issues of diversity. However, I propose that engaging teachers in writing that draws on the two major modes that bring teachers' past, present, and future perspectives together, the processes of analysis and synthesis, will help teachers begin to conceptualize how to teach diverse students in fresh and exciting ways (Emig 13). As a result of their engagements in thoughtful and reflective writing along with teacher research projects, the teachers are able to bring theory and practice together in ways that crystallize the internalization process. Teaching diverse students begins to take on personal meaning for the teachers and they begin to go beyond the initial ideas and activities presented in class and beyond their own previous levels of functioning to expand upon the concepts, relate them to new situations, and act upon their understanding with personal conviction. In this work, I found that strategically planned and executed teacher-education programs can help teachers to become more effective in their work with AAVE-speaking students. (See Ball, *Carriers,* for an extended discussion.)

Researchers

For decades, scholars and researchers from many disciplines have explored the educational issues faced by speakers of AAVE in their attempt to negotiate the codes of school-based literacy. A great deal of published work exists going back to the bidialectalism movement in education in the 1960s and, of course, even before then. But certainly since the 1960s, following school desegregation and the Civil Rights and Black Power Movements, no one can deny that volumes of literature have been produced with the aim of fostering improved literacy for African American students whose home language is a variety of AAVE.

While much of the early work focused on convincing others that AAVE was a logical and viable language and on sociolinguistic findings for reading instruction at the elementary level, composition professionals formalized their participation in the debate with the adoption of the "students' right to their own language" resolution at the CCCC in 1974. The Black Caucus of NCTE/CCCC issued a statement supporting this resolution, noting that it is not the students' language that is problematic in academic settings but the teachers' attitudes towards the students' language that constitutes the problem. In their statement, the Black Caucus urged teachers to regard their students' language as a resource. Over thirty years since the "students' right" resolution, we believe that—allowing for the exception of classrooms with exceptional teachers—the teaching corps of composition professionals has yet to live up to the challenge to reconstruct pedagogy to make the most of the literacy potentials of all students.

The primary message that we wish to leave with researchers who focus on scholarship related to rhetoric and composition includes a commendation as well as a challenge. Researchers in writing and composition are to be commended for the work they have done and continue to do to "disrupt the intellectual comfort zones" (Gilyard, *Flip the Script* 19) of those who theorize and practice in rhetoric and composition on issues of race and particularly on issues that relate to AAVE-speaking students. The challenge remains, however, for us to consider how best to move these conversations beyond the pages of our research reports and scholarly recitations, to become conversations of central day-to-day concern to other practitioners, administrators, and teacher educators such that the dialogue with research will result in the implementation of changed practice. We see three areas where such collaborative conversations and research seem important.

Teacher Authority
We need research that better illuminates the culturally nuanced ways teachers exercise or enact authority in their classrooms. How do teachers construct a teaching persona or teaching identity for themselves? How do they negotiate an ethos in relationship with their students? Observations of teachers in the community-based organizations we have discussed, along with themes emerging in studies of

teachers who work successfully with African American students (Ladson-Billings), lead us to believe issues of teacher authority in writing and composition classrooms need further exploration. Our curiosity parallels questions raised by Lisa Delpit, for instance, who has challenged an albeit simplified notion of writing process pedagogy. Delpit wanted the pedagogy to be more explicit and directive; we are interested in the teacher's enactment of authority. For example, Anthony Petrosky's study of teaching in rural Mississippi classrooms reveals the prominent role and the strong authority exercised by the teacher. Michele Foster's study of uses of performance by a female African American teacher in an urban community-college classroom similarly suggests a strong central place for her exercise of, or enactment of, authority in the success of her relationships with her students. How do teachers access and make use of authority in writing classrooms? What responsibilities do teachers implicitly or explicitly claim as their part of students' success in the classroom, in the institution, in the community?

Writing Program Assessment

Measured in terms of college grade-point average, persistence in college, and graduation rates, the achievement gap between black and white college students has been widely documented. In "The Black-White Achievement Gap in the First College Year: Evidence from a New Longitudinal Study," Kenneth Spenner, Claudia Buchmann, and Lawrence Landerman suggest this gap appears as soon as students arrive in college. The first-year writing course would be one logical place to examine the causes and perhaps reconstruct the narrative of underachievement. The study summarizes a range of explanations for achievement differences, including "status attainment variations, social and cultural capital differentials, negative stereotype threat, and the racial climate of college classrooms and campuses" (5). The study defines "climate" as "the extent to which prospective inter-actional ties of a focal environment (i.e., classroom, dormitory, social or institutional group) are perceived as welcoming and integrative, on the one hand, or hostile and exclusive, on the other" (10). "Climate" also refers to "the 'micro-politics' of the classroom such as differential treatment by teachers, school personnel and peers" (10).

Are there writing programs where African American English–speaking students not only survive but thrive because they take centrally into account the factors in achievement outlined in existing research? Are there curriculums in place that work well at making the best use of students' diverse languages and community literacies even as they effectively support students' efforts to crack the codes of academic literacy? Do data exist from any college writing program correlating race and writing achievement? Without falling into a reductionist assessment strategy, can we collect data across institutions that will show comparative levels of proficiency from program to program? We have worked with AAVE-speaking students in writing and composition classrooms for some time. Our impression and our puzzlement about why many of these students perform less successfully than students from other groups was one of the reasons we have come together to write this book. Yet we cannot find research that outright says AAVE-speaking students do as well or do better than other groups of students in a particular college writing classroom. The 1999 National Assessment of Educational Progress confirms that African American high school students are performing less well than their white counterparts. We see a need for similar performance data to be collected among first-year writing programs at the college level. But more importantly, we see a need for research within and across institutions to show what effective writing programs are doing for AAVE-speaking students.

Teacher Change
Current movements in educational reform have been based on the belief that real change comes only with the support, participation, and leadership of those who will ultimately implement the reform or change: teachers. Unless teachers play the lead role in envisioning, planning, and implementing a reform movement that reenvisions the possibilities for African American students in writing and composition classrooms, efforts toward reform in the writing classroom are unlikely to succeed. In order for reforms to be effective, programs

must have teachers who are committed to the reform process and who have the will and the capacity to implement the change.

We have found that teachers who seek a transformed pedagogy must challenge themselves to critically reflect on, analyze, and change the communication patterns through which literacy is practiced in their writing classrooms. Until teachers take race-related differences in language and literacies into account as a normal part (central and routine rather than marginal) of pedagogy and reflection, the needs of AAVE-speaking students will not be redressed, and their abilities and aptitudes for critical engagement and effective expression will remain undercounted. We regard efficacy as the most important change in reconstructing the reality of classroom teachers, offering models found in exemplary practices in community-based organizations where teachers show high efficacy and reflective optimism while at the same time integrating an explicit examination of race into the learning activities students engage in. Referring to the practice of "storying" from critical race theory to show the different possibilities for reality that exist, we likewise employ story to delve into and analyze in our own teaching lives the emergence of these alternative possibilities out of a matrix of professional, community, and personal experiences. We have found that teachers' extraprofessional identity formation plays a critical role in their vision of themselves as effective teachers and as change agents in the lives of their students. Further research in this area seems warranted.

Teachers who seek a transformed pedagogy must challenge themselves to critically reflect on, analyze, and change the communication patterns through which literacy is practiced in their writing classrooms. The vision contained in the "students' right to their own language" resolution has yet to become a broadly understood pedagogical foundation for college writing classes. Indeed, efforts to incorporate it stand out for this reason. Fine work in pedagogical theory by teacher-scholars including Kay Halasek, Jacqueline Jones Royster, Deborah Mutnick, and Laura Gray-Rosendale offer important insights in realizing the vision of the "students' right" resolution. With *African American Literacies,* Elaine Richardson adds vitally to this pool of knowledge. In the community-based organizations we discuss, we find African American students' preferred modes of expression readily incorporated in the interactive discourse among participants. We believe these modes of expression have a place in the writing classroom as building blocks for bridging African American students' experiences with academic-based literacy. We also regard these modes of expression as a source of knowledge that all students can benefit from as they broaden their abilities to express their ideas in a variety of forms. Including these devices in the writing curriculum is a strategy that is in keeping with other educational approaches that have successfully used the cultural resources of students to enrich the learning experience. Rather than avoid the students' cultural experiences, identities, and interests, other successful programs within the academy and within the extracurriculum have consciously sought them out and used them to inform the curriculum. The results are positive. More research focusing on how AAVE-speaking students and teachers coconstruct a positive writing environment for developing academic literacies is needed.

The teaching practices in the community-based organizations we have discussed give participants abundant opportunities to develop broad capacities to function within their local communities to talk, write, and develop their abilities to learn and adapt to new information and changes in their lives. This ability to develop participants' capacities is rooted in the powerful sense of efficacy and reflective optimism that program leaders possess. In addition, in each program, aspects of the community, including the participants themselves and their culturally influenced language patterns, were viewed as resources. We also believe that a shared sense of racial solidarity forms the core meaning of these community-based organizations as specifically African American sites of the extracurriculum, and a question remains as to how a similar sense of shared commitment may be activated in college writing classrooms. Or are college writing classrooms always already part of the problem? Perhaps one key to this puzzle can be found by examining the mind-set of writing teachers. Where are they coming from? What shapes their vision of their students? What empowers their faith in their capability to be a meaningful force for positive change in their students' lives?

It is important that the research in writing and composition move forward within an interdisciplinary arena of inquiry that takes significant and positive steps toward building a more powerful theoretical framework for writing research and instruction. Most critically, members of the research community must begin to communicate and collaborate with teachers rather than theorizing among themselves about what needs to happen in classrooms. Many researchers who focus on scholarship related to rhetoric and composition have been away from freshman and basic writing classrooms for many years, and among those who continue to teach in these classrooms, few can boast of having recent extended successful experiences teaching struggling African American students. Perhaps we must look to those who are challenged with the task of meeting the needs of these students on a daily basis to offer us innovations in the areas of scholarship and practice. We must solicit the support of these professionals as teacher researchers and as action researchers with whom we might collaborate and to whom we might extend support.

We also recommend that scholars initiate collaborations between writing professionals in traditional academic settings and those in community-based organizations in order to facilitate the design and implementation of innovative writing programs addressed to authentic audiences that link academic demands with community and cultural resources through the use of interactive technologies. We predict that these are the sites from which modern-day scholarship and classroom innovations will emerge—particularly within those classrooms that have adopted and implemented the principles we propose in this book.

Conclusion

The mistakes of silence are few, our grandmothers said, and easily forgotten.

As a rule, we have rarely suffered for following our grandmothers' counsel. But there comes a time we must look with fresh eyes at the world and admit the human dimensions of their fallibility. There comes a time when we acknowledge of our elders that, to paraphrase the poet, even when they were right, they were wrong (Clifton).

As writing teachers responding to complexities, complications, and conundrums when race (and racism) are acknowledged as abiding elements that shape the context of our work, we recognize that we have written and taught the mistakes of silence. Too long. Too often we have let silence take the place of conversation. Too often for our own good, too often for the good of all our students—silence, where lively conversation is needed. We want for our own good as people, as teachers, to understand our situation. We want for ourselves, with and for our students, to understand "race" as a power-infused category of social difference, to name how it operates in our relationships: to our own professional identities, to the literacies we sponsor, and, fundamentally, to each other as citizens and human beings. As one modest step toward that goal, we have focused in this book on teachers' responses to AAVE in the writing classroom.

In 1979, in the Ann Arbor "Black English" case, federal district court judge Charles Joiner's recognition of the need to acknowledge students' language was evident in the way he phrased his ruling, putting teachers' "skilled empathy" at the center of the effort to break down the barriers to learning (Memorandum). We think "skilled empathy" is a good term to use to talk about ways of reconceiving the personal and professional dimensions of teacher change. Open-ended, neither "skill" nor "empathy" is a static entity of finite quantity that a teacher can possess. Instead, skill and empathy can always be improved. Likewise, any step we take toward unleashing literacies and reimagining the possibilities for AAVE-speaking students in writing and composition classrooms is a starting point that moves us away from a state of complacency. This, too, is an effort that can always be improved. At the same time, this, like any starting point, is initially "a promise."

Adding to the call for "skilled empathy," we have found exemplary practices of teachers in community-based organizations that express a powerful sense of teacher efficacy and reflective optimism. These teachers ground belief in the capability of their students in a disposition to develop skills and attitudes necessary to teach AAVE-speaking students effectively. These teachers have developed a strong knowledge base about the cultural heritage and community literacies of their students, using that knowledge to inform curricular and pedagogical practices. Implicitly or explicitly, these teachers situate their students' learning in a context of racial solidarity that stems from participation with issues of race in their private and professional lives.

We know we will begin to see a difference in the educational lives of AAVE-speaking students in writing and composition classrooms when we no longer hear teachers say, "I respect the discourse patterns African American students use in their community, but there is no place for them in this classroom." What we have said in this book is that there *is* a place for these patterns in the writing classroom. Locating the best place for them will require the development of teachers' sense of efficacy, grounded in reflective optimism and a commitment to becoming agents of change in the writing lives of African American students.

Works Cited

Index

Works Cited

Abrahams, Roger D. *Deep Down in the Jungle: Negro Narrative Folklore from the Streets of Philadelphia*. Hatboro, PA: Folklore, 1970.

Ackerman, Diane. *Deep Play*. New York: Vintage, 1999.

Appiah, Kwame Anthony. "The Uncompleted Argument: DuBois and the Illusion of Race." In *Race, Class, Gender, and Sexuality: The Big Questions*, ed. Naomi Zack, Laurie Shrage, Crispin Sartwell. Malden, MA: Blackwell, 1998. 28–42.

Apple, Michael. *Teachers and Texts: A Political Economy of Class and Fender Relations in Education*. London: Routledge and Kegan Paul, 1986.

Ashton, Patricia T., and Rodman B. Webb. *Making a Difference: Teachers' Sense of Efficacy and Student Achievement*. New York: Longman, 1986.

Bakhtin, M. N. *The Dialogic Imagination: Four Essays*, ed. Michael Holquist, trans. Caryl Emerson and Michael Holquist. Austin: U of Texas P, 1981.

Balester, Valerie M. *Cultural Divide: A Study of African-American College-Level Writers*. Portsmouth, NH: Boynton/Cook, 1993.

Ball, A. F. *Carriers of the Torch: Addressing the Global Challenge of Preparing Teachers for Diversity*. New York: Teachers College P, 2006.

———. "Community-Based Learning in Urban Settings as a Model for Educational Reform." *Applied Behavioral Science Review* 3, no. 2 (1995): 127–46.

———. "Cultural Preference and the Expository Writing of African-American Adolescents." *Written Communication* 9, no. 4 (1992): 501–32.

———. "Evaluating the Writing of Culturally and Linguistically Diverse Students: The Case of the African American Vernacular English Speaker." In *Evaluating Writing: The Role of Teachers' Knowledge about Text, Learning, and Culture*, ed. C. R. Cooper and L. Odell. Urbana: NCTE, 1999. 225–48.

———. "Incorporating Ethnographic-Based Techniques to Enhance Assessments of Culturally and Linguistically Diverse Students' Written Exposition." *Educational Assessment* 1, no. 3 (1993): 255–81.

———. "Text Design Patterns in the Writing of Urban African-American Students: Teaching to the Strengths of Students in Multicultural Settings." *Urban Education* (1995): 253–89.

Ball, A. F., and Marcia Farr. "Dialects, Culture, and Teaching the English Language Arts." In *Handbook of Research on Teaching the English Language Arts*, ed. J. Flood, J. M. Jensen, et al. New York: Macmillan, 2003. 435–45.

Ball, A. F., and Sarah W. Freedman, eds. *Bakhtinian Perspectives on Language, Literacy, and Learning*. Cambridge, UK: Cambridge UP, 2004.

Ball, A. F., and Shirley Brice Heath. "Dances of Identity: Finding an Ethnic Self in the Arts." In *Possible Selves: Achievement, Ethnicity, and Gender for Inner-City Youth*, ed. Shirley Brice Heath and M. W. McLaughlin. New York: Teachers College P, 1993. 69–93.

Ball, Arnetha, and Ted Lardner. "Dispositions toward Language: Teachers' Constructs of Knowledge and the Ann Arbor 'Black English' Case." *College Composition and Communication* 48, no. 4 (1997): 469–85.

Bandura, A. *Self-Efficacy: The Exercise of Control*. New York: N. H. Freedman and Co., 1997.

———. "Self-Efficacy: Toward a Unifying Theory of Behavioral Change." *Psychology Review* 84 (1977): 191–215.

———. "Self-Efficacy Mechanism in Human Agency." *American Psychologist* 37 (1982): 122–47.

———. *Social Foundations of Thought and Action: A Social Cognitive Theory*. Englewood Cliffs, NJ: Princeton Hall, 1986.

Barnes, R. "Race Consciousness: The Thematic Content of Racial Distinctiveness in Critical Race Scholarship." *Harvard Law Review* 103 (1990): 1864–71.

Bartholomae, David. "The Tidy House: Basic Writing in the American Curriculum." *Journal of Basic Writing* 12, no. 1 (1993): 4–21.

Barton, David. "Globalisation and Diversification: Two Opposing Influences on Local Literacies." In *Sustaining Local Literacies*, ed. David Barton. Philadelphia: Multilingual Matters, 1994. 3–8.

Baugh, John. *Black Street Speech*. Austin: U of Texas P, 1983.

———. "Considerations in Preparing Teachers for Linguistic Diversity." *Making the Connection: Language and Academic Achievement among African American Students: Proceedings of a Conference of the Coalition on Language Diversity in Education*, ed. Carolyn Temple Adger, Donna Christian, and Orlando L. Taylor. McHenry, IL: Center for Applied Linguistics and Delta Systems Co., 1999. 81–96.

———. "Design and Implementation of Writing Instruction for Speakers of Nonstandard English: Perspectives for a National Neighborhood Literacy Program." *The Writing Needs of Linguistically Different Students*, ed. B. Cronnell. Los Alamitos, CA: SWIRL Research and Development.

Bell, Derek. *Faces at the Bottom of the Well: Permanence of Racism*. New York: Basic Books, 1992.

Berlin, James A. *Rhetorics, Poetics, and Cultures: Refiguring College English Studies*. Urbana: NCTE, 1996.

Bishop, Wendy. *Something Old, Something New: College Writing Teachers and Classroom Change*. Carbondale: Southern Illinois UP, 1990.

———. "What We Don't Like, Don't Admit, Don't Understand Can't Hurt Us. Or Can It?" *Narration as Knowledge*, ed. Peter R. Stillman. Portsmouth, NH: Boynton/Cook, 1997. 191–201.

"Black and White Relations in the United States: 2001 Update." <http:// www.gallup.com/poll/reports/bwr2001/sr010711.asp>.

Bowie, R., and C. Bond. "Influencing Future Teachers' Attitudes toward Black English: Are We Making a Difference?" *Journal of Teacher Education* 45 (1994): 112–18.

Brandt, Deborah. *Literacy in American Lives.* Cambridge: Cambridge UP, 2001.

Brooke, Robert E. *Writing and Sense of Self: Identity Negotiations in Writing Workshops.* Urbana: NCTE, 1991.

Canagarajah, A. Suresh. "Safe Houses in the Contact Zone: Coping Strategies of African-American Students in the Academy." *College Composition and Communication* 48, no. 2 (1997): 173–96.

Cazden, Courtney. "The Language of African American Students in Classroom Discourse." *Making the Connection: Language and Academic Achievement among African American Students: Proceedings of a Conference of the Coalition on Language Diversity in Education,* ed. Carolyn Temple Adger, Donna Christian, and Orlando L. Taylor. McHenry, IL: Center for Applied Linguistics and Delta Systems, 1999. 31–52.

Chideya, Farai. *The Color of Our Future.* New York: Morrow, 1999.

Clark, Romy, and Roz Ivanic. *The Politics of Writing.* New York: Routledge, 1997.

Clifton, Lucille. "Heaven." *The Terrible Stories.* Rochester, NY: BOA, 1996.

Crenshaw, K., N. Gotanda, G. Peller, and K. Thomas., eds. *Critical Race Theory: The Key Writings That Formed the Movement.* New York: New Press, 1995.

Cushman, Ellen, and Chalon Emmons. "Contact Zones Made Real." *School's Out! Bridging Out-of-School Literacies with Classroom Practice,* ed. Glynda Hull and Katherine Schultz. New York: Teachers College P, 2002. 203–32.

Delgado, R. *Critical Race Theory: The Cutting Edge.* Philadelphia: Temple UP, 1995.

Delpit, Lisa. "The Silenced Dialogue: Power and Pedagogy in Educating Other People's Children." *Harvard Educational Review* 58, no. 3 (1988): 280–98.

———. "What Should Teachers Do? Ebonics and Culturally Responsive Instruction." *The Real Ebonics Debate,* ed. Theresa Perry and Lisa Delpit. Boston: Beacon Press, 1998. 17–26.

Dorsey, Heather, and Mark Pedelty. "Moving Beyond Text and Talk: The Tableau Performance Method." <http://www.evergreen.edu/washcenter/ Fall2003Newsletter/Pg36–37.pdf>.

Duffy, Gerald G., and Laura R. Roehler. "Classroom Discussion." *Handbook of Research on Teaching the English Language Arts,* ed. J. Flood, J. M. Jensen, D. Lapp, and J. R. Squire. New York: Macmillan, 1987. 70–71.

Dyson, A. H. *The Case of the Singing Scientist: A Performance Perspective on the "Stages" of School Literacy.* Technical Report No. 53. Berkeley, CA: Center for the Study of Writing, 1991.

Dyson, A. H., and S. W. Freedman. *Critical Challenges for Research on Writing and Literacy: 1990–1995.* Technical Report no. 1-B. Berkeley, CA: Center for the Study of Writing, 1991.

Elbow, Peter. "Inviting the Mother Tongue: Beyond 'Mistakes,' 'Bad English,' and 'Wrong Language.'" *JAC: A Journal of Composition Theory* 19, no. 3 (1999): 359–99.

———. "Reflections on Academic Discourse: How It Relates to Freshmen and Colleagues." *College English* 53, no. 2 (1991): 135–55.

Emig, Janet. "Writing as a Mode of Thinking." *College Composition and Communication* 28, no. 2 (1977): 122–28.

Faigley, Lester. *Fragments of Rationality: Postmodernity and the Subject of Composition.* Pittsburgh: U of Pittsburgh P, 1992.

Fordham, Signithia. "Racelessness as a Factor in Black Students' School Success: Pragmatic Strategy or Pyrrhic Victory?" *Harvard Educational Review* 58, no. 1 (1988): 54–84.

Foster, Michele. "'It's Cookin' Now': A Performance Analysis of the Speech Events of a Black Teacher in an Urban Community College." *Language in Society* 18 (1989): 1–29.

Fox, Thomas. *Defending Access: A Critique of Standards in Higher Education.* Portsmouth, NH: Boynton/Cook Heinemann, 1999.

———. "Repositioning the Profession: Teaching Writing to African American Students." *JAC: A Journal of Composition Theory* 12, no. 2 (1992): 291–303.

———. *The Social Uses of Writing.* Norwood: Ablex Publishing Corporation, 1990.

Freire, Paulo. *Pedagogy of the Oppressed.* New York: Continuum Publishing Corp., 1970.

Garcia, Georgia, and P. David Pearson. "The Role of Assessment in a Diverse Society." *Literacy for a Diverse Society: Perspectives, Practices, and Policies,* ed. Elfrieda H. Hiebert. New York: Teachers College P, 1991. 253–78.

Gee, James Paul. *Social Linguistics and Literacies: Ideology in Discourses.* Bristol: Falmer Press, 1990.

Geertz, Clifford. "The Uses of Diversity." *Michigan Quarterly Review* 25, no. 1 (1986): 105–23.

Gere, Anne Ruggles. "Kitchen Tables and Rented Rooms: The Extracurriculum of Composition." *College Composition and Communication* 45, no. 1 (1994): 75–92.

Gilyard, Keith. "African American Contributions to Composition Studies." *College Composition and Communication* 50, no. 4 (1999): 627–44.

———. "Higher Learning: Composition's Racialized Reflection." *Race Rhetoric and Composition,* ed. Keith Gilyard. Portsmouth, NH: Boynton/Cook, 1999.

————. *Voices of the Self: A Study of Language Competence*. Detroit: Wayne State UP, 1991.

Giroux, Henry A. "Racial Politics and the Pedagogy of Whiteness." In *Whiteness: A Critical Reader*, ed. Mike Hill. New York: New York UP, 1997. 294–315.

Grant, C. A., and W. G. Secada. "Preparing Teachers for Diversity." In *Handbook of Research on Teacher Education*, ed. W. R. Houston. New York: Macmillan, 1990. 403–22.

Gray-Rosendale, Laura. *Rethinking Basic Writing: Exploring Identity, Politics, and Community in Interaction*. Mahwah, NJ: Lawrence Erlbaum Associates, 2000.

Greenleaf, Cynthia, and Sarah Warshauer Freedman. "Linking Classroom Discourse and Classroom Content: Following the Trail of Intellectual Work in a Writing Lesson." *Discourse Processes* 16 (1993): 465–505.

Griffin, John Howard. *Black Like Me*. New York: New American Library, 1961.

Guskey, Thomas R. "Teacher Efficacy, Self-Concept, and Attitudes toward the Implementation of Mastery Learning. *Teaching and Teacher Education: An International Journal of Instructional Innovation* 4, no. 1 (1988): 63–96.

Harrington, Susanmarie. "The Representation of Basic Writers in Basic Writing Scholarship, or Who Is Quentin Pierce?" *Journal of Basic Writing* 18 (1999): 91–107.

Harris, Joseph. *A Teaching Subject: Composition since 1966*. Upper Saddle River, NJ: Prentice-Hall, 1997.

Heath, Shirley Brice. *Ways with Words: Language, Life, and Work in Communities and Classrooms*. Cambridge, UK: Cambridge UP, 1983.

Heath, Shirley Brice, and Juliet Langman. "Shared Thinking and the Register of Coaching." *Sociolinguistic Perspectives on Register*, ed. Douglas Biber and Edeward Finnegan. New York: Oxford UP, 1994. 82–105.

Heath, Shirley Brice, and M. W. McLaughlin. "The Best of Both Worlds: Connecting Schools and Community Youth Organizations for All-Day, All-Year Learning." *Educational Administration Quarterly* 30, no. 3 (1994): 278–300.

————. "Learning for Anything Everyday. *Journal of Curriculum Studies* 26, no. 5 (1994): 471–89.

Hillocks, George. *Teaching Writing as Reflective Practice*. New York: Teachers College P, 1995.

hooks, bell. *Teaching to Transgress: Education as the Practice of Freedom*. New York: Routledge, 1994.

Howard, Harry, Lee H. Hansen, and Thomas Pietras. *Final Evaluation: King Elementary School Vernacular Black English Inservice Program*. Ann Arbor: Ann Arbor Public Schools, 1980.

Howard, Rebecca Moore. "The Great Wall of African American Vernacular English in the American College Classroom." *JAC: A Journal of Composition Theory* 16, no. 2 (1996). <http://jac.gsu.edu/jac/16.2/Articles/6.htm>.

Hughes, Langston. "Theme for English B." *Selected Poems of Langston Hughes.* New York: Vantage, 1974.

Jordan, June. "Nobody Mean More to Me than You and the Future Life of Willie Jordan." *Harvard Educational Review* 58, no. 3 (1988): 363–74.

Knight, Etheridge. "The Idea of Ancestry." *Born of a Woman.* New York: Houghton-Mifflin, 1980.

Kuhn, Thomas. *The Structure of Scientific Revolutions.* Chicago: U of Chicago P, 1970.

Labov, William. *Language in the Inner City: Studies in the Black English Vernacular.* Philadelphia: U of Philadelphia P, 1972.

Ladson-Billings, Gloria. *The Dream Keepers: Successful Teachers of African American Children.* San Francisco: Josey-Bass, 1994.

———. "Just What Is Critical Race Theory and What's It Doing in a Nice Field Like Education." ed. Laurence Parker, Donna Deyhle, and Sofia Villenas. *Race Is, Race Isn't: Critical Race Theory and Qualitative Studies in Education.* Boulder, CO: Westview P, 1999. 7–30.

———. "Multicultural Teacher Education: Research, Practice, and Policy." *Handbook of Research on Multicultural Education,* ed. J. A. Banks and C. A. Banks. New York: Macmillan, 1995. 747–59.

Lardner, Ted. "Item 50: Dialect Diversity and Teacher Preparation." *Situated Stories: Valuing Diversity in Composition Research,* ed. Emily Decker and Kathleen Geissler. Portsmouth, NH: Boynton/Cook, 1998. 119–27.

Lardner, Ted, and Todd Lundberg. *Exchanges: Reading and Writing about Consumer Culture.* New York: Longman, 2001.

Lardner, Ted, Barbara Sones, and Mary Weems. "'Lessons Spaced by Heartbeats': Performance Poetry in a Ninth-Grade Classroom." *English Journal* 85, no. 8 (1996): 60–65.

Lewis, Furry. "Judge Bushay's Blues." *Mississippi Delta Blues Jam in Memphis,* vol. 1. Arhoolie Productions, 1993.

Little, Judith Warren. "Norms of Collegiality and Experimentation: Workplace Conditions of School Success." *American Educational Research Journal* 19 (1982): 325–40.

Lunsford, Andrea A., and Lisa Ede. "Representing Audience: 'Successful' Discourse and Disciplinary Critique." *College Composition and Communication* 47, no. 2 (1996): 167–79.

Mahdi, L. C., S. Foster, and M. Little. *Betwixt and Between: Patterns of Masculine and Feminine Initiation.* La Salle, IL: Open Court, 1987.

Marshall, Ian, and Wendy Ryden. "Interrogating the Monologue: Making Whiteness Visible." *Journal of the Conference on College Composition and Communication* 52, no. 2 (2000): 240–59.

Matsuda, Mari. "Public Response to Racist Speech: Considering the Victim's Story." *Michigan Law Review* 87 (1989): 2320–81.

McCarthy, Cameron. "The Problem with Origins: Race and the Contrapuntal Nature of the Educational Experience." *Review of Education/Pedagogy/ Cultural Studies* 17, no. 1 (1995): 87–105.

McCarthy, Cameron, and Warren Crichlow. *Race, Identity, and Representation in Education.* New York: Routledge, 1993.

McCracken, Nancy. "Muted Dialogues: Seeking a Discourse for Preparing to Teach across Race, Class, and Language." *English Education* 32, no. 4 (2000): 246–50.

McIntosh, Peggy. "White Privilege and Male Privilege: A Personal Account of Coming to See Correspondences through Work in Women's Studies." Working Paper no. 189. Center for Research on Women. Wellesley, MA, 1988.

McLeod, Susan H. *Notes on the Heart.* Carbondale: Southern Illinois UP, 1997.

Meier, Terry. "The Case for Ebonics as a Part of Exemplary Education." *Making the Connection: Language and Academic Achievement among African American Students: Proceedings of a Conference of the Coalition on Language Diversity in Education,* ed. Carolyn Temple Adger, Donna Christian, and Orlando L. Taylor. McHenry, IL: Center for Applied Linguistics and Delta Systems Co., 1999. 97–114.

Memorandum Opinion and Order. Martin Luther King Junior Elementary School Children v. Ann Arbor School District Board. Civil Action No 7-71861. 473 F. Supp. 1371 (1979).

Michaels, S. "'Sharing Time': Children's Narrative Styles and Differential Access to Literacy." *Language in Society* 10, no. 1 (1981): 423–42.

Miller, Richard E. "The Arts of Complicity." *College English* 61, no. 1 (1998): 10–28.

Milofsky, C. "Neighborhood-Based Organizations: A Market Analogy." *The Nonprofit Sector: A Research Handbook,* ed. W. W. Powell. New Haven: Yale UP, 1987. 277–95.

Mishler, Elliot G. *Storylines: Craftartists' Narratives of Identity.* Cambridge, MA: Harvard UP, 1998.

Morrison, Toni. *Playing in the Dark: Whiteness and the Literary Imagination.* Cambridge, MA: Harvard UP, 1992.

Mutnick, Deborah. *Writing in an Alien World: Basic Writing and the Struggle for Equality in Higher Education.* Portsmouth, NH: Boynton/Cook, 1996.

National Assessment of Educational Progress. "The Writing Report Card: Trends in Writing, 1998." Princeton, NJ: Educational Testing Service, 1999.

Okawa, Gail Y. "'Resurfacing Roots': Developing a Pedagogy of Language Awareness from Two Views." *Language Diversity in the Classroom: From Intention to Practice,* ed. Geneva Smitherman and Victor Villanueva. Carbondale: Southern Illinois UP, 2003. 109–33.

Olson, Gary A. "Ideological Critique in Rhetoric and Composition." *Rhetoric and Composition,* ed. Gary A. Olson. Carbondale: Southern Illinois UP, 2002.

Omi, Michael, and Howard Winant. "On the Theoretical Concept of Race." In *Race, Identity, and Representation in Education,* ed. Cameron McCarthy and Warren Crichlow. New York: Routledge, 1993. 3–10.

———. *Racial Formation in the United States: From the 1960s to the 1990s,* 2nd ed. New York: Routledge, 1994.

Pang, Valerie Ooka, and Velma Sablan. "Teacher Efficacy: Do Teachers Believe They Can Be Effective with African American Students?" Annual Meeting of the American Educational Research Association, San Francisco, April 1995.

Parker, Laurence, Donna Deyhle, and Sofia Villenas. *Race Is, Race Isn't: Critical Race Theory and Qualitative Studies in Education.* Boulder, CO: Westview P, 1999.

Parker, R. B. "Theories of Writing Instruction: Having Them, Using Them, Changing Them." *English Education* 20 (1988): 18–40.

Petrosky, Anthony. "Rural Poverty and Literacy in the Mississippi Delta: Dilemmas, Paradoxes, and Conundrums." *The Right to Literacy,* ed. Andrea Lunsford, Helene Moglen, and James Slevin. New York: MLA, 1990.

Phelps, Louise Wetherbee. "Practical Wisdom and the Geography of Knowledge in Composition." *College English* 53, no. 8 (1991): 863–85.

Prendergast, Catherine. "Race: The Absent Presence in Composition." *College Composition and Communication* 50, no. 1 (1998): 36–53.

Raudenbush, Stephen W., Brian Rowan, and Yuk Fai Cheong. *Contextual Effects on the Self-Efficacy of High School Teachers.* Stanford, CA: Center for Research on the Context of Secondary School Teaching, 1990.

Richardson, Elaine. *African American Literacies.* New York: Routledge. 2003.

———. "Race, Class(es), Gender, and Age: The Making of Knowledge about Language Diversity." *Language Diversity in the Classroom: From Intention to Practice,* ed. Geneva Smitherman and Victor Villanueva. Carbondale: Southern Illinois UP, 2003. 40–66.

———. "'Where Did That Come From?' Black Talk for Black Student Talking Texts." MA thesis. Cleveland State University, 1993.

Rickford, John R. "Language Diversity and Academic Achievement in the Education of African American Students: An Overview of the Issues." *Making the Connection: Language and Academic Achievement among African American Students: Proceedings of a Conference of the Coalition on Language Diversity in Education,* ed. Carolyn Temple Adger, Donna Christian, and Orlando L. Taylor. McHenry, IL: Center for Applied Linguistics and Delta Systems, 1999. 1–30.

Ritchie, Joy, and David Wilson. *Teacher Narratives as Critical Inquiry: Rewriting the Script.* New York: Teachers College P, 2000.

Roediger, D. *The Wages of Whiteness: Race and the Making of the American Working Class.* London: Verso Press, 1991.

Roithmeyer, Daria. "Introduction to Critical Race Theory in Educational Research and Praxis." In *Race Is. Race Isn't: Critical Race Theory and Qualitative Studies in Education,* ed. Laurence Parker, Donna Deyhle, and Sofia Villenas. Boulder, CO: Westview P, 1999. 1–6.

Rose, Mike. *Lives on the Boundary: A Moving Account of the Struggles and Achievements of America's Educational Underclass.* New York: Penguin, 1989.

Rosen, Lois Matz, and Dawn Abt-Perkins. "Preparing English Teachers to Teach Diverse Student Populations: Beliefs, Challenges, Proposals for Change." *English Education* 32, no. 4 (2000): 251–66.

Rosenwald, George C., and Richard L. Ochberg. *Storied Lives: The Cultural Politics of Self-Understanding.* New Haven: Yale UP, 1992.

Royster, Jacqueline Jones, and Rebecca Greenberg Taylor. "Constructing Teacher Identity in the Basic Classroom." *Journal of Basic Writing* 16, no. 1 (1997): 27–50.

Royster, Jacqueline Jones, and Jean C. Williams. "History in the Spaces Left: African American Presence and Narratives of Composition Studies." *College Composition and Communication* 50 (June 1999): 563–84.

———. "Reading Past Resistance: A Response to Valerie Balester." *College Composition and Communication* 52, no. 1 (September 2000): 133–42.

Sanchez, Claudio. "Black-White Achievement Gap." *Talk of the Nation.* National Public Radio. December 24, 2003.

Scott, Jerrie Cobb. "Literacies and Deficits Revisited." *Journal of Basic Writing* 12, no. 1 (1993): 46–56.

Scribner, Sylvia. "Literacy in Three Metaphors." *Literacy: Language and Power,* ed. Daniel L. Vipond and Ronal Strahl. Long Beach: California State UP, 1994. 13–28.

Seibles, Tim. "The Case." *Hammerlock.* Cleveland: Cleveland State University Poetry Center, 1999.

Shaughnessy, Mina P. *Errors and Expectations: A Guide for the Teacher of Basic Writing.* New York: Oxford UP, 1997.

Shor, Ira. *Critical Teaching and Everyday Life.* Boston: South End P, 1980.

Sleeter, Christine. "How White Teachers Construct Race." In *Race, Identity, and Representation in Education,* ed. Cameron McCarthy and Warren Crichlow. New York: Routledge, 1993. 157–71.

Smitherman, Geneva. *Black Talk: Words and Phrases from the Hood to the Amen Corner.* Boston: Houghton Mifflin, 1994.

———. "'The Blacker the Berry, the Sweeter the Juice': African American Student Writers and the National Assessment of Educational Progress." *The Need for Story: Cultural Diversity in Classroom and Community,* ed. A. H. Dyson and C. Genishi. Urbana: NCTE, 1994. 80–101.

————. *Talkin and Testifyin*. Detroit: Wayne State UP, 1977.

Somech, Anit, and Anat Drach-Zahavy. "Understanding Extra-role Behavior in Schools: The Relationships between Job Satisfaction, Sense of Efficacy, and Teachers' Extra-role Behavior." *Teaching and Teacher Education* 16 (2000): 649–59.

Spenner, Kenneth I., Claudia Buchmann, and Lawrence R. Landerman. "The Black-White Achievement Gap in the First College Year: Evidence from a New Longitudinal Case Study." <http://www.soc.duke.edu/~cbuch/web/spenner_buchmann_ landerman.pdf>.

Steele, Claude. "Stereotype Threat and African-American Student Achievement." In *Young, Gifted, and Black: Promoting High Achievement among African-American Students,* by Theresa Perry, Claude Steele, and Asa Hilliard. Boston: Beacon, 2003. 109–30.

Stenberg, Shari, and Amy Lee. "Developing Pedagogies: Learning the Teaching of English." *College English* 64, no. 3 (2002): 326–47.

Stock, Patricia L., and Jay L. Robinson. "Literacy as Conversation: Classroom Talk as Text Building." In *Conversations on the Written Word: Essays on Language and Literacy,* by Jay L. Robinson. Portsmouth, NH: Boynton/Cook, 1990. 163–238.

Street, Brain V. *Literacy in Theory and Practice*. Cambridge: Cambridge UP, 1984.

————. "Struggles over the Meaning(s) of Literacy." In *Worlds of Literacy,* ed. M. Hamilton, D. Barton, and R. Ivanic. Clevedon: Multilingual Matters, 1994. 15–20.

"Students' Right to Their Own Language." Special issue of *College Composition and Communication* 25 (Fall 1974).

Tatum, Beverly. *"Why Are All the Black Kids Sitting Together in the Cafeteria?" and Other Conversations about Race*. New York: Basic Books, 1997.

Trainor, Jennifer Seibel. "Critical Pedagogy's 'Other': Constructions of Whiteness in Education for Social Change." *College Composition and Communication* 53, no. 4 (2002): 631–50.

Trepagnier, Barbara. "Deconstructing Categories: The Exposure of Silent Racism." *Symbolic Interaction* 24, no. 2 (2001): 141–63.

Troyka, Lynn Quitman. "How We Failed the Basic Writing Enterprise." *Journal of Basic Writing* 19, no. 1 (2000): 113–23.

Villanueva, Victor, Jr. *Bootstraps: From an Academic of Color*. Urbana: NCTE, 1993.

Vygotsky, L. S. *Mind in Society: The Development of Higher Psychological Processes*. Cambridge, MA: Harvard UP, 1978.

————. *Thought and Language,* trans. Alex Kozlin. Cambridge, MA: MIT Press, 1986.

Welch, Nancy. *Getting Restless: Rethinking Revision in Writing Instruction*. Portsmouth, NH: Boynton/Cook, 1997.

————. "No Apology: Challenging the 'Uselessness' of Creative Writing." *JAC: A Journal of Composition Theory* 19, no. 1 (1999): 117–34.

Werder, Carmen, P. J. Redmond, Jeff Purdue, and Kathryn Patrick. "Creating a Reflective Space: The Teaching and Learning Academy at Western Washington University." <http://www.evergreen.edu/washcenter/Fall2003 Newsletter/Pg38- 40.pdf>.

West, Cornell. *Keeping Faith: Philosophy and Race in America*. New York: Routledge, 1993.

————. *Race Matters*. Boston: Beacon, 1993.

West, Thomas. "The Racist Other." *JAC: A Journal of Composition Theory* 17, no. 2 (1997): 215–26.

West, Thomas, and Gary A. Olson. "Critical Negotiation(s): Transformative Action in Cultural Studies and Border Pedagogy." *Review of Education/ Pedagogy/Cultural Studies* 21, no. 2 (1999): 149–63.

White, Bukka. "Christmas Eve Blues." *Mississippi Delta Blues Jam in Memphis*, vol. 2. Arhoolie Productions, 1993.

Williams, Patricia J. "Aren't We Happy Yet?" *Nation* August 6–13, 2001, 11.

Woods, Sash. "Putting an Asset-Based Perspective into Practice: The Collaborative Learning and Instruction Center at South Seattle Community College." <http://www.evergreen.edu/washcenter/Fall2003Newsletter/Pg41– 44.pdf>.

Worsham, Lynn. "Going Postal: Pedagogical Violence and the Schooling Emotion." *JAC: A Journal of Composition Theory* 18, no. 2 (1998): 213–45.

Wright, Richard. *12 Million Black Voices*. New York: Thunder's Mouth Press, 1941.

Zemelman, Steven, and Harvey Daniels. *A Community of Writers: Teaching Writing in the Junior and Senior High School*. Portsmouth, NH: Heinemann Educational Books, Inc., 1998.

Index

AAVE (African American Vernacular English): attitudes toward, 17, 49, 68–69; developing a knowledge base of, 167; discourse patterns in, 42, 44–48, 166–70; as distinct linguistic system, 31, 42, 99; oral influences in written text, 100; pedagogical applications, 36, 174, 193; rhetorical style, 145; sociolinguistics of, 36–37; teacher familiarity with, 48–49

AAVE-speaking instructors, 64, 81, 82

AAVE-speaking students: attitudes toward, 57; in community-based organizations, 112; influences on linguistic practices of, 42; self-perceptions of, 15, 27–28

Abrahams, Roger, 152–53

academic achievement: of African American students, 28, 190–91; barriers to, 16–17, 177–78

academic American English, 68–69, 99

academic standards, external, 184

academic writing, 49

achievement gaps, 28, 190–91

Ackerman, Diane, 7

affect: changes in, 102–3; creating space for, 150–53; and efficacy, 60, 65–66, 126–27, 136; meaning of, 151; in responses to student writing, 56

affective dimension, 20

African American discourse patterns in preaching tradition, 159–60

African American oral and literary traditions, 26–27, 94, 149, 151–53. *See also* AAVE

African American students, 28, 100, 143. *See also* AAVE-speaking students

African American Vernacular English. *See* AAVE

agency matrix, 110

alternative literacies, 100

analogy, use of, 81

analysis and synthesis, in effecting change, 187–88

Ann Arbor "Black English" case, 31, 146–47, 148, 195

Appiah, Kwame Anthony, 23

Ashton, Patricia T., 58, 178

assessment, approaches to, 167, 170–72

assignment goals, 171–72

assimilationist teaching, 50

attitudes: as barriers to academic achievement, 16–17, 19, 107; as barriers to teacher efficacy, 56–57, 174; as focus of Ann Arbor case, 146–47; readjustment of, 146–49; toward AAVE, 17, 49, 68–69, 98

Ayana (Troop graduate), 61

Bakhtin, M. N., 137–38

Balester, Valerie M., 43

Ball, Arnetha: church life of, 119–20; family of, 114–16; formal education of, 117–19; as parent, 127; as researcher, 138–39; as teacher, 128–29; as teacher educator, 130. *See also* personal narratives of Arnetha Ball

Bandura, A., 59–61

Baugh, John, 19

teaching, assimilationist, 50
teaching, critical aspects of, 96–97
Teaching and Learning Academy (TLA), 183
teaching identities. *See* identity negotiation and transformation
transformative change, 102–3, 142, 186–88
transition devices, 48
Trepagnier, Barbara, 25–26
Troop (dance program), 30, 61–66

Ujima program: as community-based organization, 30; literary practices in activities of, 93–94; mentors and leaders of, 90–93; participants and activities of, 86–90; as site of extracurriculum, 79
umbrella collision, 134, 136
Umoja program, 88
underachiever students, 113–14
Upward Bound, 30, 79, 82–86

verbal-social persuasion, as efficacy source, 60–61
verb forms, AAVE rendering of, 44
vernacular resources, students', 96
vibrant learning relationships, 112
vicarious experience, as efficacy source, 59–60
voice, shifts in, 49
Vygotsky, L. S., 138

Wanika's journal entry, 90–91
Webb, Rodman B., 58, 178
West, Thomas, 23–24

Western Washington University Teaching and Learning Academy (TLA), 183
What Happened Yesterday at Ujima (Wanika), 90–91
whiteness, 21, 25, 37, 106–7, 111
Williams, Mr., 71–73
Williams, Patricia, 13, 110
Wilson, David, 58, 107–8
Woods, Sash, 181
Worsham, Lynn, 24
WPAS. *See* writing program administrators
Wright, Mindy, 182
Wright, Richard, 33–34
writing: as activity, 69–70; affective responses to, 56; cultural experiences as resources in, 149; evaluation of, 167, 170–73; fluency in academic, 49; instruction in, 81–82; journal, 90–91; oral language as precursor to, 100, 166–67; as rapture, 7–8; significant tendencies in, 22–25; variations in patterns, 42–43
writing conferences, reconceptualization of, 161–62, 167, 170
writing program administrators (WPAS): and staff development, 182–85; and support for collaboration, 177–82
writing programs, assessment of, 190–91
Writing Workshop, Ohio State University, 182

Zemelman, Steven, 143–44

Arnetha F. Ball is an associate professor of curriculum studies, teacher education, and educational linguistics in the School of Education at Stanford University, where she teaches courses in literacy studies that focus on writing and writing instruction, the oral and written literacies of culturally and linguistically diverse populations in the United States and South Africa, and the preparation of teachers to work with poor, marginalized, and underachieving students. She has published widely, with numerous book chapters and articles in journals that include *Linguistics and Education, Applied Behavioral Science Review, Teaching and Teacher Education,* and *Written Communication.* Ball is one of the editors of two recently published books: *Black Linguistics* (with Sinfree Makoni, Geneva Smitherman, and Arthur Spears) and *Bakhtinian Perspectives on Language, Literacy, and Learning* (with Sarah Freedman). She also has written a forthcoming book, *Carriers of the Torch: Addressing the Global Challenge of Preparing Teachers for Diversity.* Ball received the Richard Braddock Award with Ted Lardner for *College Composition and Communication*'s outstanding journal article published in 1997.

Ted Lardner is an associate professor of English at Cleveland State University, where he teaches courses in composition and composition theory as well as in language diversity and the teaching of English. Having served as the director of the Cleveland State University Poetry Center, he has also participated in long-term staff-development collaborations with Cleveland public schoolteachers, Cleveland arts organizations, and language-arts educators of northeast Ohio, focusing on better preparing college-bound students for university writing courses and the application of theater-arts techniques in secondary language-arts classrooms. His poems have appeared in *Luna, 5am, Caliban,* and other journals. A poetry chapbook, *Passing By a Home Place,* was published in 1987. With Todd Lundberg, Lardner published a first-year writing text, *Exchanges: Reading and Writing about Consumer Culture* (2001). With Arnetha Ball, he coauthored the Braddock Award–winning essay "Dispositions toward Language: Teachers' Constructs of Knowledge and the 'Ann Arbor' Black English Case." *African American Literacies Unleashed* represents a continuation of the inquiry first begun in "Dispositions toward Language."

Studies in Writing & Rhetoric

In 1980 the Conference on College Composition and Communication established the Studies in Writing & Rhetoric (SWR) series as a forum for monograph-length arguments or presentations that engage general compositionists. SWR encourages extended essays or research reports addressing any issue in composition and rhetoric from any theoretical or research perspective as long as the general significance to the field is clear. Previous SWR publications serve as models for prospective authors; in addition, contributors may propose alternate formats and agendas that inform or extend the field's current debates.

SWR is particularly interested in projects that connect the specific research site or theoretical framework to contemporary classroom and institutional contexts of direct concern to compositionists across the nation. Such connections may come from several approaches, including cultural, theoretical, field-based, gendered, historical, and interdisciplinary. SWR especially encourages monographs by scholars early in their careers, by established scholars who wish to share an insight or exhortation with the field, and by scholars of color.

The SWR series editor and editorial board members are committed to working closely with prospective authors and offering significant developmental advice for encouraged manuscripts and prospectuses. Editorships rotate every five years. Prospective authors intending to submit a prospectus during the 2002 to 2007 editorial appointment should obtain submission guidelines from Robert Brooke, SWR editor, University of Nebraska–Lincoln, Department of English, P.O. Box 880337, 202 Andrews Hall, Lincoln, NE 68588-0337.

General inquiries may also be addressed to Sponsoring Editor, Studies in Writing & Rhetoric, Southern Illinois University Press, P.O. Box 3697, Carbondale, IL 62902-3697.